YOUR MONEY
How to Make It Stretch

SYLVIA AUERBACH

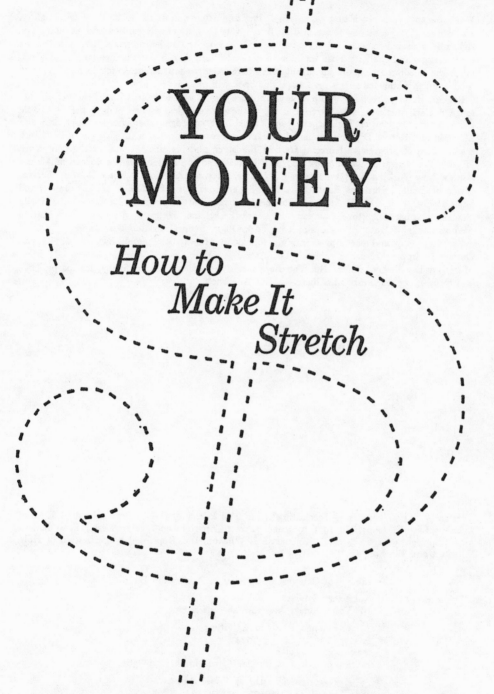

YOUR MONEY

How to Make It Stretch

DOUBLEDAY & COMPANY, INC., GARDEN CITY, NEW YORK 1974

Acknowledgments

Managing money is not a sexy topic, nor is it a topic that's supposed to be dealt with lightly. Ask anyone in the money game and he'll tell you that money is serious and economics is rightfully a dismal science. All right, we can all buy that. But learning about money can be challenging—and challenges can be interesting. Best of all, learning to manage your money can mean the freedom and, more important, the wherewithal to pursue sexier and less serious pursuits—and this knowledge is what I hope this book will offer its readers.

For me, writing this book would have been more dismal and less fun without the help of my son, Dr. Carl Auerbach, who introduced me to the psychological aspects of how people handle their money; Dr. Herbert Fensterheim, who shared his knowledge of behavior therapy; Christian M. Dahl and Robert D. Schumacher of the Irving Trust Company, who gave me insights into the thinking of progressive bankers; Herbert Bienstock and his efficient staff at the New York office of the Bureau of Labor Statistics; Jean Drissell and the Better Business Bureau of Metropolitan New York; Arnold Wonsever, Car/Puter/International Corp.; Mitchell Weil, Service Corps of Retired Business Executives; Kay Sauerbrunn, Esquire, Office of Interstate Land Sales Registration, United States Department of Housing and Urban Development; Adelle Nemser, Dunbar Furniture Company; Richard Prokriefke, National Association of Mutual Savings Banks; Salvatore Sangiorgio, New York Office, Federal Trade Commission.

For their help and encouragement, my thanks to Murray Richmond, Esquire; Sheila and Gerald J. Zipper; Judith Serebnick; Dr. Alexander Van Daele; Seymour Richmond; Ellen Muzi; my Doubleday editors, Elsa Van Bergen and Jean Bennett, and finally, for his patience and forbearance, my husband, Albert.—Sylvia Auerbach

Portion of "The Hardship of Accounting" from *The Poetry of Robert Frost* edited by Edward Connery Lathem. Copyright 1936 by Robert Frost. Copyright © 1964 by Lesley Frost Ballantine. Copyright © 1969 by Holt, Rinehart and Winston, Inc. Reprinted by permission of Holt, Rinehart and Winston, Inc.

Library of Congress Cataloging in Publication Data

Auerback, Sylvia.
    Your money: how to make it stretch.

    1. Finance, Personal. I. Title.
HG179.A93   332'.024
ISBN 0-385-00351-X
Library of Congress Catalog Card Number 73-83611

Contents

YOUR MONEY
How to Make It Stretch

· 1 ·

You Are What You Spend, Or: Dr. Freud, Red Ink, and All Those Aggregates

"Young people nowadays imagine that money is everything. And when they get older they know it."

—Oscar Wilde

You're smarter than you think you are. You go through life paying the rent or the mortgage, staying one step ahead of the Internal Revenue Service, managing occasional vacation trips as well as regular trips to the supermarket, the drugstore, and the hardware store. You contribute to united charity appeals and the collections at the office for assorted wedding and baby gifts, and buy presents for your twelve nieces and nephews at Christmastime. You support a car, pay off bills for furniture, and help your dentist and your doctor take their annual trip abroad.

And yet you say you can't manage money.

The fact is you can and you do.

When you say you can't manage money you do yourself an injustice. What you may mean is that:

a) you can't buy all the things you'd like to buy, or

b) you can't buy all the things *you* think you should be able to buy on your income; or

c) you can't manage as well as your colleagues, your neighbors, or your first cousins on your in-laws' side; or

d) you can't manage as well as the people in the ads who have money for second homes, mutual funds, or trips to Europe despite moderate incomes.

The fact is that "managing money," like everything else in our lives, is not a simple matter. It's not just keeping track of the dollars and cents once we have what economists call "discretionary income," which, translated into English, means having a few dollars and cents to make some spending choices with after the butcher, baker, and landlord have been paid. It's making choices, long *and* short run, that, inevitably, are going to set spending patterns and then bring both pleasure and pain: pleasure at the lovely moment when we succumb to the temptation of a shop window, a persuasive salesman, an easy-credit, buy-now pay-later plan; pain when the inevitable bill comes due. Often, too, there is the unexpected feeling of anxiety that somehow or other the control of the money has gotten away from us in a way we don't quite understand. We've been tempted to buy in spite of our brand-new resolve to put more money in the savings account. Or we've found out, too late, that there was a better way to buy a car, or a better place to get insurance, or even a better way to save money. All of which leads to something psychiatrists and psychologists have been observing for a long time—and something you may have suspected.

Why we spend money the way we do is not a simple matter. Each of us, whether we know it or not, has a style of spending based on an attitude about money and the things it can buy that is based as much, if not more, on our emotions and our perceptions as on our rational planning. Spending money not only reflects income and needs and desires; it also reflects personality traits and psychological attitudes. It can even reflect problems that have their roots, said the good Dr. Freud, in early training and family relationships from infancy to the time we got our first allowance or the first paycheck.

Dr. James A. Knight, professor of psychiatry and associate dean of the Tulane University School of Medicine, puts it this way: "Each of us may understand the typical meaning of money, but simultaneously endow it with special significance. Hidden from the individual's conscious mind will be some of the factors that shape its psychological meaning for him . . ." In his book *For the Love of Money*, Dr. Knight describes some of the things that money symbolizes for us:

A substitute for mother: Mother, or rather the comfort and (literally) the support for survival that mother love provides in an infant's life, probably influences the child's later attitudes toward money. "The same conditions that make the infant long for a mother's love continue to exist, although on a different level, when he becomes an adult. If the individual could find *mother* for the rest of his years, life would be relieved of many of its uncertainties and misfortunes. It is no small surprise then that man is driven to pursue this mirage and find in money a substitute for mother."

Expanded portions of self: "In the deeper layers of the mind money, like all other possessions, assumes the role of the parts of the body that one could lose, or, after the fantasy that they have been lost, wishes to regain . . . nearly everyone refers to his savings account as a nest egg."

Psychoanalyst Theodor Reik, in his book *Of Love and Lust,* notes that to some men money is a *symbol of potency.* In discussing "man and money" he says that men who consider their wives spendthrifts and resent their wives' spending habits are sometimes "motivated in unconscious reality by the impression that the woman deprives the man of power—especially of sexual potency . . . the unconscious content of the accusation is that the wife is emasculating her husband."

Dr. Reik goes on to say that "A great number of wives behave as though— and in this 'as though' is the unconscious meaning contained—the fears of their husband concerning money spending were psychologically well-founded on reality. These women unconsciously conceive of money as a *substitute for love.* They squander money, spending it foolishly and in this fashion get even with their husbands who are withholding love from them . . . women feel that a man who spends money on them instead of giving them his love is offering them only a second best. But that appears to them as a poor substitute and not good enough —or only good enough to be carelessly spent."

These are just a few of the hidden psychologically symbolic meanings of money. And there is a natural outgrowth of these hidden motives—the equally hidden reasons for spending money. Here too the psychologists and psychiatrists have probed our psyches and come up with some interesting types. Though few of us go to these extremes, there's a little bit of each of these spending traits in us at times.

There's the compulsive spender, for instance, who is "comfortable emotionally [according to Dr. Knight] only when he feels free to spend." Compulsive spenders vary and so do their motives: to make a show of wealth that will offset their basic feelings of inferiority; to squander money in order to become *dependent* again when they are poor again; to show their "bad" parents or husbands or wives or lovers that they want to be treated kindly and generously; to punish a parent for not giving enough love by forcing the parent to worry about his child's excessive spending; to buy affection or even love; to offset feelings of self-pity or depression. (Could that be why you succumbed to that beautiful window display?)

"For many charge account spenders," says Dr. Knight, "charge account buying is even more exciting than money. They equate the charge account with temporarily unlimited spending power. Their pleasure from spending exceeds the pleasure obtained from the items or services purchased."

Even bargain hunting can have its hidden motives. Why do bargain hunters buy things they don't need, just because they are cheap? On a conscious level they convince themselves that they are saving money, but, say the psychologists, on an unconscious level it's playing the game of outsmarting the seller that provides the real excitement. (We're not talking here, of course, of purposeful bargain shopping to stretch a limited budget.) According to Dr. Knight, "The bargain hunter is treating the world as the perpetually refusing mother. To win a bargain is not only to wrest symbolic affection from her but also to wrest by one's wits more than the perpetually refusing mother would ever give."

And it isn't only psychiatrists and psychologists who understand these unconscious motivations. Fund raisers consciously appeal to the status seekers, the guilt-ridden, the affection-starved. Merchants set out their bargain wares on tables where we can see, touch, and indulge ourselves in winning some long-lost or denied affection. Manufacturers appeal to repressed desires for the visible display of power and self-esteem that comes from owning merchandise. And all are helped by master motivators who analyze these repressed desires and then demonstrate to their clients—manufacturers, distributors, retailers—the best method for appealing to these desires.

Consider, for instance, Dr. Ernest Dichter, founder and president of the Institute for Motivational Research, and often thought of as the granddaddy of the whole field of motivational research. Dr. Dichter advises sellers to "sell 'sinful' products with a psychological sizzle. Give people an excuse for enjoying them." Liquor, therefore, should be promoted not as a help in letting you get drunk (if that's your subconscious desire) but rather as an aid in celebrating a festive occasion. Candy doesn't indulge your taste for sweets but gives you quick energy to work better. A bawdy play is a "sociological experiment in the theatre."

There's also the new "art" of "psychographics," which claims to be able to identify your personal values, attitudes, emotions, and beliefs, so it can send a laser beam of an advertising message right to your very core. There are ads to appeal to the rationality of the coolheaded, and ads to appeal to the feelings of the emotional. The subconscious authority seekers are the targets for the ads with a fatherly-looking figure in a white coat giving advice on what to buy, and of course there are other ads aimed at those who long to dominate. Whatever your psychological makeup, the advertisers have a message designed to get you where your defenses are weakest.

It would seem as if you hardly have a fighting chance to hold onto your dollars.

And yet, for the most part, you do.

In general, you manage your affairs well enough to get along in the world, and that's not easy in the face of inflation, rising taxes, an unstable economy, and a world that gets increasingly complicated as it offers more and more choices, and therefore requires more and more decisions. (Should you buy regular, no-knock, lead-free, premium, or super gas? Are the best buys at a discount, specialty, suburban, downtown, import, boutique, or unisex clothes shop? Which are the longest-wearing pantyhose—three for $2 or $3.50 each? Are you better off buying them in the supermarket or by mail order? Should you buy life insurance through your savings bank, your employer, mail order, your favorite brother-in-law, a credit union? Choices, choices. The mind boggles.)

But you do have some things going for you.

Let's go back, for a moment, to where we started from—the fact that you're smarter than you think you are. You may say, "I can't do math, I can't even add two and two," but you are "doing math" every day without giving it a thought. Each time you pay a bus fare, buy a commuter's ticket, divide a recipe for six down to two-and-a-child for dinner, or pay for groceries at the checkout counter, you're "doing math."

You may say, "I can't manage money." But ever since your favorite uncle gave you money to spend as you wished—and you had to make the agonizing choice between saving for next Saturday's matinee vs. the on-the-spot joy of a double-decker ice cream cone—you've been managing money. And since that time you've had to make an infinite number of spending choices, many of them just as agonizing as the movies vs. your stomach. The apartment with a view but the kitchen in the closet vs. the apartment with a gorgeous kitchen and a view of the alley. The run-down house surrounded by huge old trees vs. the development house surrounded by crab grass. The sure promotion to a new job in a strange city vs. the maybe promotion if your boss gets promoted. Steak vs. hamburger. If you've survived these traumas and remained reasonably solvent, you've "managed" your money.

But, you say, I would rather have had an apartment with a view *and* a gorgeous kitchen; two weeks in Spain instead of two weeks at the seashore; more steak, less hamburger. And as you say it you have the nagging feeling that—if only you had managed your money better—you could have had them. So what you're really saying is not that you can't manage money, but that you can't manage it to your satisfaction. Now, starting from this new premise that you *can* manage money, but not as well as you would like, let's take a look at some of the obstacles in your way.

First, there's your unhappy childhood. Too late to do anything about that.

Next, there are the limitations set by where you live and sometimes when you got there. If you live in a part of the country where good housing is scarce and rentals are high, there's not much you can do about that. If you were unlucky enough to buy a house in the late 1960s or in 1970, when mortgage rates peaked, you're paying more for your house than your sister, who bought her house in 1971 when rates had declined. And you're paying much more than your cousin, who bought her house in the early 1960s. Not much you can do about that.

Then there's the general price level of the area in which you live. Your roommate from college who lives in the East, for instance, pays less for clothes than you do, but you don't want to move to the East so you're not going to do anything about that.

And then there are sometimes sources of income other people have that you don't know about—but that lead you to think they manage better than you do.

New York magazine wrote about two families, one suburban and one Manhattan-based, that managed incredibly well on the husbands' salaries in the academic world. The Rosses, with a combined income of about $15,000 and two children, spent about $1,000 annually on a vacation, went to movies and concerts frequently, entertained and ate out without their children at least once a week. How did they do it? Good money management—*plus* free medical care for the children from an uncle who was a pediatrician; partial scholarships from the private school their children attended; and a $7,000 annual trust fund.

The Langstaffs didn't have a trust fund, but they managed a color television set, fine clothes for their daughter and son, and two recent trips to Europe. How did they do it? Again, simple. The TV, most of the children's clothes, and the trips to Europe were gifts from their parents.

(With these little boosts you too could be a superb money manager.)

So you can see that managing money isn't a simple job, a question of stiff upper lip, everybody into the budget pool or anyone can make trillions in his spare time. But you do have things going for you that you may not have thought about.

You're *motivated*. You have the will to do something about your dissatisfactions, or you wouldn't have bought this book.

The timing is right. Ever since Ralph Nader as David aimed his slingshot at General Motors, the Goliath of the automobile industry—and scored a hit—the outlook for consumerism brightened. In recent years we've had the Truth-in-Lending bill, the Fair Credit Reporting Act (more of these later), a more aggressive Federal Trade Commission checking on advertising claims, and consumer groups springing up around the country to fight for their rights. All help us to get our money's worth.

You have some skills. You've been managing all this time, so you have—though you may not believe it—what psychologists call an "entering repertoire." You have a basic body of knowledge, even if it's only your past mistakes, on which to build. You're not really starting from the bottom. You may not soar to the heights, either, and be able to spend every penny wisely and well. But who said that was a necessary goal in life?

Furthermore, you can take advantage of a new tool that's been developed by psychiatrists and psychologists to help you overcome your incorrect or "bad" habits and develop a whole set of new habits and attitudes that will make your job easier. That's what Chapter 2 is all about.

2

How to Cope with
Spending Hang-ups

"A man always has two reasons for doing anything—a good reason and the real reason."
—J. P. Morgan, multimillionaire banker par excellence.

Behavior therapy. It doesn't sound like the kind of language you associate with money management—and, in fact, it isn't. Behavior therapy is a method used by psychiatrists and psychologists to help individuals overcome the personality problems that show up as neurotic behavior, without going through a lengthy psychoanalysis. Dr. Herbert Fensterheim, assistant professor of psychiatry and co-director of the Behavior Therapy Training Program at New York Medical College defines behavior therapy (briefly and necessarily oversimplified) "as the psychological process whereby bad habits may be changed or new and appropriate ones established." The therapy is based on a theory derived in part from the research of the Russian psychologist Ivan Pavlov, and in recent times from the American psychologist Dr. B. F. Skinner, a Harvard professor.

Pavlov's dogs, during his pathbreaking experiments, were trained to associate the ringing of a bell with getting food, since food always followed the ringing. After some time the ringing of the bell would start the dogs salivating, even before the food arrived, since they associated the sound and the food. These experiments were followed by others, where the bell was rung but no food was forthcoming. For a while the dogs continued to salivate at the sound of the bell, but after some time had elapsed, and the dogs learned that the bell no longer meant food, they stopped salivating at the sound. In effect, they *unlearned* their previously learned response.

According to Dr. Fensterheim, this illustrates that learning is a "two-way street." Just as a dog can learn—"be conditioned"—to respond to a stimulus, he can also be conditioned *not* to respond to the same stimulus. Through conditioning people too can learn to respond or not respond to a certain stimulus, and behavior therapy is largely based on this response or no-response premise.

"The behavior therapist treats the symptoms because they are the form of the behavior," he says. "If the symptoms are neurotic it's not because of unresolved unconscious conflict [as a Freudian psychiatrist might interpret it] but because of 'inappropriate learning,'" and behavior therapy says that whatever has been improperly learned can be unlearned and replaced by a more suitable behavior pattern. Dr. Fensterheim has had considerable success using behavior therapy in helping people overcome many problems, from the irresistible impulse to steal automobiles to sexual aberrations. He believes some of the techniques he uses can be used successfully by individuals who have spending problems that prevent them from controlling their finances. Furthermore, the theory can be applied in a common-sense way that is practical, uncomplicated, and without outside professional help. Here is how Dr. Fensterheim suggests you go about it:

1. *Define the behavior to be changed,* i.e., define the problem specifically. Certainly you know that you want to manage your money better, but what is your specific problem? Do you find you can never leave a store without buying something? Do you have a tendency to spend more than you planned, because you can't resist a salesman's pitch? Are you very good at planning budgets but very bad at sticking to them? Do you feel under great pressure to acquire the things that your roommate or your neighbors acquire?

When you define what your particular soft spot is you will then be able to apply the proper remedy.

2. *Define your goals clearly.* There should be no ambiguity. You are going to stay within such and such a portion of your salary and save the remainder, not— you are going to start saving some money.

3. *Decide on the particular program you will follow* to change the behavior you want to change—and plan it on a step-by-step basis, with rewards for each step along the way. Make the reward contingent on the response. (The behavior therapists call this "shaping"—leading the patient step by step in the direction of the desired behavior by a combination of suggestions and reinforcements.)

4. *Keep a careful record* of the step-by-step program you have set up. Once you have defined your goals so that you know what you want to accomplish there can be no equivocating.

5. *Don't expect to go from complete chaos to perfection.* Don't think you can successfully go from big Saturday night dinner-theater-dancing to eating peanuts in front of the TV set; from scooting around in a red Alfa Romeo to walking to work; from shopping only in the best stores to shopping in bargain basements. Have a gradual approach, reward each step of the way, and don't expect to accomplish your aim overnight.

Incidentally, the goals, the rewards, and the "give-ups" can play a very large part in how successful you will be, especially if it is to be a joint decision. Each partner should have individual responsibility and there should also be joint responsibility. And in deciding on the goals each partner should be honest, and really try to communicate his honest thoughts and feelings. In a budget discussion, for instance, each partner must be open and direct in saying what he wants, feels, thinks. And he must be prepared to respect the other person's feelings.

This means that if your goals are questioned by your partner, you have to say, "BUT you have no idea how important it is to me to be able to splurge once a week," or "to have those camera attachments," or "to have a baby sitter one evening." *These questions have to be resolved before the behavior therapy is begun.*

Now to get down to some specifics.

Let's say your problem is budgeting. (More on this in Chapter 3.) First you stop and decide what you want to do about the problem; then where you want to go, in terms of budgeting; then the steps you're going to take to get there.

Let's say further that you are married and would like to save to make a down payment on a house, that you've been trying to put aside some money but so far you've been quite unsuccessful. You're not sure where the money goes, but it goes.

You would start in a very small way, perhaps setting aside a certain amount of money each week to be spent for food. Suppose the wife is the family food shopper. She plans the meals and the shopping so that she stays within the budget for a month. At the end of the month she gets a reward, which has been specified in advance. It could be, for instance, dinner out in a good restaurant, or a bouquet of fresh flowers, or a book she's been anxious to read. Whatever it is the goals are set and abided by and the reward is set and given.

Suppose it is the husband who wants to contribute to the savings fund. Suppose he has gotten into the habit of stopping off with the men at the office for a drink two nights a week. Suppose he decides to come straight home those nights and put the money into the "hope chest." His reward might be a bottle of his favorite wine, or a record, or even something as homely as no hassle if he wants to watch the ball game with no interruptions from spouse, children, or dogs.

You might even want to use visual aids (after all, if it's good enough for the sixth grade and for General Motors it's good enough for you). You could have a chart showing your progress and awarding each other gold stars when you've met your goals for the week. You could put the money in a big glass coffee jar and have visual proof of progress.

A single person applying the same technique would, of course, abide by the same rules: setting a realistic goal, planning a step-by-step program, suitable rewards along the way, and following the program faithfully with no backsliding.

Perhaps you have a different problem—one that can be a real troublemaker —the "keeping up with the Joneses" syndrome. The Dictionary of American Slang dates this term from about 1926, but probably Eve's first neighbor had to go out and get some fancy fig leaves and sew them on her bra as soon as she saw Eve doing it. And her husband must surely have felt he had to get a bigger apple as soon as he saw Adam going around munching and spitting out apple seeds.

There are several aspects to this problem. The first is deciding you *have* to have what the Joneses get, a really conscious competition. Few of us are this openly competitive or such conscious social strivers. Much more dangerous, because it's subsurface, is allowing yourself to drift into the decision: The Joneses got a new car, or a patio, or finished their recreation room in pickled driftwood so I guess we'll have to. And more disconcerting is drifting into the decision not to keep up, but at the same time feeling very dissatisfied. None of these alternatives is satisfactory because *all of them mean a spending decision that is a result of outside pressures rather than internal will or judgment.* And none is conducive to the essence of managing money—the decisions to spend or not to spend should be conscious decisions, so that the *money is under your control.*

Life-style is, after all, a series of alternatives and so is the spending of money. You have to make the original decision that you are going to make conscious choices among the available alternatives—what you want and also what you are willing to forgo. You have to feed vitamins to the inner Jones, the you inside who says and practices: "It's my life and I'm in charge of all my decisions, particularly my spending decisions." Each time you make such a choice, even if it's on a minor matter, you will find the inner Jones getting stronger and more self-confident. In time, it will become an established thought pattern.

Keeping up with the Joneses may affect big spending decisions—but *impulse buying of small items* can have just as devastating an effect on a budget and on your feeling of confidence about your ability to manage your affairs.

If this is your problem set up an absolutely ironclad rule for yourself: I will not buy anything the first time I see it. You may pass up some unbelievable bargains: that black and silver tray that would have looked absolutely superb in your liquor cabinet; a British raincoat at half price; a super dress that's been sold when you come back to the store with your winnings from the baseball pool. Never mind. You learn to resist the blandishments of the stores that know your weakness. You learn to control your impulsiveness, and you are, with each success, reinforcing your confidence in your will power. You will feel much better about yourself, and you will gain self-respect, a very powerful reinforcer.

Suppose you have a different problem—you can't go into a store and just look around without buying something. Take the case of Jill M., a very attractive dancer, who for a time toured with a well-known dance troupe and then settled down in a career as a consumer relations specialist with a major utility company. Jill is no stranger to shopping, to stores, or to dealing with people. And yet she says when she goes shopping, particularly in a good store, she just can't walk out without buying something.

Jill's problem is similar to the problems of many of Dr. Fensterheim's patients. They lack assertiveness and have never learned to say no, even to unreasonable requests. (Dr. Fensterheim cites as an extreme case the patient who, when asked to do something ridiculous, such as crawl across the office floor on his stomach, will agree to do it, saying, "If you think it will help, Doctor.") Such people have to learn to say no. If you have this problem you have to practice saying no by going into stores, trying things on, and not buying them. To develop this skill you then have to practice handling merchandise, staying in stores five minutes, and then going out without buying something. Soon you will learn that the assistant manager doesn't tackle you as you leave and that the worst that will happen is that you will get a grimace from a salesclerk. You will never win a most lovely customer contest, but since that isn't your goal in life, who cares?

A more serious problem is the tendency to be a compulsive shopper—you have twenty-five pairs of shoes in your closet, say, and you feel an irresistible urge to buy number twenty-six. Stop where you are. Silently, to yourself, shout "calm, calm, calm." Relax, take a deep breath, exhale it slowly while letting your muscles go limp, and then continue on your way. If you shop with your best friend it may startle him a bit, but just explain that you are practicing will-power isometrics.

A NEW KIND OF LITTLE BLACK BOOK

Let's say you have none of these problems, but you do have a case of off-and-on spending problems arising from special situations.

Let's say, for instance, that whenever you have a new love affair you know (from past sad experience) that you have a tendency to overspend. And let's say you know further that you're not going to be aware of how much you're going into debt (until it's too late) because you're going to give Cupid and your credit cards a workout. This is the behavior you want to change, and here is one method you can use.

It is, alas, very unromantic. Go forth and invest in a little black book—but not the kind that used to contain interesting addresses and phone numbers. This black book, or red or blue or plaid, is going to be your spending record. Every time you dash out of your office at lunchtime and add another slinky dress to your wardrobe you are going to add another slinky sum to your record of expenditures in your little black book. And every time you skip the special of the day in the company cafeteria to take the beautiful new addition to the staff out for lunch at the elegant restaurant nearby, you're going to add a beautiful new number to your running total of expenditures. It should certainly give you pause.

Remember, though, that this is not a punishment-based theory. Therefore, you are going to allow yourself some leeway. You might set an upper limit on your spending for a week, for instance, and reward yourself appropriately each week as you stick within your limits. In this way, even allowing for affairs of the heart, you are still in control. It's this ability to control that is the major fringe benefit in the process of learning to be a tightwad and to overcome your spending hang-ups. But there are other benefits as well. Developing your will power in managing your money will extend to other areas of your life as you gain confidence and self-respect. Doing without "store-boughten" things and learning to make do with what you have on hand may bring out hidden talents you never knew you had.

The ability to communicate with your partner in money-managing decisions—so often a contentious subject—may make it easier to communicate honestly in other ways. You may fight until you arrive at a compromise, as you discuss goals and assumptions, but at least it won't be a fight about the symbol, money, but about the more basic idea, life-style. And the compromise will be a more realistic one. If you have children, in the course of your own learning—avoiding impulse shopping, developing a resistance to compulsive buying, building a feeling of self-worth and confidence—you are setting an excellent model for them to imitate.

So, single, married, or somewhere in between, this part of the money game pays off in more than dollars and cents.

3

Budgets, Conventional and Otherwise, Or: The Trouble with the Soybean Solution

> "Nobody was ever meant
> To remember or invent
> What he did with every cent."
> —Robert Frost

Now that you've acquired some insight into your obvious and not so obvious spending motivations, and some methods of dealing with your money-managing hang-ups, where do you start?

One possibility is a budget.

A budget can be a wonderful device for relieving anxiety, especially when you've been overspending. Nothing will make you feel better than to draw up a list of all the things you spend money on—and decide to eliminate new clothes, vacations, hairdressers or barbers, cigars, peppermints, coffee breaks, beer drinking, bowling, dinners out, and anniversary cards. You make a solemn pledge to live on nothing but soybeans for one week of every month, and you're immediately convinced this is positively the last time your bank account will be overdrawn. This makes you feel so virtuous you bring out the bottle of champagne you've been hoarding since New Year's Eve, and you celebrate the dawning of a new era of financial splendor and solvency.

But of course this kind of budget won't last, because the kind of person who could stick to such a self-denying way of life wouldn't have gotten into such a mess in the first place. Most of us, even if we love soybeanburgers, are not disciplined enough to adopt the "soybean solution"—but we're not totally without inner resources either. The trick is to find an approach to money matters that is not masochistic but gives some control based on personal preferences, personality, short- and long-term goals. Is this possible? With some thought and planning on your part, plus the right-for-you psychological attitude, the answer is yes.

Consider, first of all, whether you're more inclined to be a grasshopper or an ant.

In the Aesop fable, you'll remember, the grasshopper played all summer and didn't bother to store food for the winter. He had a marvelous time while the busy ant worked and worked with no time off to play, storing food for the winter. When winter came the grasshopper appeared at the door of the anthill, shivering and starving, and tried to get a crumb or two. The ant chased him away, saying he should have thought of providing for the winter during those long summer days.

If you're inclined to be almost 100 per cent grasshopper the very word "budget" may turn you off. It's probably a waste of time for you to draw up a detailed budget or even an extensive "plan." Your chances of staying with your plan are minimal; your chances of being depressed if you fail are maximal. You may even go out and buy something extravagant, to relieve your feelings of depression and hopelessness. If this is how you feel, based on past experience, and you think that even the suggestions in Chapter 2 won't help you much, you may be quite right in your personal assessment. Dr. Fensterheim frequently gets calls from would-be patients who ask him if he will help them give up smoking. Dr. Fensterheim replies that he would love to—but he hasn't been able to give up smoking himself! However, you have alternatives.

Consider Ellen W., who earned a good salary as a researcher in a large bank in a metropolitan area. Surrounded as she was by talk of money and thrift Ellen was very self-conscious about her runaway spending habits. She tried very hard to follow the suggestions in the "manage your money" pamphlets available at the bank, but the suggestions didn't do her much good. She just couldn't seem to resist spending her whole salary, and clothes were her particular weakness. Nor could she bring herself to work out a budget—she'd tried once or twice but the whole idea had been just too distasteful and she'd given up. Yet she was worried about not having a "cushion" to fall back on if she had some emergency and needed money. And she found herself getting positively snappish when she was teased at lunchtime about being the last of the big-time spenders.

Finally Ellen saw that she wasn't going to change her personality, she liked being able to splurge, but she also wanted to have some financial security. She decided she needed some help, which she got in a very simple way. She had the bank automatically deduct a small sum from her paycheck every month and deposit the money in a savings account. She deposits the remainder of her paycheck in her checking account, pays her share of the rent on the apartment she shares with another young career woman, and keeps enough to cover her daily expenses. What's left is her "to hell with it" money.

If she sees a dress in a shop window that she absolutely adores she buys it with no feeling of guilt. If it means she doesn't get to a movie that month—tough. Some months she sees lots of movies, some months she splurges in other ways. But her basic needs are taken care of, she finds she manages eventually to get all the things she really wants, and, most important, she has a savings account. She's lost the feeling she can't control her own affairs, she no longer feels guilty about her extensive wardrobe, and she takes the lunchtime teasing with good humor.

Kathe and Jim M. had a different problem. Kathe came from a comparatively poor home where living on a budget had been refined to an art. It was natural for her to count pennies, shop carefully, handle her clothes so they would last, walk to save carfare. (To this day, she says, she can still hear her mother's voice saying, "You can only wear one dress at a time.") Jim, however, came from a more comfortable home where the word "budget" was never mentioned. He detested worrying about money, but was as anxious as Kathe to save for the baby they hoped to have some-day. After many arguments they realized their outlook on money was incompatible —but they were not. They decided who would pay for what out of their joint income, set up allowances for each, and then arranged that each would contribute a set amount to their joint savings account. Kathe decided she would accumulate her share by practicing the little economies that were really second nature to her. Jim, however, decided it was easier for him to contribute his share by bartending on Friday nights. He enjoys the feeling that he doesn't have to count pennies and— since he's naturally gregarious and his regular job involves little dealing with peo-ple—he also enjoys the friendly contacts at the neighborhood bar.

Though neither Ellen, Kathe, nor Jim was aware of it, they were following the sound psychological principles discussed in Chapter 2: adapting a particular kind of budget to a particular life-style. Each recognized his own strengths and built on them, allowing for the spending attitudes and habits that had been acquired pre-viously—what psychologists call the "entering repertoire." Each arrived at the same end—control over expenditures in order to achieve a goal—by different means. None of these means are either "right" or "wrong"; they are simply different to accommodate different personalities. In keeping with the "positive reinforcement" principle each has short-run rewards: Ellen, her freedom to splurge; Kathe and Jim, watching their savings account grow monthly—without feeling "put upon" and without the quarrels and recriminations they'd had before as each tried to impose on the other his own rules about how money should be handled. The budgets were no longer strait jackets, confining the individuals to a rigidity they resented; instead, the budgets were stretch suits, designed to "give" a little here and there while holding their basic shape.

Can you do it too? Of course you can. You'll need to decide, if you haven't done so already, where you fit on the grasshopper-ant scale, whether you will enjoy a more structured arrangement, without keeping track of every penny, or whether you pre-fer a more casual approach. Then you will need some kind of budget plan. You might even think of it as a game plan, with the object to get to the finish line— control of your finances—despite all the obstacles (a boss who doesn't appreciate your true worth and therefore doesn't immediately double your salary; ridiculous prices for everything you want; an unfortunate penchant for beef rib roasts and scotch liquor instead of lamb shanks and low-calorie soda). You'll play the game in your own way at your own pace, alone or as a team. And since it's a game of skill, not luck, you'll get more proficient as you get more practice.

You won't need much in the way of game equipment—just some things in which to "keep score," such as a notebook, a pen or pencil, and maybe some envelopes for stashing away receipts. "Keeping score" will consist of learning how your money is spent and then making any changes you think are necessary in order to arrive at the finish line—control—sooner. You'll want to set up some system of record keep-ing; it can be as simple or elaborate as you choose. But, regardless of your system, there are some basic elements in planning a budget.

You need to know the amount of money you have to spend. It's nice if you must use an adding machine to total your income from stocks, bonds, rental of your yacht, and fees for your advice on a variety of subjects, from the best way to chill champagne to how to supervise the upstairs maid. If this isn't your problem, just take a pencil and paper and total your annual income from salary or salaries, bonuses, commissions, interest on savings accounts, tips, dividends. From this total subtract what you have to pay in taxes. The remainder is what you actually have to spend—the pie that you're going to cut up.

You need to know your expenses, both fixed and flexible. Fixed expenses are those you really can't change—at least not in the period of a year. They include what you spend annually for such things as: housing, various kinds of insurance, utilities (heat, gas, electric, phone), installment payments, tuition, transportation, union or professional association dues, contributions to pension plans, etc. *Flexible* expenses are those that vary, and some of the variability is under your control. (We'll get back to this point in a minute.) Flexible expenses include money spent for such things as:

Food
Services—laundry, dry cleaning, personal care (barbers and beauticians), gardeners, window
     washers
Household maintenance—repairs on house and appliances, upkeep on house and grounds
Clothing
Car maintenance
Health care, not covered by health insurance plans—doctors, dentists, opticians, medicines
Allowances for daily living expenses—coffee breaks, newspapers, cigarettes, etc.
Recreation—from movies to vacations
Gifts
Charitable contributions

One of the first things you realize, when you look at this list, is that while some of these expenses are "flexible," i.e., subject to change, the flexibility isn't under your control. This is particularly true of doctor bills, automobile repairs, and household repairs, such as a complete breakdown of the heater (usually on a weekend during a record-breaking cold spell). This leads to the next point:

You need to have an emergency fund. Ideally it should be 10 per cent of your income, put in a savings account so you can withdraw funds as needed, but, in the meantime, the money is in the bank earning interest. You shouldn't think of this savings account as your little nest egg for vacations, a new color television set, or a moving-picture camera. It is an emergency fund to cope with unexpected medical bills, major household disasters—or to tide you over if you lose your job. Many people found to their intense surprise during the mini-recession of 1969–70 that so-called "lifetime jobs" meant the lifetime of a government contract, not the lifetime of an individual. An emergency fund guarantees a breathing spell, a time in which to look around, to think, without having to jump into the first job that comes along just to meet bills coming due. *This breathing spell can make a difference in your lifetime career.*

How can you establish what your expenses are? There are several ways. Going back over your old checkbooks will give you a pretty good idea of where some of your money went. Charge account payments will also help, particularly if they were made to stores that sell only clothes, or household goods. Credit card payments will show how much those nights out amounted to; doctor and dentist bills will remind you of your bellyaches and toothaches. You can take some pretty educated guesses on the amounts you spend at the supermarket or the butcher's. And you can probably do fairly well estimating how much you give away to charity and how many engagement, wedding, baby, and graduation gifts you'll have to give and how much they'll cost. What may surprise you is adding up all your daily expenses and suddenly realizing how much money you nickel, dime, and quarter away.

Suppose you are just starting out—first job, or first apartment on your own, or new marriage—and you really haven't the slightest idea what anything costs or how much you spend for any of the flexible items, except that you never have any money left at the end of each paycheck. What do you do? Then you have to keep fairly detailed records, admittedly a chore. But you don't have to do it forever; a month should be enough time to get some idea of what things cost and how you spend your money. You might carry around a little book with columns headed food, carfare, clothing, extravagances, etc. and make your entries. You don't have to bother really to keep track of the pennies. Round off the figures, making all the $1.49 expenditures $1 and all the $1.51 expenditures $2, and you'll come close enough for your budget purposes. When you've been virtuous like this for a month you'll have enough data to get a budget going.

You need to decide on realistic goals. A budget has to have a purpose, since the choices to be made depend on what's to be achieved. (If you're planning to invest in a yacht, for instance, you'll have to decide to save more than $5 a month.) If you want to save for a down payment on a house you may be willing to cut down drastically on your vacation plans. If you want a longer than usual vacation you may decide to get along without a new winter coat. If you want to go to school at night to increase your earning potential you may forgo a new couch. These are the choices to be made and they're not easy.

This is a good time to reiterate some of the psychological aspects of spending and budgeting that I talked about in Chapter 2. When deciding on your goals and how to achieve them there's little point in attempting the soybean solution (i.e., depriving yourself of just about everything you enjoy) just because you're dissatisfied with how you've handled money in the past. Your object is not to punish yourself because you've been a naughty boy or girl, but to get on with the job in the best, most-likely-to-succeed way. If two of you are involved in the planning each has to be prepared to accept (cheerfully, if possible) the feelings of the other about what is and what isn't important. Nothing is easier, for the non-smoker, than to economize by giving up a cigarette allowance. And the smoker who habitually reaches for a cigarette instead of a sweet finds it correspondingly easy to forgo hot fudge sundaes and Danish pastries with the morning coffee. While it's true that non-smokers and thin people have longer life expectancy, that's not what's relevant here. The real argument against this approach is that it won't work.

What will work is making decisions that are reasonable for you, after you've looked at your spending profile and the places where you really have some choice. Then you can decide where it's feasible to cut down, to postpone, or to eliminate altogether. Before you make these decisions, a little simple arithmetic is in order. You start with your after-tax income, subtract from it your emergency fund and the total of your flexible expenses, and the remainder is available for the special goals you have in mind. If it all works out to your satisfaction you already have a well-balanced budget. You may have very little more to do except to decide that you want to cut a little here and add a little there.

But what if a slight problem arises? You follow the method faithfully. You write down your after-tax income. In a separate column you total all your flexible expenses based on old bills which you firmly believe are pretty realistic. You set aside 10 per cent of your income for an emergency fund. You subtract the flexible expenses and the emergency fund from your income, and make a basic discovery. You're *sure* you can't afford an emergency fund, gifts, movies—and you even have doubts about clothes and eating. How can you have a budget on that basis?

Obviously you can't. You have several possibilities at this point.

1. You may find it feasible and not too difficult to make some changes in your flexible expenses to bring you the results you want. Just to be sure you don't miss any options, check the list of "Money-Saving Questions" on page 17.

2. You may, since you started with educated "guesstimates," have to go back and keep more accurate records. Don't forget, you have an unseen enemy in this battle of the budget: inflation. Your actual expenditures may have gone up more than you realized because of rising prices. Or you may be spending more on impulse items—gadgets, records, jewelry—than you're aware of, particularly if you're picking up these items while just strolling through a store on your lunch hour. In other words, there's a leak in your spending plan somewhere, and you've got to find it.

Finding it will require some record keeping. I've tried two methods and both worked. One was to keep a running record of expenses in a little book—as recommended for people just starting out (see page 10). The other method, and the one I like a little better, is to cash a check at the beginning of the week, divide the cash in little envelopes labeled food, entertainment, household expenses, personal allowances (including money for children's allowances) and see how far the money goes. After a given period of time, say a month, using either method, you have a pretty good idea of precisely how you spend your money.

One of the fringe benefits of doing either of these things is that you get immediate feedback, i.e., you suddenly become much more conscious both of prices and of how and where your money goes. You begin to think twice before you succumb to the temptation to buy something on impulse.

3. With a more current picture of your spending you can draw up a much more realistic budget; you may very well remake it with a new slant on what you can and cannot afford. Oddly enough, though making these decisions may seem confining, the opposite is true. You will feel more free because you've established some kind of routine and some limits. Then within the limits, there's no need at all to count pennies, or to be troubled by "can I or can't I afford this?" You may be a prince at the beginning of the week and a pauper at the end, but you won't be out of control.

And that's very important in acquiring confidence in yourself and your ability to handle your affairs.

4. You may have to accept the real possibility that on your current income, *no matter how well you manage,* you really can't save any money, have an emergency fund, or do more than barely meet your current expenses. If this is the case you may be relieved to discover it's not poor management but just plain not enough income that is causing your problems. Obviously, then, you've got to consider another job that pays more, a part-time job in addition to the one you have, or a job for the wife of the family if she hasn't been working up to this point.

There are still some unanswered questions. The first is—what period of time should a budget cover? Most people feel that a year is a feasible period. It's a comparatively simple starting base, since so many of the figures you start with, salary, taxes, insurance, are already on an annual basis. Furthermore, at this stage in your life you will probably want to re-evaluate where you stand, what you want, where you're going at the end of about a year. However, there is nothing, absolutely nothing, that says you have to stay with a budget for a year if it doesn't suit you. You may find three months or six months is right for you. It may prove, in fact, to be the best time period if you're just starting on your own, if you're recently married, or if you've never attempted to budget before.

The second question is, who should manage the money? Usually there's one person in the family who is better at it, or who has more time. Fine. Motivation or ability plus time is a dandy combination—up to a point. But I firmly believe that the non-manager should get some experience also—even if a little gentle coercion is needed. Everyone should have to do the grocery shopping once in a while, maybe just once a month or every two months, just to see how much money it takes to fill a few grocery bags. And everyone should have to sit down and write the checks and make the deductions in the checkbook, just to see how easy it is to deplete what looked like a respectable-size bank balance. I believe in one person having the major responsibility, since that's the most efficient way to handle the question. But I also believe that the roles should be shifted on some kind of regular basis. It will result in fewer arguments about money, and easier-to-arrive-at and easier-to-balance budgets.

(If you have children, and they are old enough to understand, they should sit in on the budget discussions and learn early in the game that money doesn't grow in pay envelopes. And if they're old enough to have allowances they should be permitted to handle them as they want to, making mistakes just as adults do, so that they too will learn how to manage money.)

Money-Saving Questions

Food: Can you bring your lunch from home? Not every day of the week, because that would cut you off from contacts that you need both professionally and also because it's more fun—but say on Mondays and Wednesdays. Can you get together with friends and decide you'll only give dinner parties with limited menus, saving money and trouble all around? Can you get together with another "single" and save money by buying for two, helping to use up each other's leftovers?

Services: Can you be just a little less fastidious and cut down on your cleaning and laundry bills? Can you form a baby-sitting pool so that you pay for sitters in corresponding time, not money? Can you learn to cut your spouse's hair?

Household Maintenance: Can you paint the outside yourself? Can you postpone putting in rosebushes until next year? Can you learn how to do simple plumbing jobs yourself?

Clothes: Can you plan your purchases so that you take advantage of sales? Can you shop in stores that have fewer services but lower prices? Can you get together with other families with young children and arrange for a central exchange for outgrown clothing?

Recreation: Can you wait to see popular movies until they're at your neighborhood movie house, instead of at the more expensive first-run theaters? Can you postpone buying best-seller books until they come out in paperback? Can you plan an off-season vacation to take advantage of lower rates? Can you look into what's free or cheap in your city and have an evening in a little ethnic cafe instead of a big, expensive nightclub?

Gifts: Can you start cuttings of your favorite house plants, and plant them in pretty, inexpensive pots as hostess gifts? Can you knit, crochet, carve, or bake Christmas presents?

Finally, a few suggestions for making the whole scene easier.

1. Keep the budget and the record keeping simple and easy.

2. Don't try to account for every penny. Once the spending limits have been set, relax and enjoy the fruits of your day's work.

3. Have some kind of filing system. And if two of you use it, have a system that both understand. Set aside one drawer, or one file box, or one space in a closet, and keep in it receipts, bills, canceled checks, bank statements, installment loan books, tax records, and a copy of your budget. It will make the job easier, and you'll love yourself at income tax time. Your checkbook—and be sure you get one from the bank that has lots of space in which to keep records—can be a running account book if you will write in it a brief note stating what the check was for, e.g., Jones' Department Store, $20.22 (bath towels).

Keep in mind that the first budget is the most difficult. But if you plan it well on sound psychological principles, adapt it to changing circumstances, and live with it for a predecided length of time, you'll find that the new approach will become almost second nature. In a while you will find that you are really in control, and that will be satisfying both to your ego *and* to your bank balance.

The Case of the Compulsive Gambler, Or: Where to Turn If You Are Hopelessly in Debt

Consider the extreme case of Murray L., whose earnings as a manufacturer's representative increased until he made well over $40,000 a year. The L.'s lived modestly with their two young children in a four-room apartment in a good neighborhood in Brooklyn. Yet they were forever in and out of debt because Mr. L. couldn't resist the lure of nearby race tracks. He never lost control completely, or the family would have been bankrupt. But he did lose enough money to keep the family in debt.

For several years a friendly banker who worked with Mr. L.'s business account would periodically help clear up Mr. L.'s personal debts. But once they were cleared Mr. L. would get into trouble all over again. (A psychiatrist might say that Mr. L.'s problem was that of many gamblers: "engaged in a desperate struggle to force fate, or Lady Luck, to show them favor—perhaps because as children they felt their own mothers weren't nice to them, didn't favor them.) Finally, the banker pointed out to the L.'s something they had begun to realize themselves: a more drastic solution was necessary. On the advice of the banker they put all their finances in the hands of an accountant who managed their money, paid their bills, and doled out to Mr. L. the funds he needed.

If your problems are as serious as Mr. L.'s you too may need professional help. One place to get it is through one of the more than a thousand Consumer Credit Counseling Services located throughout the country. They are very often sponsored by the National Foundation for Consumer Credit and are specifically geared to help families who have debt problems they cannot solve themselves. The Foundation is supported by funds donated by local business, banking, and other financial firms as a public service. Frequently the services themselves have the co-operation of local attorneys, the Better Business Bureau, trade associations, and merchants. Since creditors are just as anxious as debtors to clear up the bills, the services can usually work out long-term arrangements that are helpful in getting families back on their feet.

Foundation-sponsored services usually display their distinctive logo, see illustration below, which you should look for before committing yourself, to be sure you are dealing with a legitimate agency and not a commercial debt consolidation service that may simply get you into more debt.

To get the address of a Foundation-sponsored counseling service near you write to the National Foundation for Consumer Credit, Inc., Federal Bar Building West, 1819 H Street, N.W., Washington, D.C. 20006.

Copyright 1962, 1964, 1965, 1968
National Foundation for Consumer Credit, Inc.

The symbol or "certification mark" shown above is owned by the National Foundation for Consumer Credit, and will be used to identify the Consumer Credit Counseling Services participating in a nationwide program under the sponsorship of the Foundation and its co-operating associations. The use of this symbol is confined to those organizations which the National Foundation for Consumer Credit can certify are participating in this unique program. Use of this seal or symbol by others is prohibited.

4

Does It Make a Difference Where You Save Your Millions? Yes.

"Money is like manure—good only when spread around."
—Carl Sandburg

Are you worried about where to keep that million dollars you just won by cleverly having the right code number on your magazine subscription?

You didn't win? It was someone with a name like yours? Sorry about that.

Well then, do you have a somewhat smaller sum on hand that you would like to deposit or save in the most advantageous way? Would you believe $1,000?

Just to make life simple let's assume that you have the tidy little sum of $1,000, and you plan to use $500 for your day-to-day expenses and for paying bills. The remaining $500 is going into savings.

Expenses and bills first. You want to pay bills by check because it's the most convenient way. In addition your canceled checks are proof of payments, the checkbook stubs let you see where your money has gone and, when income tax time comes, are a record of expenses that are tax-deductible. So there are many advantages to opening a checking account. The question is where? Since, by law, only commercial banks can offer checking accounts it has to be in a commercial, not a savings bank. Safety is no problem, because just about all bank accounts, whether savings or checking, are insured up to $20,000 by various government agencies. (Look for the sign that says your account is insured.)

The next question, if you have a choice among several commercial banks, is which one? Banks, like other privately owned businesses, compete with each other, and offer different terms. So, if dollars and cents is your prime consideration, you'll want to shop around and get the best terms. (There are other considerations, such as convenience, which we'll get to later, but for the moment, let's concentrate on the money side.)

One way in which commercial banks differ is their service charge for checking accounts. Most banks have two kinds, regular and special. *Regular accounts* are supposedly "free," but the price of this "free" service is maintaining an average minimum balance in the account, usually a minimum of several hundred dollars, and up. If you don't maintain this balance there is a sliding scale of charges—the lower the balance, the higher the charge, up to several dollars per month.

In contrast to this type of account is the *special account,* which requires no minimum balance. Instead, you pay for each check as used plus a minimum monthly service charge. Here again banks differ; some charge less per check and more for the service charge and vice versa. Some banks don't bother with a service charge if you use more than ten checks a month, some have a different minimum. Again, you have to shop around to see which bank offers the most service for the lowest charge.

How can you decide whether a regular or special checking account is best for you? It will depend on how many checks you write—how much "activity" there is in your account, as the bankers say. If you don't write many checks you'll probably be better off with a special checking account; if you're forever cashing checks and paying bills you'll probably do better with a regular account. Since we're talking about $500 one possibility is to keep $300 in a savings account; at 5 per cent simple interest* it would earn about $15 a year, and the remainder of your $500, or $200, would be reserved for running expenses in a special checking account that might cost you $1.75 per month for ten checks, or $21 a year. If you subtract from this $21 the $15 earned interest you see that your special checking account would cost you about $6 a year. Contrast this with the cost of keeping a balance of $500 in a regular account in order to write as many checks as you please at a yearly cost of about $16 a year. You're ahead with a special account by about $10. (I use "about" when discussing earned interest because it is taxable, which has to be considered.)

All of this high finance points up one very important fact in discussing banking accounts, savings accounts, and interest rates. Unhappily, unless there are thousands of dollars involved, the savings in actual dollars and cents usually don't add up to much more than the price of a new shirt or one good restaurant meal. This doesn't mean that the shirt isn't better on your back than on a banker's back, or that the meal isn't tastier in your stomach—but, bank advertising to the contrary, nobody gets rich from interest on bank accounts unless he's rich to start with. If there are exceptions to this rule they are the advertising agencies that do bank promotion or the newspapers and the radio and television stations that publish or broadcast the bank's messages.

That Old Devil Bank Statement

You're all set to confound your roommate, your boss, and the second-grade teacher who failed you in finger painting by becoming a millionaire next Tuesday. There's one small drawback, however.

After all those pencils sharpened, and erasers worn away, and hours spent adding, subtracting, and swearing—you finally realize you just can't make your checkbook agree with your monthly bank statement.

Relax. Neither can lots of other people, including some who should find the task easy.

---

* "Plain" interest, or interest that isn't compounded.

Take my friend Sylvia P., for instance, who teaches advanced mathematics, statistics, and calculus at a fine liberal arts college. She's had trouble doing it for years. Finally she asked the head of her department—a renowned mathematician— how he did it. Simple, he said. Whenever his checkbook gets too mixed up he has a quick solution: he changes banks.

Even people who do at least try to reconcile their checkbooks monthly have very different views on what balancing means. Conscientiousness ranges from one prosperous matron I know who balances the joint account "down to the last penny," to a busy X-ray specialist who says, "It's OK if it's within a hundred bucks." Some bankers estimate that from 50 to 75 per cent of depositors reconcile their statements to no closer than two to three dollars, judging that their personal time is worth more than the time it would take to find the error, and judging also that the bank is probably right.

If this is how you feel or if you are in the 2 to 5 per cent of individuals who have no difficulty always reconciling the statement down to the last penny, turn the page.

But if you would like to do a better job, you'll be interested in the things that bank customers do wrong. How do banks know these are the common errors? From their experience with customers who come in and say the bank has made a mistake in their balance and they're not really overdrawn. Then an employee of the bank goes over the checkbook. Usually (but not always) it is the customer who loses the argument.

Here are the common errors, and the things you should watch out for, when entering checks or trying to reconcile your checkbook.

Never borrow deposit tickets. Sure, you cross off your friend's account number and write in your own number in bold letters. But the computer can't "read" your nice neat handwriting; it can only read encoded letters. So the deposit is credited to your friend, who becomes temporarily richer; you become temporarily poorer, both accounts are messed up, and you hate yourself in the morning.

Watch out for transposed figures. Your balance is $247.67 but when you transfer the balance to the next page in your checkbook you write $274.67. The error happens, of course, during a month when you're short, and you are overdrawn before you know it.

Have a system for reminding yourself to enter loose checks. You don't want to be bothered carrying around your checkbook so you carry a few checks, which you use but forget to enter. What a shock when you see you're $92 poorer than you thought you were! If two of you have a joint account the possibility of error seems to be quadrupled, instead of doubled. Tie a strong string around your finger, slip a rubber band around your wrist, make an entry in your datebook, write a note on the calendar, put a note on the baby's car seat, on your desk—do anything but *don't trust to your memory.*

Don't forget to deduct bank service charges or per check charges. These aren't big sums, but their effect is cumulative if you neglect to enter them—and first thing you know you're discouraged because your figures are so different from the bank's.

Examine your statement to be sure all the deposits have been entered, and then that all the checks sent to you really belong to you. This is one of the first things banks do when customers ask them to check their accounts, since this is where bank errors may be made.

One way to avoid errors is to stop after every three checks, add them up, subtract the sum you get from the balance in your checkbook *before* you deducted the same three checks. The number you get should be the same as the running balance in your checkbook. Here's what I mean:

Checkbook		Doublecheck		
balance	$420.00	balance	$420	
check A	60.00			$420.00
	$360.00		$60.00	101.15
			25.15	$318.85
check B	25.15		16.00	
	334.85		$101.15	
check C	16.00			
	$318.85——————agrees with——————$318.85			

If the numbers do agree you can proceed; if they don't, you can stop and look to see where the mistake is, and you only have to go back three checks to find it.

Doing this doublecheck has made my job much easier: it may do the same for you.

Incidentally, if you get into a real mess, and you can't straighten it out yourself, you can go in and ask the bank to help you. They may not be keen to do it, and you may have to leave your checkbook with them until the job is done, but it is a real possibility. And once you are off on a fresh start you may enjoy the challenge of keeping your checkbook current.

INTEREST, INTEREST, WHO PAYS MORE INTEREST?

Another way in which banks differ is the rate of interest they pay. Banks are businesses and what they sell is money; money which they lend at a price in order to earn the profit that enables them to stay in business. But they have to have their stock in trade, money, in order to earn their profit. Where do they get the money? From you, when you make a deposit in the bank. If you put your money in a checking account the money is in and out, as you deposit and withdraw, and the bank is never sure how much it will have on hand to lend. But if you put it in a savings account for a specified period of time the bank can lend a portion of it with some certainty that you're not going to ask for it. The bank is willing to pay you an annual fee, *interest,* for this certainty, which you can think of as the price or rate paid to you for renting your money for a year. (Just to add to the confusion it may also be called the annual yield, or annual rate of return, or effective annual rate.) The interest is calculated as a percentage of your account; a 5 per cent annual interest rate on a deposit of $500, for instance, would pay you $25 at the end of the year, if you leave your money in the bank for the year. If you withdraw it before the year is up you get a part of the 5 per cent annual rate—how big a part depends on how long the money was in the account. If it was left for half a year you would get half of the $25, or $12.50; for a quarter of a year a quarter of the $25, or $6.25.

The interest rates are set by the Federal Reserve Board, and they vary from time to time as the "Fed," as it's popularly known, attempts to adjust the supply of money to the needs of the economy.

The Fed's regulations say that commercial banks cannot pay as high a rate as the mutual savings banks and the savings and loan associations, also known in the banking trade as the "thrifts." (The savings banks and the savings and loan associations are somewhat different in structure, but for our purposes we can treat them as one.) The difference in rate varies about ½ of a percentage point, perhaps 4½ per cent at a commercial bank and 5 per cent at a thrift. (The idea behind this rate differential, by the way, is to keep money flowing into the thrifts, since they use much of the money to finance home mortgages. While commercial banks also finance some mortgages, this is not their main business. Why is it important to keep money in the thrifts? Because if such deposits decline, as has happened sometimes in the past when savers could get more interest just as safely elsewhere, mortgage money "dries up." Then home buyers find it very difficult to get mortgages at a price they can afford.)

Obviously, if you have your choice between a passbook account at a commercial bank or at a thrift you'll earn more interest at a thrift. However, these aren't your only choices. As I mentioned before, money is the banks' basic stock in trade and just as an apple farmer without apples to sell would go out of business, so a bank without money to lend would go out of business. In order to get money, your money, banks have come up with many different attractions. (During the weeks that I was writing this chapter, as a premium for opening a savings account I could have gotten a variety of gadgets to brighten my kitchen, curl my hair, make serving dinner easier, or help my husband shave. I could also have made a donation to the local library that would have been matched by the bank, or received six months of free checking.)

A more common way banks use to attract depositors is to vary the interest rate they pay. One of the methods you're probably most familiar with is compounding of interest, i.e., the bank will take the $500 you've deposited, pay interest on it at the specified rate, and then, as subsequent payments come due, pay interest on the original sum plus interest on the interest that's been added. Since interest piles on interest, when banks say they compound interest daily or even every second, it sounds like a lot of money. Unfortunately, as I've noted before in my cynical way, unless you start with lots of money, the big difference that comes from earning the much-advertised "big 6.2 interest" compared with the (little?) 6 per cent usually won't do more than buy you a seat on the bus or several ice cream cones.

There are other differentials: some banks have grace days so that money deposited before the tenth of the month will earn interest as if it had been deposited at the beginning of the month, or money withdrawn three days before the end of a quarter will earn interest as if it had remained in the bank until the very last minute of the quarter. Again, unless really substantial amounts of money are involved the difference in dollars and cents is very small.

WHAT'S IN A NAME, OR:
OTHER KINDS OF SAVINGS ACCOUNTS

The differences don't stop here. In addition to the passbook account there are other ways in which you can save, at either a commercial or a savings institution, and earn various yields. These longer-term accounts have various names: certificates of deposit, investment certificates, savings certificates, and maybe some new names by the time you read this book. The yield changes depending on the length of time involved and your freedom to get the money back either quickly or slowly, with or without forfeiting some of the interest. The lowest rate of return, naturally, is for the shortest period of time offering you the greatest freedom. If you, for instance, want to be able to withdraw your money at a moment's notice, but have it earning interest while it's in the bank, you will prefer a day-of-deposit to day-of-withdrawal account, which has the lowest interest rate. If you are willing to leave your money in the bank for a longer period—a year, perhaps, or two, or longer—you will get a higher rate of return.

The bank guarantees that it will pay you a given rate of return for the specified period, say 6 per cent for fourteen months; you in turn guarantee that you won't ask for the money until the fourteen months has passed. If an emergency arises and you find you must withdraw the money before the time limit the bank won't throw you out in the snow with a hungry baby. It will, however, penalize you for your poor crystal-ball gazing by deducting some interest.

If you feel bewildered by all these different arrangements, types of accounts, ways of computing interest, variety of grace days, etc. don't for a minute think you are stupid, or that the subject is beyond you. Several years ago Jackie Pinson, a graduate student at Kansas State University, spent months researching the ease of comparing different types of savings accounts. She took a hypothetical savings account, made hypothetical deposits and withdrawals, *and* worked out the yield in forty accounts using five ways of calculating interest and four other variables: frequency of compounding, frequency of crediting, number of grace days, and possible penalties for some withdrawals. Then she asked eight savings institutions to compare their methods with hers, and make their own calculations if they used some methods different from hers. None of the institutions arrived at the same yield, though each used the same six-month time span and the same rate. Ms. Pinson and her professor, Richard Morse, head of the Family Economics Department at Kansas State, agreed that if a graduate student doing intensive research couldn't make comparisons easily, the average saver would find the task just about impossible.

THINGS TO PONDER WHEN YOU CHOOSE WHERE TO SAVE

How then are you to decide which type of account is best for you? Consider the factors listed below in making your decisions. Keep in mind that although in the beginning you may not have much money to save, and differences in accounts may not amount to huge sums, you are acquiring good experience and knowledge in handling your monetary affairs; in the long run this may prove more valuable than the interest you earn on your bank accounts. Then, when you do have more money it will all be so easy you'll be able to devote most of your time to sailing your yacht, furnishing your home with antiques, or collecting rare butterflies in exotic places. So here are the things to consider before you choose the lucky bank that is going to get your account.

1. *Consider your time.* If you know you'll make deposits much more faithfully if the bank is around the corner from your home or office, or if you have to go into the bank anyway to cash a check and deposit your pay, this may be more important than, or as important as, a differential between an interest rate of 5¾ per cent

vs. 6 per cent. In other words, it's better to be getting 5¾ per cent on $10 deposited every week than 6 per cent on $25 deposited whenever you have the time to get to the bank, which may be never.

2. *Consider whether you may or may not need the money in the near future.* If you don't, as mentioned before, you can earn more with a longer-term investment, especially if this is a way of forcing yourself to save. How long should the "longer" term be? At this stage of your life probably about two years would be long enough. For one thing, your plans are liable to change and you will need the money for something you can't foresee at the moment. For another thing, tying up your money for any length of time is in some ways a gamble, since interest rates do change. If you have a 6 per cent savings certificate for two years, for instance, and the interest rate in the meantime drops to 4 per cent, you've won. On the other hand, the rate might just as easily go up to 8 per cent, and you've lost. So flexibility may be your best bet.

If you are going to be making fairly frequent deposits and withdrawals, however, you are better off with a day-of-deposit to day-of-withdrawal account.

3. *Consider the services you might want from the bank in the future.* If you think you will want a house and a mortgage it may pay you to have a savings account in a bank that gives mortgages. As a regular customer you are more apt to get preference and help than as an "outsider." On the other hand, if it's important to have the bank do your saving for you you may prefer a commercial bank that will automatically take money out of your checking account and put it in a savings account.

After taking these factors into consideration here are some other things to check off:

1. Get the most frequent compounding of interest—you might as well, even if it is a very small amount.

2. Take advantage of grace days accounts if they coincide or are easily adapted to your own deposit days.

3. Unless you have a day-of-deposit to day-of-withdrawal account, don't withdraw money without asking how much interest you will lose. You may lose all the interest for a quarter even though you are withdrawing the very last minute of the very last day of the quarter. It may sometimes even pay to borrow the money from the bank if you only need the money for a few days, since the cost of such a short-term loan could be less than the interest loan.

4. Don't hesitate to change your type of account as your needs change.

Finally, though it's part of financial jargon to talk of the "privileges" you have at a bank, the fact is that the bank couldn't exist without you and your money. You are both customer and supplier and as such you have a perfect right to get all the information you want about what's best for you. So if you have any questions, don't hesitate to walk right in and ask for answers from an officer of the bank. As you'll learn in Chapter 8, whether "he's" a Mr. or a Ms. he wants your business.

Love and Honor, Yes!
But a Joint Checking Account?

Do you prefer the old-fashioned "togetherness" marriage style, the most recent "open marriage," with each of you free to pursue separate interests and careers, or something flexible in between? Whichever your choice there are some dollars-and-cents reasons for forgetting romance in deciding whether to have a joint checking account.

Admittedly, a joint account has advantages: a single record of where you stand; a single expense for the one account; only one bank statement to reconcile at the end of the month; each of you able to see at a glance where the money is going; and each of you able to draw on the account at any time.

But there are drawbacks. Just because each of you can draw on the joint account there's the possibility that both of you will splurge on the same day—with an overdrawn account the result. And recriminations. And a dollar and/or more charge from the bank. And some dubious looks and maybe a loss of credibility to the unlucky receiver of the overdrawn check. A joint account can be a real headache unless *you make and abide by some strict rules* on how to keep the records and perhaps who is going to keep them. If each of you is carrying around and cashing loose checks, you could be in for some nasty surprises at the end of the month if either or both of you forget to enter checks.

A joint account implies joint, and equal, responsibility on both sides. But suppose one of you is naturally thrifty and good at managing money, and the other is not. Why fight it? Why not let the born money manager take over and run a single account, thereby freeing the other partner to paint gorgeous butterflies over the dark spots on the kitchen wall, or make glasses out of old bottles, or cook shrimp Szechuan for company dinner.

However, since the butcher, the banker, and the subway-change maker may not appreciate these creative talents, the butterfly painter still has non-creative expenses. And he should be free to choose an arrangement for meeting these expenses. There are several possibilities, depending on the temperament, the personality, and the free time of the person involved.

If you are the partner who wields the paintbrush or the glass cutter you might like a weekly allowance without further headache except making sure you've kept enough on hand to guarantee you won't have to dine on toothpicks, paper napkins, and lots of water on Friday. Maybe you would find this too confining, and prefer a small but separate account that you would reserve for your limited daily expenses. Still another possibility is sharing of responsibilities on a more or less natural division of labor, but with two accounts. Then the food shopper pays for the groceries, and the person who drives pays the monthly installment on the automobile loan. Either of these two-account methods means double expense, of course. But both partners get experience in the handling of money, without too much strain—and in the long run this may prove a money saver.

So much for the cheery (more or less) aspects of a joint account. Now let's look at the dismal side.

Joint accounts are started when the dew is still wet on the orange blossoms, or the ink is still wet on the marriage certificate. But what happens when the parchment begins to crinkle, and the sweetness and light is turning to thunder and lightning? As many a horrified spouse has discovered, the partner who's fastest on the draw can empty the joint account before the trusting partner has even realized one of the checkbooks is missing.

And while we're being dismal you should know that banks have a legal responsibility to stop withdrawals from joint accounts if one of the partners dies, since the money in them may become part of the taxable estate, until the funds are released by the tax authorities. So the survivor may find himself without ready cash. Banks do often arrange for an advance, but there is red tape and various time-consuming procedures involved. So a separate account for each of you can make life easier at a difficult time.

· 5 ·

What's the Best Credit Buy, Or: How Much Should You Pay the Piper?

"Solvency is entirely a matter of temperament, and not income."
—Logan Pearsall Smith

Can you imagine a world in which you'd have to pay cash for everything? No more borrowing, charge accounts, installment loans, credit cards, pay-as-you-go plans? The mind boggles—and the world we live in would boggle as well. After all, cities and states, large and small, do their financing with credit; the federal government is always borrowing to pay for all kinds of things, from a war to building housing; and business borrows to bring the latest fashion to your local boutique or the newest car to your local automobile dealers. Without credit we would all be reduced to using a primitive barter system (your homemade ties for my homemade spaghetti) and a not so primitive poverty. You too live on credit, and without it you might have to wait until winter was over before you could afford a winter coat, you might lose a job because you couldn't afford a car for transportation, and you could never buy a co-operative apartment or a house.

So credit is a good thing, but like so many other good things in life it has its limits. If you stay within the limits that are reasonable for your income, you can not only enjoy all the advantages of credit, you can also feel noble because you're doing your bit for local, national, and international trade. (And the day will surely come when we'll all be zooming around in our spaceships, stopping to fill them up at a chain of interplanetary space stations, using our space credit cards.) But if you exceed the limits you'll hate the day you learned to sign your name to a contract, and the pleasure you get from spending (it is fun while it lasts!) will be overwhelmed by the pain of being in debt beyond your means. Part of the pain will be doing without the things you really need but can't afford; another and worse part will be getting dunning letters and nasty phone calls from credit collection agencies. With all the other pressures in your life, who needs it?

What then are the sensible limits to credit? Financial experts, family service organizations, and credit counseling groups, who've had many years of experience dealing with individuals and families who've gotten into really serious trouble and who overstepped their credit bounds, offer two guidelines, or two approaches.

One approach is that no family or individual should owe more than 20 per cent of annual, after-tax income. Let's say that you bring home $10,400 per year after taxes, or $200 a week. First thing you have to do is allow about 25 per cent for housing, which leaves you with $7,800 for everything else. About 20 per cent of this $7,800, or about $1,500, or about $125 a month is your debt ceiling. When you commit yourself to more than this you are pushing up against the ceiling and the very least you can expect is a big, bad headache.

Another more conservative approach is that you shouldn't owe more than 10 per cent of your income, which you could pay off within twelve to twenty-four months. Now let's give you a raise and a promotion and say you are bringing home, after taxes, $12,000 a year. This more conservative measure says that you can carry about $1,200 in debts for the year, or about $100 a month. Of course these are only approximate figures; if you are fortunate enough to have inexpensive housing you may be able to carry more debt. On the other hand if you are a gourmet who entertains frequently with only the finest meats, the most exquisite wines, and the best in superb pastries you're going to have a lower debt limit.

A corollary to these two approaches is the time question. True, you are sure when you sign for something that at the moment you can afford it—but how about next year or the year after? When you're buying a car, for instance, are you smart to buy it under a three-year credit plan, which adds considerably to your costs and means that you will still be paying for it when you think it should be traded in, when with just a little stretching you could pay it off in two years? And when you set your debt limit within the bounds of your current income, are you sure that will be your income next year, the year after, or the year after that? If you're all tied up financially you may not be able to take advantage of an opportunity to change jobs, or have a family, or even buy something else that you need or want. Remember too that people get into trouble with credit usually not because they indulge in one great big mad spending orgy, but because they add on a small payment here and a small payment there, without realizing that the sum of all the little parts can get to be greater than the whole income available.

WHERE TO LOOK
FOR CREDIT BUYS

Naturally, once you've decided how much credit you can afford you want to know where to get it, how much it will cost, and what the best buys are. Like anything else you buy, credit has to be shopped for: there are different ways to get it for different purposes from many different sources. The answer to the question, what's the best buy, isn't easy—especially if you're convinced you can't do math, or you've committed yourself to finishing the playroom next week, or you're tired of trying to turn out gourmet meals in a closet. Then it's very tempting to go and get what you want, and take the easiest credit plan available. If you're shopping in a store, for instance, you'll use the store's revolving credit plan; if you have the option of using your bank credit card you'll use that; if you're having some repair work done you may use the contractor's finance plan.

As a matter of fact any of these choices may or may not be the best. But how are you to know? And on what facts should you base your judgment? To make your job easier look at Chart 1 on pages 32–36. You'll see immediately that getting credit depends on many things besides having an honest face, and the more you know about the options you have, or don't have, the better position you'll be in.

Just to see what we're talking about in dollars and cents let's take two nice round sums, $500 and $1,000, and see what they would cost if you were to borrow them at three different rates, for several different time periods.* (See Chart 1, pages 32–36. Obviously, it does make a difference; how much of a difference depends on the sum, the rate, and the time period involved.

Take a look now at the two following examples.

Example 1
$500 for one year at 12 per cent=$533.04
$500 for one year at 7 per cent= 519.12
$ 13.92

1.16
For 12 months (one year) 12√13.92 or $1.16 per month
12

19

19

72

72

Example 2
$1,000 for two years at 18 per cent=$1,268.88
$1,000 for two years at 7 per cent= 1,074.48
$ 194.40

8.10
For 24 months (two years) 24√194.40 or $8.10 per month
192

24

24

00

You can see that the difference between $500 for one year at 7 per cent compared with $500 at 12 per cent isn't great; $13.92 or $1.16 per month, about the price of a hamburger. On the other hand, the difference between $1,000 borrowed for two years at 7 per cent compared with $1,000 borrowed for two years at 18 per cent is $194.40 or $8.10 a month. That's *not* an inconsiderable sum; it could pay for lots of steaks and roasts of beef.

All of which leads to some fairly obvious conclusions. If the difference between borrowing $500 for a year at 12 per cent or at 7 per cent is the difference between making a simple phone call and signing and mailing a form at 12 per cent vs. getting in your car, driving, parking, waiting to see someone, having to fill out more forms, waiting for approval, and so on at 7 per cent, you may very well think—and you may very well be right—that your time is worth more than the $13.92 and you'll

*The monthly payments are based on interest payments from various formulas used by creditors. In general, unless specified otherwise, they are based on a percentage of the declining balance; you owe less each month as you pay off more of the loan. But the payment figures should be considered only as a guide, since creditors use different methods of computing interest rates and charges.

be better off with the quick, easy-to-get loan. But when the difference is $194.40, you will, quite correctly, think differently.

THE RIGHT CHOICE?
AN OBSTACLE COURSE

Why do people borrow at higher costs than they "should"—with "should" in this case meaning when they have cheaper credit available to them? The Survey Research Center of the Institute for Social Research at the University of Michigan has looked into this question and has found that most consumers aren't well informed about credit—where to get it, the going rate, and so on. This is scarcely surprising. Can you remember, in all your years of schooling, ever taking or even being offered a course in consumer economics? If you've had the time and initiative to educate yourself, you're an exception.

Because of this ignorance, people often don't ask the right questions when it comes to credit. They don't ask what choice they have or what the money will cost over the long run. They are most interested in how much they will have to pay each month, because they want to know if they can manage the monthly payment; the annual interest rate and the finance charges either aren't asked about or aren't considered.

For many years lenders understood all of this very well, and interest rates were put in eye-straining small print, or were on the last line of the last page of the contract, or were given as a monthly rate, "just 1½ per cent per month," which sounds like so much less than 18 per cent a year. But in this age of consumerism and the Truth-in-Lending law, such practices aren't allowed. All you have to do now is look at the bill or contract and see where it says "annual percentage rate" and "finance charge." And you should be able to see it plainly, since one provision of the law says it has to be printed in plain, clear, easy-to-read type.

Knowing the annual percentage rate isn't enough, however, if you are part of a revolving or continuous credit plan, i.e., one where you can keep charging new goodies as soon as you've paid for part of the old goodies. You also have to know, a percentage of what? Department stores, credit card accounts, mail order houses, and other merchants that offer revolving credit plans have various methods for applying the annual percentage rate. Some take a percentage of the total owed on your account *before* deducting some of your payments. Others have billing cycles that make it difficult for you to pay before you begin incurring service charges. Still others compute the finance charge on the entire previous balance of your bill, even if you've paid off most of the bill. And still others credit your account with payments before figuring the interest, so you are only charged interest on the unpaid balance. Suppose you charge $500, and within your billing cycle pay $400, so you are left with a bill of $100. If the lender charges interest on the $500, because you still owe them money, at the 1½ per cent monthly rate (18 per cent annual rate) you would be charged $7.50 in interest. On the other hand, if you charged the same $500, paid $400, and the lender credits your account before computing the interest, you would be charged 1½ per cent of $100, or $1.50. After all, the $6 difference is better in your pocket than theirs, right? So before committing yourself to a revolving credit plan, check to see how the interest rate is computed. If you can't get a copy of the plan before you sign, so that you have a chance to read about it, you

CHART 1

(Figures are given as of 1973. Interest rates change so they may be different as you read this — but other facts still hold.)

SOURCES OF CREDIT	REQUIREMENTS	ADVANTAGES	DISADVANTAGES	QUESTIONS TO ASK	COST (Based on $500 repaid in 1 year)
COMMERCIAL BANKS **TYPES OF LOANS:** **SECURED**				1. What is the effective annual rate — the interest rate you really pay. 2. How much is the regular monthly payment?	
The borrower guarantees repayment of the loan by pledging an asset as collateral. Then, if the borrower defaults, the bank has a legal right to the asset pledged as collateral.	The borrower must own an asset of value — such as a car, stocks and/or bonds, real estate — which the bank will accept as collateral.	Usually cheaper than an unsecured loan made under similar circumstances.	If you default you can lose the collateral. While the loan is outstanding, you cannot sell, give away, or destroy the collateral.	Who will physically and legally have possession of the collateral? (Customarily the bank will keep the bonds, for instance, and be free to sell them if you default. And it's not unknown to have a car repossessed by an agent of a lender who "jumps" the ignition and drives the car away.)	Range of interest rates 7% – 10% at 7% Monthly payment $ 43.18 Total amount repaid 518.16 Dollar cost for the year 18.16
UNSECURED An ordinary loan which requires no collateral.	An excellent credit rating.	In case of default the bank has no specific or extraordinary claim against any of your assets.	Usually more expensive than a secured loan.	Does the promissory note have to be endorsed by anyone besides yourself?	Range of interest rates 7% – 20% at 12% Monthly payment $ 44.42 Total amount repaid 533.04 Dollar cost for the year 33.04

PASSBOOK

A secured loan in which the money in your savings account is pledged as collateral.

A savings account.

The lowest interest rate available.

Your savings continue to earn interest.

You're forced to maintain your savings account balance.

You pay interest for the right to borrow your own money.

You cannot withdraw your savings.

Range of interest rates
6% — 8%
at 6%
Monthly payment $ 42.55
Total amount repaid 510.96
Dollar cost for the year 10.96

READY CREDIT

(Also known as "instant cash," "no-bounce checking," or other snappy names, depending on the imagination of the bank's vice-president in charge of public relations.)

An excellent credit rating.

Money is always available without further arrangements; you are only charged for what you use.

You are tempted to use it and overextend yourself, just because it is available once you establish the credit.

Range of interest rates
7% — 18%
at 9%
Monthly payment $ 43.73
Total amount repaid 524.76
Dollar cost for the year 24.76

SAVINGS BANKS, MUTUAL SAVINGS BANKS

(The difference between these is in their corporate and ownership structures.)

TYPE OF LOANS:
PASSBOOK

A savings account.

The lowest interest rate available.

Your savings continue to earn interest.

You're forced to maintain your savings account balance.

You pay interest for the right to borrow your own money.

You cannot withdraw your savings.

Range of interest rates
6% — 8%
at 6%
Monthly payment $ 42.55
Total amount repaid 510.96
Dollar cost for the year 10.96

SAVINGS AND LOAN ASSOCIATIONS

TYPE OF LOANS:
PASSBOOK

(Continued)

SOURCES OF CREDIT	REQUIREMENTS	ADVANTAGES	DISADVANTAGES	QUESTIONS TO ASK	COST (Based on $500 repaid in 1 year)
CREDIT UNIONS **TYPES OF LOANS:** Unsecured or signature loans, i.e., lent to the member on the basis of his signature on a promise to pay. The limit will depend on whether the union has been chartered by the state or the federal government and by the assets of the union. Each member can borrow a fixed amount of the capital of the union, within the limits of the charter. It is in a range of no more than a few per cent for signature loans. Secured loans. The same rules apply, except that the percentage that can be borrowed is higher, perhaps 10 per cent of the credit union's capital, for secured loans.	For members only.	Very low rates. Maximum legal rate only 1% per month or 12% per year on outstanding balance.			Range of interest rates 9% — 12% at 9% Monthly payment $ 43.73 Total amount repaid 524.76 Dollar cost for the year 24.76
FINANCE COMPANY **TYPES OF LOANS:** SECURED UNSECURED	Must be employed, or have a regular source of income.	Will lend to people with relatively poor credit ratings.	Very high interest rates.	Does the promissory note have to be endorsed by anyone besides yourself?	Range of interest rates 20% — 36% at 21% Monthly payment $ 46.70 Total amount repaid 556.90 Dollar cost for the year 56.90

DEPARTMENT STORES

TYPES OF LOANS:

(You may not think of your revolving charge plan as a loan — but by giving you the toaster or winter wardrobe or TV without money they are making a loan.)

REGULAR CHARGE ACCOUNTS

Good credit rating.

(Also known as 30-day charge accounts.) The consumer charges purchases during the month and pays in full within 10 to 30 days after being billed, depending on the store's system.

Convenience.

Free credit if paid promptly.

What are the store's credit rules on such accounts?

REVOLVING CREDIT

A plan whereby the consumer makes a regular monthly payment on his account and can charge an amount equal to his monthly payment each month. The amount of the monthly payment is based upon the consumer's ability to pay.

You pay within the limit set by the store.

Comparatively high interest rates.

(Varies by state sometimes.)

How is the finance charge applied toward the outstanding balance? (See text.)

When are your payments credited toward your account?

To what balance is the finance charge applied?

Range of interest rates

12% — 25%

The department stores use many different procedures in handling charge plans, and the cost to the consumer can vary widely. The effective annual interest rate, however, will always give you the actual cost of credit.

at 18%

If finance charges are calculated on the balance which appeared on last previous statement:

Monthly payment $ 45.84
Total amount repaid   550.08
Dollar cost for the year   50.08

(Continued)

SOURCES OF CREDIT	REQUIREMENTS	ADVANTAGES	DISADVANTAGES	QUESTIONS TO ASK	COST (Based on $500 repaid in 1 year)
CREDIT CARDS INDEPENDENTS Examples: . American Express Diners Club Carte Blanche Credit cards have their own extended credit plans, comparable to banks'. The plans vary depending on the credit card. For information, check the company that issued the card.	Membership fee. Excellent credit rating, good salary and employment history.	Convenience. Free credit if bills paid promptly, after initial fee is paid.	Membership fee paid annually.		
"instant cash" plans. The					
BANK CARDS Examples: Master Charge Bank Americard	Available from your commercial bank. Good credit standing.	Free credit if paid promptly.	Finance charge of 18%. Temptation to use the credit available instead of paying in full.		Range of interest rates about 18% Monthly payment $ 45.16 Total amount repaid 541.92 Dollar cost 41.92
INSURANCE COMPANIES Holders of life insurance can borrow against their policies.	Consumer must have a life insurance policy that has a cash value.	A low-cost loan — customarily at a lower rate than the current interest rate.	The amount of insurance is lowered by the amount of the loan.		About 5% to 6% Payment schedule varies and may be added to premium. Inquire from agent.

can call and ask, but unfortunately it may not be easy to get an answer right away. Very often the clerks in the billing department don't know themselves, as I found out when doing a little checking. (They are usually polite, but flustered, and you can just tell they're thinking, "Why do all these calls from kooks have to get put on my line?") But a little persistence will get you the answer.

PSYCHOLOGICAL BLOCKS TO GIVING YOURSELF CREDIT

The persistence is important, because there are psychological blocks that hinder getting the best credit buy. First is the path of least resistance, which many sellers of "big ticket," i.e., expensive, items, understand very, very well. They know you'll be so tempted when you see the gleaming car on the salesroom floor, or the washer and dryer right there, so shiny and so much prettier than the pair you have at home, that you'll want to close the deal that very moment even if you thought you were "just looking." The way to avoid this, of course, is to do your homework and inquire about loan sources while you really are in the "just looking" stage. And very often a phone call or two—plus examining the chart on page 32—will give you a good standard of comparison.

Second, there's the feeling that it's indecent, somehow, to discuss your money affairs with a stranger. (Researchers into money matters report that it's often easier to get people to talk about their sexual problems than their money problems.) You dread the thought of going to the bank and filling out those long forms and having someone pry into exactly how much you make, which rarely sounds as if it's enough for survival when you're telling about it. So it seems easier to deal directly with the showroom salesman in a casual atmosphere than with a more formal bank officer in a more formal bank.

But stop a minute and think. Why should you care about this? Especially if caring will cost you money. If you really find that you dread the thought of laying bare your financial soul go back to Chapter 2 and get reacquainted with Dr. Fensterheim and behavior therapy. Practice a few situations where you deliberately incur the snide remarks and annoyed looks of someone who thinks you are shopping beyond your means.

You might, for instance, go into a posh clothing store, finger the merchandise lovingly, but murmur "No thanks, just looking" when the duke or duchess of a salesclerk approaches you. After a while you'll find that you couldn't care less about their condescension. (If they feel the need to act like visiting royalty who are just working to wear out their old clothes they are terribly status-conscious, and that's their problem.)

Or you could buy a newspaper and pay for it with a $5 bill. Or ask for change for a $10 bill without buying a package of gum. You'll learn to be indifferent to the "drop dead" stare of the man who gives you change. (You can sympathize with him, too—his feet are killing him.) These are all techniques recommended by Dr. Fensterheim to help develop assertiveness so that you can do what's best for you without worrying too much what people will think of you. (If you feel bad you can always go back later and buy something with the money you've saved by being a smart consumer.) But in the meantime you will be fortified, in control of your finances, and a credit shopper, or shopper for any service, par excellence.

6

How to Pick the Winning Card in the Credit Card Game

"Creditors have better memories than debtors."
—Benjamin Franklin

Now that you know more than you ever thought you'd want to know about the cost of credit, let's take a look at the modern equivalent of Aladdin's lamp. You remember Aladdin, of course, the poor boy who found a dirty lamp, shined it, and was surprised to have a genie appear and say the ancient equivalent of "Name it, pal, and it's yours."

We have our charge and credit cards and something Aladdin didn't have: constant temptation and constant urging to get a charge or credit card and then to use it, use it, use it. (Of course, Aladdin didn't have to pay the bills at the end of the month, either, but life never was like a fairy tale.)

There's much to be said for using credit, as we mentioned before. No need to carry cash; the opportunity to leave money in the bank earning interest while you buy; a chance to take advantage of sales; increasingly diverse services, from being able to buy theater tickets by phone to being able to charge tuition payments; no worry about being unable to pay for a meal in a strange city—or even your own city. And new possibilities seem to be springing full-blown in the minds of bank executives and merchants almost daily. The next step, in fact, seems to be a son of supercard that will do away with some of the drawbacks of the existent charge and credit arrangements by giving everyone a card and a secret code number, so that even the fear of credit card theft is virtually eliminated.

But all credit cards aren't equal—and some are more equal than others.

The trick is to take advantage of the best features of the various credit card plans offered, and to avoid the pitfalls. Or, to put it another way, to outwit the credit merchants at their own game.

First step is to get the right kind of charge or credit card. The most advantageous charge card is the regular thirty-day charge account. When you open an account for the first time this is the type of account that you should ask for. You may very well get an interviewer who encourages you to take a deferred payment or budget account, with revolving credit. Though this kind of account may be more profitable for the store, not only for the interest they earn but also because it makes it easier for you to continue to buy, it isn't the most profitable for you. The credit interviewer may particularly urge this on you if you are not, at the moment, in the "we only buy large yachts, doesn't everyone?" class.

Never mind. Say that you want the regular charge account. This means that you have free credit between the time you buy something and the time that you receive your bill, plus at least a week or more of grace period, though you are asked to pay immediately. If you find that you can't pay immediately you always have the option of paying out your purchase at the going interest rate. But in the meantime you have that "free ride" of credit from the day you buy those nifty patio pajamas to the day you have to pay for them. And you avoid the psychological hazard that the offer of revolving credit gives you. Sure you're hardy, strong, brave, trustworthy, and true with a backbone made of newly welded steel. But why push your luck? Save the will power for double-decker chocolate ice cream cones, double martinis, and salted peanuts. Think of yourself as a miser when it comes to paying interest unnecessarily.

Next, the credit card crunch. You're probably aware of the differences, but just to refresh your memory there are, generally speaking, two broad classifications, the bank credit cards and the travel and entertainment cards, commonly called the T & E's. Each has its pluses and minuses.

Plus for the bank credit cards is that they have no membership fee, they have somewhat lower minimum income requirements, and their use is broadening all the time. In Manhattan, for instance, you could eat all your meals, travel around by limousine, send flowers to your love, buy a new outfit, go to grand opera, or buy a tent without ever soiling your hand with a coin or a dollar bill. Then at the end of the month, you have only one bill to pay, instead of a long, dreary bill-writing session.

Minuses include, above all, that bland phrase, "You pay no finance charges on purchases if you pay your balance by the due date each month."

Deep in the upper left ventricle of your heart you *suspect* that you may weaken occasionally and pay only the minimum balance due instead of paying the full amount and avoiding the 18 per cent finance charge. (But bankers *know* you'll weaken, because they studied the market before they began issuing credit cards, and time has proved their market studies were correct.) Your noble resolve will melt under the pressure of other bills, other obligations, and maybe a bit of a shock as you see how much the small bill here and the small bill there have mounted to by the end of the month.

And even that 18 per cent interest charge isn't the whole story. True, your monthly statement tells you, at a quick glance, what annual interest rate you are paying. But you may forget that there can also be a minimum finance charge per month, and a new charge every time you add another major purchase, which is considered another new loan.

The T & E cards—American Express and Diners Club are the major ones and Carte Blanche is less well-known—operate quite differently. They charge an annual membership fee, which may or may not include an extra charge for a subscription to their magazines. They ask for immediate payment, and you have to make a special commitment if you want extended credit. They require somewhat higher income levels before they will grant you a card.

The T & E's have two major selling points, which you may or may not consider pluses. They are considered the "status" cards—supposedly using them shows that you've achieved a certain financial level and therefore a certain status. (This doesn't buy much in the way of groceries.) And they don't set limits on your total spending, as the bank credit cards do, so theoretically, the sky's the limit. The trouble is, as you well know, the sky is not the limit unless you have a parachute in the form of a rich uncle who adores you madly and thinks it's a rare privilege to pay all your bills. So this is a dubious advantage.

A more positive advantage is the timing of the payment. Though it is due as soon as the bill arrives the fact is that the T & E billing departments usually don't begin to get insistent until thirty or at the most sixty days have elapsed. However, this is a sometimes thing and is not recommended as a constant practice, since it doesn't pay to get a credit record as a slow bill payer. But it is better than having an automatic service charge at an annual rate of 18 per cent tacked onto your bill as soon as you fall behind. Furthermore, the extended credit rate on T & E cards usually is 6 per cent lower than the rate on bank or charge account credit cards.

The special advantage of the T & E's used to be their literally universal acceptance, so they were a boon to the overseas traveler. And when the exchange rate favored the American dollar the tourist abroad could get gifts cheaper by paying with his American credit card. And they were useful for cashing checks abroad. But these advantages are diminishing with time as bank credit cards extend their operations overseas.

There are also some charge account specials you want to keep in mind. Even with the regular charge account some stores will allow major appliances to be sold on an interest-free plan for sixty-to-ninety-day payment. And around Christmastime some stores offer special promotions—ninety-day interest-free payments on certain merchandise. No matter what kind of charge account you have, or don't have, in the store, it pays to take advantage of these promotions, if the prices in the store are competitive.

So much for the more obvious pluses and minuses of the various charge and credit card plans. But there are some not so obvious hazards that you can be sure are not pointed out in the sign-and-join brochures.

Suppose you have decided to buy a convertible sofa bed from a store that doesn't have charge accounts, but will accept your bank credit card. You put the bill on your credit card, the store gets paid by the bank (less the service fee the bank charges the store for being part of the plan), and everybody is happy—especially your cousin from Pennsylvania who stays with you when he visits and is too tall for your fold-away cot.

The first time your cousin tries the bed the mechanism jams and you have a terrible time both getting the bed to open and closing it again.

You call the store and learn that the salesman who took your order has gone off to homestead in Alaska, the factory that made the bed went bankrupt, and the manager just started last week and doesn't want to know what happened before he came—he has enough of his own headaches. To sum it all up, the store has its money and couldn't care less.

What recourse do you have? Legally, and depending on the state in which you live, perhaps not much. But you're not totally without rights, and you should press your case.

You will of course go through the usual routine of phone calls, letters, a complaint to the Better Business Bureau, keeping a record of your calls and a copy of your letters. But you also have, if you use it, an ally in the bank which issues the credit card. The bank has no great desire to become identified with a merchant who has a reputation for not being reliable. According to spokesmen for the major credit cards banks will look into your complaint. Since both you and the merchant are their customers they will try to mediate the dispute. But if you can prove that justice is on your side they will, say these spokesmen, intervene to see that justice triumphs. In extreme cases they will, they say, not only pressure the merchant but also, if he doesn't act, charge him for the goods and make a reasonable refund to you, the customer.

Note this word—"reasonable." To go back to the sofa bed, if it breaks down within several months, for instance, and has already been used, the adjustment might have to allow for wear and tear, that is, depreciation. What happens can very well depend on the individual bank, since state laws differ, individual banks differ, and each case may very well differ.

Which brings up another point. Standard wisdom has been that you have your credit card with one bank and your savings and/or checking account with another. The reasoning behind this is a principle based on common law, called the "right of offset," that banks in many states claim. This means that if they are holding money for you and you owe them money and they have reason to believe that you aren't going to pay, they have the right to offset your debt by withdrawing from your account the amount that you owe them.

Again, spokesmen for the major credit cards were quick to say that banks are loath to use this right, which is bad public relations, and will use it only as a last resort—making sure, for their own protection, of course, that they cover themselves legally.

And it's this public relations and customer relations angle that you can take advantage of. If you do have an account with the bank that also issues your credit card, you have some leverage with them. If they want to get your future loan business, and your savings account, and your mortgage, and maybe the account of your club or your business, it's to their advantage to see that you aren't dissatisfied with your credit card. Especially if they know you aren't shy and will make lots of public noise about your dissatisfaction.

However, you have to make your troubles known. Don't think you don't have a case, and don't be reluctant to press it. Call the bank, write to them, offer your proof of damage done to you by the merchant, and say why you think you are entitled to a replacement or a refund or a credit. (Remember that the bank also has the right of offset against a merchant's account, if he's a local merchant, so that the bank has some leverage against the merchant.)

If there is a question in your mind about the bank—and there is a possibility of having your savings account dipped into for a bill that is in question—you would be better off keeping your savings account in a different bank from the one in which you keep your checking account. (In fact, your savings account probably should be in a savings bank, not a commercial bank, because the savings bank pays higher interest.) If you are still concerned about chances of error and adjustment, particularly with big expensive items that you'll have for a long time, such as furniture, you would be better off buying from a store that counts on your good will as a regular charge customer—even if it costs you a bit more.

Were You Born to Pay Cash?
"I can resist anything but temptation."
—Oscar Wilde

There is a little-recognized disease that sometimes afflicts credit card users. Since it hasn't yet been otherwise identified I call it *credit confabulation.** The disease has specific sex characteristics. The male of the species is affected with *credit card croup,* from an excess use of credit cards, particularly high-status cards like American Express, while the female of the species suffers from *charge card colic,* characterized by an excess use of charge account cards, particularly in high-fashion, expensive stores.

Consider the case history of Miss Southern Belle, twenty-seven, who came to New York to succeed in business, armed with such assets as a banker father, a master's degree in economics from a fine southern university, an excellent figure, and a pretty face. After several years she had acquired a job in an advertising agency that paid her $15,000 annually—and debts of over $7,000, consisting of equal parts charge and credit card accounts, an overdrawn bank account, and a loan taken to consolidate previous charge account bills.

Miss Southern Belle (with no apologies to Women's Lib) brought out a battery of short skirts and see-through blouses, and personally applied for a loan from her local bank. Each loan officer she saw knew she wasn't eligible but succumbed enough to pass the application along, thinking maybe someone higher up might be willing to make an exception—particularly in view of her good salary. When the application reached the highest-ranking officer she supplemented her appeal with assurance that she wouldn't get into the same mess again, liberally interspersed with much flapping of her naturally long eyelashes and "But, Sugah, you don't understand . . ."

The banker, who says he's as lecherous as the next man, feels he did her a great favor when he said absolutely no. Some people, he says, just can't handle credit and will never acquire the necessary discipline.

What are the symptoms? (You'll recognize some of them from Chapters 1 and 2.)

Impulse buying—unconsciously or subconsciously putting out of your mind how much you are spending.

Feelings of inferiority, maybe, so that you constantly need new things to bolster your ego; very often clothes for women, a flashy car or new expensive camera or other gadget for men.

A need to keep up with the Joneses—because their acquisitions threaten your feelings of status.

The feeling of power that comes from spending, and the feeling of almost unlimited power that credit cards give, since with them you have no *visible* reminder of a dwindling supply of cash or a declining bank balance.

Overcoming feelings of depression by treating yourself to something you'd like to

---

*CONFABULATION: The patient who is suffering from a disorder of memory may fill up the blanks in his recollections with experiences invented for the occasion; this process is called confabulation. (French's Index of Differential Diagnosis, ninth edition, p. 183.)

have; or overcoming feelings of loneliness simply by the very act of getting out, going to a store crowded with people, dealing with salespeople.

You could also be avenging yourself on your mother, your father, your aunt Tanya who made you wait for your piano lesson out in the cold hallway while she took care of the paying pupils, your last lover, your husband, your wife, or the teacher who poked fun at you all during first grade.

The reasons don't matter once you're in the hole. The important thing you can do for yourself is to recognize that at this point you just can't handle credit. Later, when you've won the lottery, you'll get psychoanalyzed and find out why. In the meantime, do a few simple things that aren't going to hurt.

Shed a few tears for times gone by. Then write a "Dear Credit Card Department" letter, requesting that your account be closed permanently. Have it duplicated and send a copy—with your handwritten signature on it—to the store, bank, boutique, sauna, or whatever that has given you credit. Then, with strong hands and steady nerves, put a scissors through the heart of each of your cards and discard them. To heck with fighting temptation—just don't have it.

This, of course, leaves you with a shopping problem. You certainly can't go walking around with a wallet full of bills, so you're going to have to make some other arrangement. One possibility is to treat yourself (good for the morale) to one of those pretty engraved small-size checkbooks that you can carry around. This may, however, give rise to a different kind of hassle, if there are two of you using the same checking account. One of you will have to tie a string around your finger, slip a paper clip over your watchband, keep a little notebook, or whatever your favorite device is, to remember to enter the checks.

Another possibility is traveler's checks. They have several advantages: first and foremost you set an immediate limit on what you can spend by the dollar amount of traveler's checks that you buy, so you're setting up some kind of system for controlling your spending—which is, after all, the basic problem. Second, they are acceptable in most places; in fact they may be more welcome than credit cards since the store or restaurant doesn't have to pay the card issuer a fee that can range from 4 to 7 per cent. Third, they usually don't require any identification, which can be a problem with a check. Fourth, if you're using a special checking account that costs 10 to 15 cents a check plus a monthly service charge traveler's checks may turn out to be cheaper. (Cook's traveler's checks are usually a few pennies cheaper than the others, Barclay's International are sometimes available at no charge.)

CREDIT CARDS AND GIGO†

Here is another all too prevalent credit card problem in the age of the computer. As long as your bill is routine and you do nothing to disturb the form in which you are (though you may find the thought depressing) just an electronic speck in the computer's memory bank, everything is fine.

But suppose you don't pay your bill, and for a very good reason—it's incorrect.

† GIGO: Garbage in, garbage out. A common phrase in computerland, meaning that the computer is *not* human, and will only do what it's told to do by a human writing a program of instructions. If that human writes a poor program (garbage in), particularly one that doesn't allow for changes, only poor information (garbage out) will result.

Here are some excerpts from an actual case history of what happened when something "unusual" should have been put into the computer's program but wasn't.

June 8, 1970

Mr. George Faunce
President
Diners Club
10 Columbus Circle
New York, N.Y.

Dear Mr. Faunce:

It is necessary for me to send this registered letter as the situation I find myself in regarding dispute over airline charges on my husband's account has proven impossible to resolve in seven months of telephone and letter contact with various departments in your firm. My husband is self-employed, a marketing consultant to large insurance firms, mutual funds and stock brokerage firms across the country. He travels and charges continuously and has, as of recent months, stopped using his [Diners Club] card until this matter is settled.

Since disputing some airline charges for last August, which appeared on my November statement, I have spoken with at least seven employees in departments ranging from Collection, to Member Services, to Lost Control, to Airline Representatives—including among others a Mr. Conception, Mrs. Bowie, Mrs. Thorn, Miss Heckel. These people plus others over the course of this nightmare confrontation with a non-responsive, incompetently mechanized system have promised to get back to me with the simple verification I need that my husband did indeed make the flights it is claimed he did but our records show doubt about. (When having a problem of this sort with an American Express airline charge, it was looked into and a credit was issued within two months.) I have been told by your employees that it would take the incredible amount of four to five months for Diners Club to get this information checked by the airlines. We are beyond that in time now.

As I have chosen to pursue this matter, not liking the automatic late charges that start appearing, I was asked on two occasions to send, at my expense, photostatic copies of the four different charges in dispute. No one ever acknowledged receipt of these copies, nor have they ever been found, nor does evidence of my ever having complained seem to have been registered—but those late charges are regularly added and I am told by your employees "not to worry about them, they will be adjusted when the matter is settled."

When I talk with an employee, take his name and try to get back to him in two weeks to see why I have not heard from him I am told there is no way I can get to the same person again, or that "he or she no longer works here."

Before this IBM system bills us into bankruptcy, is it at all possible to have one intelligent human being adjust this matter? Possibly the power of your office could be used to locate past photostatic copies, correspondence, record of complaints—anything?

Hoping to hear from you or your offices I am,

Very truly yours,

Sheila Zipper

Gerald Zipper
No. 1718-0344-8

About a week later the Zippers got a telegram from the Legal Department of the Diners Club. The telegram said it was important that the club gets its "past due balance of $1181.72 immediately." Gerry was asked to get in touch by phone with a Mr. Hamilton of the Legal Department as soon as he received the telegram, and he was warned that the "status of his account" was pending.

Gerry then sent the following letter:

June 29th, 1970

Mr. George Faunce
President
Diners Club
10 Columbus Circle
New York, N.Y.

Dear Mr. Faunce:

On June 8th I sent you a registered letter concerning an eight-month-old dispute with your organization over airline bills that I would like verified as they do not seem to jibe with our records.

I received a form subsequently, dated June 12th, with the name E. Muratore on it saying that my letter would be given "prompt attention."

The next correspondence received from your company was a telegram on Saturday . . . signed by L. Hamilton.

I called Mr. Hamilton at 9 A.M. on Monday morning, rather upset that before receiving any further word after my letter and your form reply that it was being investigated I should receive such a telegram. I asked him if there was anything in my file and he checked first, then said there was no indication of either my letter to you, or any past record of calls, letters, etc. My agitated pleas concerning the impossibility of this situation elicited from Mr. Hamilton what I find to be an incredible question from a responsible business organization—"What is your Zodiac sign?"

I have rechecked past statements back to last November. The following airline charges are disputed:

8/18/69	$286.65	Nov. statement
8/19/69	357.00	" "
8/18/69	25.20	" "
11/19/69	67.20	Jan. 1970 statement
10/4/69	341.70	May 1970 statement

On that original disputed bill, I regret to find that after advice from your company not to pay the charges (Nov. statement) I neglected to pay the other charges on the bill. I am therefore enclosing a check for $378.62. If there are late charges due on this amount we understand the need for paying them. As to the disputed airline charges, as I have stated in the past, I have on two occasions sent photostatic copies of them, which upon arriving at Diners Club seem to vanish.

Once again, we wish to see verification of the above airline flights so that we can pay them in good conscience. If you continue to add late charges and do nothing to help clear this matter I will have to send copies of my next letter to the Better Business Bureau, the District Attorney's office and to our attorney.

Hoping to hear from you promptly, I am

Very truly yours,

Sheila Zipper
(Mrs. Gerald Zipper)

In desperate self-defense the Zippers did get a lawyer, Murray Richmond, who tried to clear up the matter. Though he couldn't make much of a dent on the

Diners Club bureaucracy he did at least take most of the burden of answering off the Zippers' shoulders. The affair of the Diners Club vs. the Zippers continued with more letters, photostats, apologies, missing employees, payments from the Zippers to Diners and from Diners to the Zippers until October 1, 1971.

At that point, since Mr. Zipper had resigned from the club, Diners promised that "Mr. Zipper will not receive any further statements."

But on October 13, 1971, Gerry received a brief letter from National Credit Records of America to the effect that a good credit reputation makes many good things in life available and such a reputation depends on prompt payment, that Diners had made a "number of attempts" to settle the Zipper account before referring it to National, and that the Zippers should pay promptly or explain what was holding up payment. If they explained the problem they would find National "ready to work out mutually satisfactory arrangements."

Gerry sent his lawyer a copy of this letter, along with a note that he had penned many times before:

October 27, 1971

HERE THEY GO AGAIN!!
I received this yesterday . . . and, man, they are craaaaaaaazy!

Gerry

Then the lawyer, Murray Richmond, sent to Diners and the National Credit Records a threat to start a court action on the basis of possible libel, and the business ended.

Of course, this is an extreme example, but it is not at all unusual, although Diners Club, which has since improved its billing system, was one of the worst offenders at the time of this correspondence. The Senate Banking Subcommittee on Financial Institutions and the White House Office of Consumer Affairs have bulging files on similar cases. The man-hours spent on letters and phone calls, the money spent on lawyers' fees and on photostats, stationery, stamps, and phone calls, and the value of the time spent by everyone from state Supreme Court justices to housewives would probably add a neat little sum to our gross national product.

There is a moral to the story: put your faith in a Supreme Being, in your country, in your local police force, in your daily horoscope—but never in the expertise or the record keeping of your charge and credit card offices. Credit cards aren't all pleasure and no pain aside from paying the bill at the end of the month. As a smart credit user you have to—for your own protection—save those slips to be sure that you're being billed correctly. If the Zippers hadn't had records they might have passed on to their children or even their grandchildren a Diners Club file and debt.

However, withholding payment on any charge or credit account, when your bill is in question may get you a bad mark on your credit record, with all kinds of unforeseen results, such as denial of future loans, or a bad job reference, or refusal of an insurance policy. So it's a good idea to know your rights under the Fair Credit Reporting Act, which is the subject of the next chapter.

7

The Credit Bureau Is Watching You: How to Stare Right Back

"A good reputation is more valuable than money."
—Publilius Syrus (about 42 B.C.)

Remember that credit application you filled out so carefully? Right now it's in the hands of a pretty clerk in a short white skirt, a tight black sweater, and knee-high white boots. With a bored look (she's been doing this all morning) she punches the information in your application onto a small strip of bright yellow tape. The tape goes into what looks like an electric broiler with a dome on top—and in a second a query about you is transmitted three thousand miles to a computer where more details about your life than you thought were known are stored in a sleek gray computer. And in a few minutes the message comes back: you're OK.

And so you get the loan for the new car and drive happily ever after.

Or do you? Suppose your name is John Doe and by some ridiculous coincidence there's another John Doe in your town. And suppose that while you are a model citizen, he gives pot parties, guns his motorcycle on his way home at 3 A.M., and never pays his bills. And suppose your credit file gets mixed up with his at a credit bureau.

What happens? When the pretty clerk punches the message into the transmitter and sends it cross-country it comes back with a coded version of "This fellow is a deadbeat. Don't lend him a dime and watch your expensive desk set if he's sitting in your office." The bank officer who interviewed you is surprised—he could have sworn you looked even more trustworthy than his cousin Harry—but the records don't lie, and you don't get your loan. (And the same thing could happen if you were Ms. Jane Doe and you were confused with a girl whose favorite lunchtime occupation was running up charge bills she never paid, for clothes she took on cruises she never paid for either.)

Or consider the Zippers, whom you met in Chapter 6 while they were engaged in dubious battle with the Diners Club for more than a year, trying to get their account straightened out. As far as Diners Club was concerned the Zippers were poor credit risks, and this would certainly have been recorded in their credit file.

The fact is there are about 2,500 credit bureaus and local merchants' associations around the country and their files have credit records on just about every adult American who has ever applied for credit in any form: charge accounts, credit cards, bank loans, or automobile loans.

Where does the information in the files come from? Much of it comes from you—the information you supplied when you applied for the credit. But other bits, or tidbits, come from a variety of sources that may amaze, annoy, or even enrage you, depending on what's in the file. In addition to the information that you give when you apply for credit, the credit bureaus also keep tabs on court dockets, county clerks' files, and other public records. All of these are sources of information about individuals who may be in, or getting into, financial difficulties. Unfortunately, two problems can arise: there can be a case of mistaken identity (our two John or Jane Does) or there are difficulties in following court cases to their conclusion. There are often delays asked for by attorneys for both sides, then rescheduled trials, maybe further delays until the case is finally settled. Credit bureaus admit they don't always follow the cases through, so a report that someone was sued for non-payment of a debt may go into the file, but a later report—and it could be as much as a year later—saying that the debt was adjusted satisfactorily may never get into a person's file. And, even if the credit bureau were able to follow up every court case, and did so superconscientiously, some cases are settled out of court. This settlement may never be put in a file, just because there is no mechanism for doing so.

A different situation arises when it comes to employment reports. Suppose you are being considered for a promotion in your company, or for a job in a different company, and no one is telling you until you're investigated. Suppose there's incorrect or derogatory information about you in your file at a credit bureau, but you don't know about it. You're suggested for the job, the unfavorable report comes through, and you're vetoed—without your knowing anything about it.

And there is still a different situation when it comes to insurance companies' investigations. Insurers get an "investigative consumer report," which, according to the Fair Credit Reporting Act, is "a consumer report or portion thereof in which information on a consumer's character, general reputation, personal characteristics or mode of living is obtained through personal interviews with neighbors, friends or associates of the consumer reported on or with others with whom he is acquainted or who may have knowledge concerning any such items of information."

In reporting on a case of five major insurance companies who had allegedly violated the Fair Credit Act, *Consumer News* (published by the Federal Office of Consumer Affairs) was even more explicit in describing the purpose of insurance companies' investigations and noted that "When a person applies for insurance, the insurance company, as part of its underwriting process, often will order an investigation to determine the applicant's morals, reputation, personal characteristics and style of living."

Translated into action this means that so-called investigative reporters may and very often do come around and ask your neighbors details about your personal life, and take notes on what's said, without really knowing if the information is accurate, or if the neighbor hates you since your wash was whiter than hers or you stopped lending your electric lawn mower. The information is supposed to be confirmed from other sources before it is included in the report, but the law doesn't in any way spell out specific standards for such verification.

Who are the reporters who gather these rosebuds of information? Usually they are regular employees of inspection companies whose business is to compile such information under a service agreement with an insurance company. But they may also be independent or free-lance reporters. They are paid about $1 or $2 per completed report, and, according to a story in *Writer's Digest* (June 1972), such a reporter can, with experience, "average four reports an hour." (The reports are rewritten by a professional report writer before being submitted to the client insurance company.)

It's not hard to envision all kinds of errors getting into such reports. Forget nasty neighbors who hate children and dogs and never forgive anyone whose child and dog have ever wandered across a freshly planted flower bed. How about neighbors who misunderstand when your gorgeous redheaded cousin from Dubuque comes to visit unexpectedly while your wife is away, shrieks "darling" as she gets out of the cab, and kisses you madly while the neighbors are watching with fascination. Or your old school chum drops in on his way down to Washington while your husband's away and stays overnight. Or just the simple fact that with so many people handling reports and files—typists, clerks, writers, computer programmers—it's almost inevitable that errors will creep in, despite the best intentions and best neighbors and best management possible.

And that, in fact, is precisely what has happened to some individuals. They have had their car insurance canceled, their credit card application rejected, have been turned down for jobs, or have been denied insurance on the basis of false or incorrect reports. They've been accused of not paying bills to record clubs they never joined, or not paying for sheets that were never delivered, of having a "hippie-type" son who is "active in various anti-establishment concerns and suspected of using marijuana." (The son in question was called a "model student" by his high school principal, had won a scholastic award, was a track star, campaigned both for the Republicans and against the Vietnam war, and had experimented with marijuana once.)

Each of these consumers learned about the derogatory or incorrect information in his file because he knew about and insisted on getting the full benefits of his rights under the Fair Credit Reporting Act, so this might not be a bad time to list those rights, and the credit bureau's responsibilities.

1. *You have the right to review your credit file.* Suppose you are turned down for credit, or charged for it at a higher rate. Suppose you are denied insurance or charged for it at a higher premium or turned down for a job—all because of a bad credit report. In each case you must be given the name and address of the source of the report. Then you have a right to go to the bureau and insist that they tell you the substance of the report and the sources of the information, with two exceptions. You don't have to be told the medical information in your file, and you don't have to be told the sources of the report about your character, reputation, and personal life—the part of the report that's based on opinions or observation by people who know you as a neighbor or former employee, for instance—unless you sue to find out these sources, on the grounds that the credit bureau and its users are violating your rights under the act.

The credit bureau, in addition to telling you the substance of the material in your report, must also tell you the names of everyone who got an employment report about you within the past two years, plus the names of anyone else who got reports about you within the past six months. Furthermore, the bureau has to have people on hand to give you this information during regular business hours. In fact, though the assumption is that you will go in person, if you write to the bureau and take steps to ensure the proper identification you can ask to have the information given to you over the phone.

2. *You can correct errors in your file.* Suppose you question some of the material in your report? The bureau reinvestigates any item you question, and if it's found to be inaccurate or no longer true, you can insist either that the unfavorable notice be taken from your file or that your side of the story must be added.

Suppose, and it's been known to happen, you buy a dishwasher that turns out to be a real lemon. You refuse to pay Super-Duper Applicance Acres until they either repair or replace the machine. They refuse to do anything; you refuse to pay. They say you are a bad risk and that goes in your file—you can enter a statement of one hundred words (or more if you need more) detailing the sad story of your misadventures with Super-Duper and your willingness to pay when they live up to their part of the contract by providing you with a dishwasher that works dependably.

Your side of the story, or a summary of it, will go into any future reports about you. And if an item has been removed from your file or your statement added you can insist that the credit bureau tell any employers about the change if they've received a report about you in the past two years. And you can also ask the credit bureau to pass on this same information to anyone else who's received a report about you in the previous six months.

If you go to the credit bureau within thirty days after receiving the report they can't charge you for telling you what's in your file or for sending out any corrections or deletions that you ask for. After thirty days, however, they are permitted to charge you for giving you information about what's in your file, but no more than they would charge a merchant, for instance, who asked for the same information—and the charge has to be told to you in advance. However, the bureau cannot make a charge for notifying anyone that material in your report was taken out because it was inaccurate or could no longer be verified.

There's more, but we don't have to go into the fine points here. The important thing to know is that you do now have rights, and if you suspect they've been violated you can do something about it. But "doing something" to set the record straight isn't always easy. People who've tried haven't always been successful.

Sometimes the credit agencies have said, perhaps legitimately in some cases, that they were simply trying to prevent the revelation of their confidential information to unauthorized persons. Sometimes, however, the bureaus have said the files were out of the office for posting and wouldn't be available for a week or more, apparently to discourage people from looking at their file by making the chore a nuisance. One bureau, checked by a newspaper reporter posing as an ordinary citizen, said it didn't have a credit report on him. But the reporter got a copy of his file from another source, and the material in it showed him the file had been compiled before he inquired.

In other instances where credit bureaus have been willing to show their files they have insisted first that the individual sign extensive waivers authorizing the bureau to give out information and stating that he won't sue the agency for libel, invasion of privacy, or negligence in reporting false information. (This despite the fact that the law itself prohibits such suits unless there is proof that the false information was "furnished with malice or willful intent to injure such consumer.")

And in still other cases credit bureaus have imposed excessive charges for searching their files, although they are supposed to charge nothing or, after certain specified periods of time, no more than they would charge an ordinary business or company using their service.

By the time you read this chapter many of these difficulties may have been ironed out as the various credit-reporting agencies, who at first vigorously opposed any regulation, accept the limited restrictions placed on them. (When the law was first passed I called the Credit Bureau of Greater New York Inc., the New York City office of the national association Associated Credit Bureaus, Inc., Houston, Texas, to get information about the law for a consumer column I wrote. A pamphlet the national office sent out had said "your credit bureau would be glad to answer any further questions you might have about your credit record or your rights," but the manager of the New York office told me frankly he was "very much opposed to the law" and that he preferred not to be bothered with problems.)

As the law stands the FTC's powers are very limited—it cannot issue rules that "have the force of law" but can only set guidelines that are "advisory." Industries in question, such as credit associations, banks, or insurance companies, are then expected to comply with these guidelines or risk the expense of an investigation and some kind of penalty from the FTC.

You can see that lots of people know more about you than you thought—and that you may be under investigation without knowing anything about it. Furthermore, if you have problems the FTC can't help you out as an individual, since it's not empowered to act on behalf of an individual consumer, but only, with some exceptions, against companies that do business in more than one state. You can at least register your complaint with the FTC and if there are enough of these complaints the FTC may decide to investigate the company—which may make you feel better but won't do you much good in the short run.

If you have a serious problem you will probably need a lawyer to press your case, though critics of the law feel that the ground for a civil suit, that false information has been given with "malice and willful intent to injure you," is a difficult thing to prove. You can also sue on a charge that a violation of the act, while not intentional, caused you demonstrable financial damage, again a difficult thing to prove. In the case of a denial of a job, for instance, there may also have been other factors that worked against you—no one is ever exactly perfect for any job—and certainly a clever lawyer could show that in addition to your dubious credit record you also lacked experience in operating left-handed coffee machines, or something like that.

Some individuals have enlisted the aid of a local chapter of the Civil Liberties Union and won their case, forcing credit bureaus to open their files. Others have appealed to their congressmen. If neither alternative is feasible, you can only hope that your records stay in good order and your neighbors and former bosses always stay friendly.

· 8 ·

The Fine Art of Borrowing

"Let us all be happy and live within our means, even if we have to borrow the money to do it with."

—Artemus Ward

Would you believe that your banker loves you? You really do mean more to him than you may think as you face him across that polished desk. Like all lovers, though, he doesn't love without some reservations, and he doesn't love you all the time.

If you're in your twenties or thirties—the swinging years—your banker may very well save his sunniest smile for you.

For one thing, he may be about your age or not too much older, and may share your taste for sailing, skiing, movies by new directors, or the latest style in shirts and ties. But it goes deeper than that and, as you may have suspected, involves your pocketbook and your spending and borrowing needs.

The fact is you're at the age when your needs and desires are at their peak, and you have the possibility of earning the income to achieve many if not all of them. So a more important thing may be not how he looks at you but how he "sees" or perceives you.

You, suffering pangs of self-doubt brought on by the knowledge that you have a low bank account, have only been on your job a few months, have to pat your car on the head and tickle it for five minutes before it will start in the morning, think you wouldn't lend yourself money if *you* were the banker. He or she, however, perceives you as a likely new business prospect for years to come, faithfully paying off loans for a car, vacation, mortgage, honeymoon, braces for the kids' teeth, an extra bathroom, etc.

So he's more than willing to get to know you as a customer, to listen to your problems, and to accommodate you when you need loans—especially when you are a good credit risk so he can be friendly without fear of penalty. After all, friendship or no, he is in business to earn a profit and he never really forgets that.

What makes a good credit risk? Here's what most bankers say:

1. *Past credit performance*—how promptly you've paid off previous loans.
2. *Collateral*—what security is being offered to guarantee the loan. A car loan

has excellent security—the car itself. If the borrower defaults the bank can, and does, come and get the car. It can then be resold so the bank isn't a complete loser.

3. *Total indebtedness in relation to income*—If you want to buy a 40-foot cabin cruiser, a villa in Spain, or a Rolls-Royce equipped with an English chauffeur and your monthly payments will leave you $18.23 in your bank account, forget it. Though some bankers these days are young and decidedly un-stuffy, they still hold to the more conservative banker's viewpoint that a good ratio between total indebtedness and income is 20 per cent. The absolute maximum would be 30 per cent.

HOW TO PUT YOUR BEST FOOT FORWARD
WHEN APPLYING FOR A LOAN

Wear shoes. Though banking standards have changed considerably since the days when tellers sat behind iron bars and slipped money through slots, and though young bankers may now wear Pierre Cardin suits or head their local political reform club, when it comes to money they are still a pretty old-fashioned crew. You don't have to wear "banker's gray" but no matter what you wear it helps if you look as if you paid some attention to your appearance. Neatness counts. Grooming is important, and dirty fingernails may get you on the sidewalk in no time at all.

Have a plan. Don't wander in and say, "I'd like to borrow $2,000 for some things I have in mind that I—uh—think I'd like to have. We're considering a trip on a banana freighter if we don't decide to redo our kitchen in fuchsia and chartreuse." Make a really first-class impression by saying "I want to borrow X dollars specifically for . . . , which I estimate will cost . . ."

Borrow for a worthwhile purpose. This term "worthwhile" can be pretty broadly interpreted, depending on your life-style and budget. The loan can be for an automobile, a vacation, some home remodeling, or furniture—not necessarily luxuries but certainly things you could live without.

A loan to study or to prepare yourself for a new occupation is considered a good investment both for you and for the bank.

However, and it's a big however, if you want to borrow to consolidate some other debts your application will be looked at very, very carefully; for this purpose it's not just a good idea to have a plan, it's *essential.* To make a really good impression for this kind of loan you must be prepared not only to justify the loan and prove you can pay it off, but also to explain how you got into such a situation in the first place.

(Incidentally, be prepared to substantiate your purpose. If you say you are going to use the money to buy a new stove and refrigerator, don't be surprised if your banker asks where you've shopped and how much you expect to spend. He trusts *you*, of course, but in the past he's been fooled by people who may have had the best of intentions when they borrowed the money, but were tempted on the way home from the bank by various characters who persuaded them to buy other things, like get-rich-quick stocks. And since bankers too have their own home mortgages to pay off and don't get promotions if they pile up a record of bad loans, they have to exercise due caution.)

GETTING CREDIT
THE FIRST TIME AROUND

There is a popular idea that, even though you don't need the money, you should borrow from a finance company, and repay it promptly in order to establish credit references. Finance companies have less stringent standards for extending credit, and because of this charge interest rates that may be twice as much or more than those charged by banks. Then, the theory goes, when you do need money, and you want to borrow from a bank, whose rates are lower than the rates charged by finance companies, you'll have no difficulty. The ploy will of course cost you time and money. Some bankers don't buy this idea. "You can't 'con' a banker into giving you a loan" is what they say. They suggest that if you anticipate needing a loan you can prove your credit-worthiness by maintaining a checking account for a year with no record of being overdrawn, or by incurring a really necessary debt, such as buying furniture, and paying it off. Or, having a savings account for a length of time consistent with your earnings, perhaps eight months or so if you've been working for a year. Any one of these things will prove you're financially responsible, which is what bankers are interested in.

Incidentally, the kind of account you open when buying furniture can help establish your credit rating. What you do is borrow an idea used by small business companies that want to establish a good credit record. If you're buying furniture costing about $500 or more the store will probably encourage you to buy on a budget rather than a thirty-day account. On a budget account you'll pay interest if you take longer than thirty days to pay the bill; on a thirty-day account even if you stretch your payments over several months the store can't collect interest, though you may get some dunning letters, and it's not a practice to be recommended.

If you say you don't want to open an installment account and prefer a thirty-day account many clerks have been instructed to say, "If you buy on the budget account and pay in thirty days, no interest will be charged. Therefore it's the same thing." However, it's *not* the same thing. If you buy on the budget account, even though you pay in thirty days, the purchase will be recorded as a budget purchase. On the other hand, if that same $500 is charged to your thirty-day account, and then the bill is paid within thirty days, it will show that you were granted a large amount of credit and you paid it in thirty days.

In the first case, it appears that you had no choice but to buy on a budget account, even though you paid the account in thirty days. In the second case, instead of having a $25 or $100 limit on your thirty-day account, your records now show that you incurred a debt of $500 or more and paid it within the required thirty days. You are therefore a better credit risk than the person who had to buy on an installment plan budget account, and then somehow got together the money to pay off the account in thirty days.

WHAT IF THE ANSWER IS NO?

It can happen and it does. Your banker loves you—but. *But,* you have a poor credit record. *But,* though you think you have the necessary income and credit record, you happen to apply the day the court notified your banker that he has to raise his alimony payments, and he's feeling sour on life and humanity. Let's consider these problems and possible solutions.

You have a poor credit record. There are two aspects to this: a poor credit record at the moment, or a poor credit record in the past, though you've been fairly prompt about paying your bills recently.

If you're in debt at the moment, and you've been hiding bills under old telephone directories because you can't pay them, or can only pay a few of them, or part of them, there's really not much you can do. (See Chapter 14 for what to do when you lose your job, however—a different situation.) Creditors have computerized memories these days. True, though banks try to keep their computers on speaking terms with other people's computers, and though there are credit bureaus who check loan applicants, computers are still programmed by people and banks are still run by people, who make mistakes and let some bad risks get by. (That's why your neighbor down the street got himself in such a financial hassle.) In general, however, if you are in debt the bank will know about it. And they'll say "no dice," unless you can offer some very sound and plausible explanation.

What would such an explanation be? An extended illness, of your own or someone in your family; a job layoff; obligations to a relative, such as an aging parent. Even with these explanations there is no guarantee that you'll get a loan. In fact, your chances are slim, but at least you will have tried.

If you can't offer valid reasons you have a chance if you can show that though you were careless in the past you have reformed. If you want to restore your credit you should start paying off your old debts. To err is human, to forgive is good for bank business. So if you can show a twelve-month good record you will probably have your credit restored. However, it will probably pay you to apply for a loan at a different bank.

There is always the possibility, if all else fails, that you can get a co-signer, who assumes responsibility for your debt if you default. His credit record has to be very good, of course.

Incidentally, if you are turned down because your credentials aren't well enough established, you may not have been working long enough, or living in a particular city long enough; try again in about five to six months. Could be that this time the banker will say yes.

You feel a loan is justified, based on income and credit, but the bank turns you down. Don't accept the verdict passively. *Demand* to see someone with more authority in the bank's loan department and insist on knowing why the loan was refused. If the refusal came from a branch office and ultimate approval comes from the main office, demand that someone in charge there review your file.

It could be that you are right and the loan officer is wrong. It could also be that there is an unfavorable, unjust, or even untrue record in your credit file. You should learn about it and clear it up. (See Chapter 7.)

· 9 ·

Finders, Keepers, Or: How to Get Help with Your Tax Return

"Tell me more about those tax loopholes you keep dreaming about."

—Psychiatrist to tax lawyer-patient

Sure taxes are inevitable, but paying more than your share isn't. So whether you call it tax avoidance or tax evasion, tax wisdom or tax dodging, the name of the game is saving money and getting help to play is your goal. And like most games it's not only a question of skill but also a question of timing and luck.

But first let's discuss a common psychological hang-up. Most of us, though we know we're going to have to part with the money, somehow can't bear to do it one moment sooner than necessary. In some ways that makes sense. You can very well say that the longer the money is in your savings account the more interest you get on it, and the longer it's in your checking account the higher the balance and the lower your service charges. However, this doesn't mean you have to let the tax preparation go until the last minute. If you can overcome this psychological block, if you can separate that 1040 form from the substance, money, and get your return prepared early, you will benefit from the closer attention of whoever helps you with your tax form, if you decide to get outside help.

The next question, then, is—should you get outside help, and if so, what kind?

If you are the not too rare person who blanches at the sight of printed forms, especially detailed ones; who sometimes has trouble recalling his birth date when filling out personnel questionnaires; who "has sort of forgotten" where the commas go when separating hundreds from thousands, you may very well benefit from help —particularly if you are filing a return for the first time. In fact, the Internal Revenue Service had you in mind when it decided to expand its taxpayer service. In previous years there has always been some help available—ranging from complete filling out of forms for those who were unable to do it for themselves because of disabilities to telephone answers for anyone who wanted a specific question answered. But most recently the IRS has promised extensive help, comparable to the help you would get at a commercial tax-preparing service.

One reason for this helping hand from everybody's favorite uncle was the revelation, in 1971, that there had been incredibly widespread fraud (up to 97 per cent) on returns prepared by some commercial tax services, forcing the government to run audits on many returns that wouldn't ordinarily have been checked. So Uncle Sam may have decided that it was cheaper to have it done properly in the first place, by people who knew their business—namely IRS men and women, called tax service representatives (TSR).

Obviously, there aren't enough such people sitting around the IRS offices during the comparative quiet of April 15 through December, and so helpers have to be hired. Who the TSRs are and how they're trained has a direct bearing on what kind of help you'll get. Some are former IRS employees, who've retired but come back every year, lured perhaps not only by the extra earnings for four months or so, but also by the chance to hold a lot of nervous hands figuratively during a time of travail and soothe many feverish and furrowed brows. They are brought up to date on the changes in the tax laws since they last spent time in the IRS offices. There are also the people brought in from other departments, who deal with other tax matters during the year and are very knowledgeable in wending their way through the thickets of the 1040.

But since even these two groups aren't enough to handle the load, there are some lower-level IRS employees and even some part-timers, including moonlighters from other jobs, housewives, and students. They receive about a week's training before going forth to help the troubled taxpayers. Asked if this was enough training a spokesman for the IRS said frankly that it wasn't, and these people are used mostly for answering the routine questions that are asked over and over again.

So, if you choose to go to your friendly Internal Revenue Service what kind of help can you expect? That depends partly on when you go, partly on where you go, and partly on what kind of luck you have in drawing an IRS man. Certainly if you go early, right after you've gotten your statement of earnings and withholdings for the tax year, your chances of getting someone's undivided attention are better than if you wait until the last two weeks before T-day. You will have a shorter wait: five or ten minutes vs. 45 or more. Because there is less pressure, if you have an unusual question you have a better opportunity to get more expert answers, or more answers from experts.

Chances are there's an IRS office near your office if you work in a major urban center. But there are also offices in suburban centers. And the hours usually coincide with the pattern of employment or shopping in the area. So if you want to go to a downtown office the thing to do is try to avoid the lunch hour, if you can swap a lunch hour for some less busy afternoon time off. If you find the neighborhood center more convenient try to go against the neighborhood time patterns. In either case the IRS says it will experiment with longer hours, Saturday openings, night openings, so check your local office by phone before going—you may not have to compete as much with the crowds.

Considering all these variables, particularly the variable in the level of training and experience of the person who may be helping you individually—or helping twenty of you in what is almost like a classroom situation—it's not surprising that there are variables in the interpretations of the law. In fact, when an enterprising *Wall Street Journal* reporter tried the identical return in five cities around the country, Atlanta, Des Moines, Rome (Georgia), San Francisco, and New York, he got five different answers as to what the taxpayer owed, and what was owed to him. The only consistent fact in all five was that the taxpayer was due a refund; the amount ranged from a low of $177.14 in Atlanta to a high of $484.18 in New York.

Of course, only you know your expenses and income, so the IRS man, whether he's a temporary employee who will go back to his kitchen or tool shop after the April deadline or a full-time, year-round pro, isn't responsible for your statements or deductions. *Most important of all, he isn't responsible for any wrong advice he gives you. In fact, no matter who prepares (or repairs) your return, ultimately the buck stops with you.*

Let's say that you need help and you decide to get it from the IRS. Like anything else if you do your homework and come prepared you'll get more from the lesson. So if you wonder about your claims for a medical deduction, for example, bring along the bills. If you want to prove that you really have been the mainstay of your local charity, bring along the canceled checks.

And even if you've never lost anything in your life, you're better off having the originals duplicated and bringing the copies. For one thing, you'll have greater piece of mind, and be able to concentrate on the question at hand, instead of worrying that that man sitting next to you with the pile of papers is going to scoop yours up along with his when he finds out he can't deduct his Caribbean vacation as a business expense.

DOES IT PAY TO PAY?

With this free help available what are the advantages of going to a tax-preparing service? What should you know about them? How can you judge their reliability and their ability? If your return is audited it doesn't much matter if the mistake was made through stupidity or cupidity—you are still responsible.

Actually there are three types of paid services qualified to help you. First are the lawyers and certified public accountants who are qualified to practice before the IRS. They may represent you if your return is audited—though again it's still on your head and out of your pocketbook if there have been mistakes. Neither the lawyers nor the CPAs are permitted to advertise their tax services. Next there are the tax preparation firms, both large and small, sometimes specializing in preparing tax forms and sometimes having tax preparation as a sideline to regular services, such as bookkeeping or lending money or tax planning for business. Third are the individuals who operate on their own—very often blooming in the spring in empty stores, corners of real estate offices, or even in private homes, and fading the day after returns are due. Neither these individuals nor the tax preparation companies are qualified to represent taxpayers before the IRS.

Surprisingly, there are no formal requirements for becoming a tax preparer. There are no standards of competence for an individual and no standards of training for people hired by companies who prepare returns. (Your twelve-year-old cousin, who is the star of his arithmetic class, could put aside his marbles and set himself up as a tax preparer and no one could stop him.)

Most of us don't have either the complications or the resources that make it worthwhile to go to a lawyer or an accountant to prepare our returns. But there are some advantages, psychological and practical, to going to a commercial tax-preparing service.

The main advantage is the individual attention that you get, in contrast to the group encounter that you may become a part of as IRS offices get busier and busier. But there are lesser advantages, depending on how you react to the tax trauma and how much time you have. *If you are busy* and time is money, it may be faster to have someone do the work for you than to do it yourself.

If you have a tendency to put the chore off until the last inconvenient moment, and feel that paying a fee will make you more conscientious about getting your records together earlier and more thoroughly; *if you are preparing the return for the first time* and think that an individual "lesson" will enable you to do it on your own next year; *if you were low man on the totem pole in arithmetic* and just know you're going to make countless arithmetic mistakes—then you can make a good case for paying someone to help you. (Under current tax laws you can deduct the cost of a tax service, but only if you itemize your deductions.)

Remember, though, that that is what you are getting—someone to help you. You still have to get your records together. And you have no guarantee (a) that the work done for you will be 100 per cent accurate and (b) that the errors made, if there are any, won't cost you time if you have to undo them, and maybe money if the IRS doesn't accept the deductions that the service said you could claim.

In the 1972 survey of 3,200 tax preparers, at least 1,800 were reported by IRS Commissioner Johnnie M. Walters as having prepared fraudulent returns. The figure didn't even include the returns that were inaccurate just because they were badly or sloppily done. And when IRS men, posing as taxpayers, submitted figures that should have showed that they owed the government $148, the tax preparers came up with refunds due the taxpayer of amounts ranging up to $750. This of course would have made the taxpayer full of a warm glow toward the service—until he was audited by the IRS. At that point he would have had to pay what was due plus interest on the money. And the tax preparer would certainly not have refunded the difference, and might or might not have refunded the interest, depending on how reliable the service was.

This is not to say that all such services are either outright dishonest, or even necessarily careless. It is to say that though your chances of getting a good service have been enhanced since the 1972 investigation, you still have to be cautious when choosing one.

To get an idea of how these services do business let's take a look at the Manhattan region of the nation's largest tax-preparing service, the H. & R. Block company. Block began as a small help-to-business company in Kansas City, Missouri, in 1946. The company grew and began to specialize in tax preparation in 1955. It now claims to prepare returns for about 8 million persons annually, does a repeat business for many of its customers, has its shares listed on the New York Stock Exchange—and has a real stake in seeing that its service is performing well. (The company president, after years of opposition, testified in favor of legislation requiring the registration of tax preparation services with the Internal Revenue Service. Henry W. Block said that a "standard of competence" should be established for tax preparers and companies should be required to disclose compliance to the standard.)

If you live in Manhattan you might, in late December or very early January, see a large display ad in your neighborhood papers for a tax preparer. If you answer the ad and have some spare time (seventy-two hours, to be exact) and $75, you could enroll in one of Block's tax preparation courses. At the end of the course you can hang out your little sign saying you are now qualified to prepare tax returns. (Patrick Manrose, director of Block's Manhattan regional office, says they often take the brightest members of the class into their office. The question that always bothers me is: what happens to the not-so-bright ones?)

Block also sometimes advertises for tax preparers in the regular classified help-wanted columns, instead of using a display ad. They train the applicants, if they pass an aptitude test, to work in Block's offices. During the training period the applicant is not paid. If he proves himself he can then work in a Block office for a minimum (in 1973) of $2 per hour base commission against his draw of 20 per cent commission on every return that he prepares.

The fees vary, depending on the complexity of the return. Mr. Manrose said the average fee is about $12.50. A really top-notch preparer can earn about $7 to $10 per hour. But the average preparer can make much less, and conceivably, at the end of the season, could have earned only $2 per hour if he wasn't very fast, or if the office he was assigned to wasn't very busy.

You can see that anyone working under this arrangement has everything to gain from preparing your return as quickly as possible. All the forms, however, are checked before being sent to you by Block; this is not necessarily true in other services and certainly not likely in the one-man operations.

What then should you ask when you're trying to evaluate a tax-preparing service?

1. How long have they been in business?

2. What kind of background and training have their employees had?

3. What kind of guarantees or references can they offer about their reliability and accuracy? Can they, for instance, give you the names of several clients who have come back for several years because they were satisfied with the service? Can they name some small (or even medium-size) businesses they've serviced?

4. What they will do about any mistakes they make that will cost you time and maybe money? Although they cannot represent you before the IRS they should be willing to go with you, if you are called for an audit, to explain how they arrived at their figures.

If it turns out that you will have to pay interest they should be willing to pay the interest if they were responsible for the disallowed deduction.

Even if you have faith in the service of your choice you will find that, if you shop around, the deductions vary and so, consequently, do the fees, since they are usually based on a sliding scale depending on the size of the return. In a survey of a variety of large and small tax preparers in Manhattan, for instance, the identical data—an income of about $12,000 derived partly from writing fees and partly from stock dividends—resulted in a surprising range of opinions and charges. Six tax advisers were visited: their estimate of fees ranged from a low of $16 to a high of $125 and their estimate of the taxes due ranged from a low of about $1,300 to a high of about $1,650.

Of course, considering the complexity of our tax laws, the accretion process by which they are enlarged (which is something like a coral reef), and the new and improved forms that the IRS seems to come up with every year, the variety is not surprising—just discouraging. If the experts can't agree, how are the rest of us to keep our confidence in our ability to pay the IRS its due and not one penny more?

There is only one bright spot: the right of administrative appeal if your return is questioned—and tax commissioners who say they are as anxious as you are to be sure that your return is equitable.

YOUR FRIEND IN THE APPELLATE DIVISION, OR: DON'T TAKE NO FOR AN ANSWER

Yes, it does happen. And on a day when it's pouring rain, and everyone around you has been snappish, and everything that could possibly go wrong has gone wrong plus a few things you never thought about even in your most depressed moments. On such a day the mailman brings you a notice that your income tax return is being audited.

Don't hold out your wrists and wonder what size handcuffs would fit you. You may find it difficult to believe, but your Internal Revenue Service agent isn't out to snatch your last piece of bread, with or without gravy. He is, he says almost plaintively, only interested in seeing that you pay your fair share of taxes. More than that, since there may be some difference of opinion as to what that fair share is, he is also interested in seeing that you receive reasonable and just treatment, regardless of your tax bracket. So, before you begin to estimate whether eating is a luxury that you may have to give up in order to pay back taxes, listen to this from the IRS:

"The selection of your income tax return for examination does not necessarily mean that you owe more tax. Your return may be selected for examination if you have not furnished enough information about some item of income or deduction, if you have reported some income that is not taxable or have deducted some unallowable expense item. In such cases the Service will also want to insure that the other information on the return is correct. Or you may have filed a claim for refund, and your refund may be examined to make sure that the proper amount of tax is refunded to you."

The important thing to remember is the philosophy that prevails at the IRS. The agency has no desire to clog the tax courts—in fact, their aim is to arrive at an agreement at lower levels of appeal so the routine cases never appear in tax courts at all. So they make every effort to dispose of each case, if at all possible, at an administrative level. Further, the IRS recognizes that many tax laws are open to interpretation, and that there are honest differences of opinion as to how much is owed. So they are willing to listen to your reasoning and to compromise if you can back up your claim. And, at each level of appeal—an audit by an examining officer, a conference with a District Conference Staff member, or a hearing with the IRS Appellate Division—you get a brand-new look at your problem. The judging of the appeal is *not* based on what has been argued before, but on how the IRS official considering the case sees its merits. In other words, the IRS men don't operate on the buddy system, even informally, They aren't bound by a previous decision and have no particular reason to uphold the judgment of the lower level. Nor are they interested in other aspects of your return—they consider only the specific question at issue.

Regardless of the reason you've popped up in the IRS files for an audit, you want to know the best way to proceed.

If your claim is more than $2,500 you may want to have professional help, particularly if large sums are involved and the tax law is complicated. But most of us fall in the small taxpayer category, with $2,500 or less as the limit. And for such cases the Tax Reform Act of 1969 and the IRS have set up procedures which are comparatively simple and informal. The 1969 act set up a Small Tax Case Division of the tax court, to handle appeals of $1,000 or less. If you were involved in such a dispute you could take your case to this division, where there would be an informal meeting presided over by a U. S. Commissioner.

If the dispute involved more than $1,000 but no more than $2,500 you would also be entitled, at least in the beginning stages, to an informal meeting or hearing. All along the line you would be, the IRS says, dealing with people who are not only experienced but also specially trained to deal with Mr. Average Taxpayer, who cannot afford to hire an accountant or a lawyer to represent him. (In fact, you are probably better off not having a lawyer or an accountant—there is a certain amount of psychology involved here, and it doesn't pay to appear too prosperous.)

So, generally speaking, the situation looks something like this. You are not automatically a scoundrel if your return is questioned, and you don't automatically have to accept the government's case. As we saw on pages 57–58, whether it was a tax preparer or an IRS man there are differences of opinion as to how the laws are interpreted and, consequently and more important, how much money is owed. If you think your claim is valid you can pursue it through several levels of appeal without having to pay fees to lawyers or accountants—providing, of course, that you can spare the time to do so. If you do press your case you will be doing so in informal meetings and hearings where you won't be under stress to accept a judgment without having the right to present your views. You may win or you may lose, but at least you have a fighting chance.

In fact, in about three quarters of the cases that involved sums under $2,500 the cases at the conference level were typically settled by agreement on both sides in recent tax years. And roughly the same proportion applied when appeals were carried one step further to the Appellate Division conference level. Each side pushed a little and yielded a little until a satisfactory compromise was reached.

So if your return is audited go prepared—and go with the knowledge that if you have a good case you won't be without a sympathetic audience. How convincing you are is up to you, but at least you can be armed psychologically with the knowledge that being the "little guy" isn't necessarily a drawback, and can even be an advantage.

(For a succinct bulletin—three pages of easy-to-understand text and a good diagram of the steps involved in an appeal—get the pamphlet *Audit of Returns, Appeal Rights and Claims for Refund,* publication 556, from the Internal Revenue Service. Available free from your local IRS office. Easiest to get if you pick it up yourself, since the offices very often have a backlog of mail requests for pamphlets, but it can be sent to you if you don't mind waiting.)

· 10 ·

Where the Jobs Will Be

"Work is the curse of the drinking classes."
—W. C. Fields

Suppose you really could look into a crystal ball and see the future. Suppose you really believed in time machines. What would you want to know about your mañanas—the times to come? That your roof will start to leak as soon as the guarantee expires? That the first time in three years you are late for work you'll meet your boss on the elevator? That as soon as you put your money into a stock that's been rising steadily it will take its first drop in five decades?

Instead, how about a look at where the jobs will be. This glimpse into the future, with the help of the Bureau of Labor Statistics, the National Planning Association, the March 1972 *Manpower Report of the President,* and other sources, could help you decide what fields to enter or switch to, what training to get, or where opportunities will be if you want to move to a different part of the country.

Actually, if you think about it (and you probably have), some trends seem fairly obvious. The problems of the cities mean more need for urban planning; the problems of the environment mean more opportunities in environmental controls. More attention to health problems means more need for health workers. An increasingly technological society means more need for practitioners and teachers of the technologies. With the shorter work week, leisure industries, from hiking equipment to second homes, are expanding.

However, present trends aren't necessarily the wave of the future. Even with all the facts and great expertise there are no guarantees that projections will prove valid. In the past, developments that couldn't possibly be foreseen have had a way of effecting profound changes. The birth-control pill, for instance, affected the age at which people marry, the birth rate, the demand for housing, and enrollments in elementary schools. The computer gave birth to a whole new industry. Atomic energy is making older power plants outdated, just as the airplane and the automobile cut deeply into the use of ships and trains. Even at this moment scientists and engineers, here or abroad, may be developing something that will give us another new industry and maybe in the process wipe out an old one. So, with the understanding that many aspects of projections should be preceded with "probably" or "other things being equal," let's take a look at the decade of the seventies and see what the future may have in store when it comes to jobs.

First, let's start with some assumptions—the very assumptions that the Department of Labor uses when it makes its projections.

1. The international climate will be an improvement over the decade of the sixties; the world will be more peaceful though still heavily armed. Our peacetime army will be maintained at a level consistent with peace—probably about the level it was before the mobilization for the Vietnam war.

2. There won't be any drastic changes in our economy or economic structure; nor any drastic changes in our social framework or the values we consider important in the jobs we hold; the education we want for ourselves or our children; the style of life and leisure that we prefer.

3. There will be some kind of reasonable—if not pleasing to everyone—balance between prices and employment. Inflation and unemployment may still be problems, but no more severe than in the fairly recent past.

4. A benign if not always enlightened Big Brother, in the form of government, will still be trying to solve the nation's problems. But Big Brother will be more likely to assign the tasks to his cousins in state and local governments than to try to do the job all by himself.

5. Though there will be more of us our *rate* of births will go down.

CHART 2

THE LARGEST NUMBER OF EMPLOYMENT OPPORTUNITIES WILL CONTINUE TO BE IN THE SERVICE- PRODUCING INDUSTRIES

Millions of workers

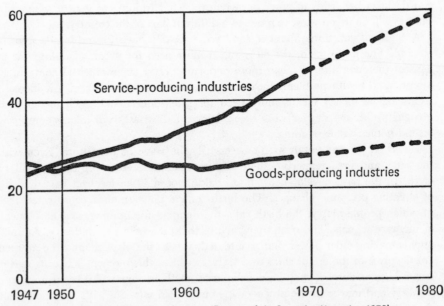

Source: Bureau of Labor Statistics (*The Manpower Posture of the Seventies*, November 1970).

CHART 3

Employment trends among major occupational
categories,[1] 1947-68 (actual) and 1980 (projected
for a services economy with 3 per cent
unemployment)

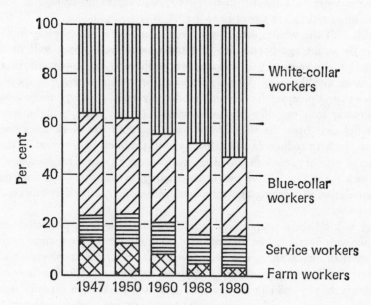

1Farm workers include farm managers.

35,000—25,000—35,000, OR:
THE SHAPE OF THINGS TO COME

Despite the declining birth rate, if the Bureau of Labor Statistics projections prove accurate there will be 167 million persons of working age (sixteen and over) in 1980—and 100 million of them will actually be on the job, for an increase of about 22 per cent, of persons of working age, above the beginning of the seventies. (This working group can be projected with more confidence than some other variables, since everyone who will be old enough to work during the seventies is already with us, and death rates and net immigration rates are reasonably steady.)

The labor force is constantly changing as individuals enter and leave. New workers will include almost 24 million young people looking for that important first job, almost 6 million women entering or returning to the labor market, plus more than a million immigrants. The dropouts will be those who die, retire permanently, or leave—sometimes only temporarily—for a variety of personal reasons.

It's interesting to know not only how many but also *who* will be in the work force, so you know who the competition will be, or who your market will be if you're thinking of going into selling or one of the service industries. The youth-quake will subside, as the huge increase of teen-agers that characterized the sixties tapers off. The rate of increase of the young twenties will also slow down. However, the number of twenty-five-to-thirty-four-year-old persons, considered by many to be in their prime working years, will increase at a very rapid rate while their slightly older counterparts, those in the so-called "mid-career years" of thirty-five to forty-four, will increase only moderately. And there will be a sharp slowdown in the number of older workers, forty-five to sixty-four, and almost no change in workers beyond the usual retirement age of sixty-five.

But this isn't the whole picture, since age alone isn't the only significant factor. White male adults age twenty-five and older, who were about half of our labor force until the seventies, will become proportionally less important in the labor market, since they'll account for only about a third of the increase in the work force (an encouraging prospect for Women's Lib). By 1980 about 73 million women, or approximately four out of every ten women (43 per cent), will be working, up about 2 per cent from the start of the seventies. And the black labor force is expected to reach 12 million in 1980, from about 3 million at the start of the decade. The annual rate of growth of the black work force, 2.4 per cent, compares with the white work force rate of 1.6 per cent—leading to a more rapid increase in the black population of working age compared with whites, especially among those under thirty-five.

Where will all these people find jobs? That too has been projected—though of course not with anything like the degree of certainty for the population projection.

The most dramatic change in recent years has been the employment shift from manufacturing (goods-producing) industries to service-producing industries. The projection is that by 1980 almost seven in every ten workers, or 68 million of us, will be in jobs connected with government, transportation, public utilities, trade, finance, real estate, or personal services. (See Chart 2.*)

A parallel and major trend of the past fifty years or so is the growth of white-collar jobs. This occupational group, which surpassed blue-collar employment for the first time in 1956, will account for about half of all employed workers (50.8 per cent) by 1980. (See Chart 3 for the mix of white-collar, blue-collar, service, and farm workers.)

Overall, the picture will look something like this: State and local governments will have the most rapid growth by the end of the decade—a 53 per cent increase. Services will grow 40 per cent, followed by construction, 35 per cent. Manufacturing will grow only 11 per cent, but it will still be our largest industry. Agriculture will continue its decline. (See Chart 4.)

Now for some specifics.

The most rapidly growing industry has been the office, computing, and accounting machines industry, with computer production the dominant factor; from 1968 to 1970 computer output grew at the "astonishing rate" of almost 40 per cent annually. The projected rate remains extremely high throughout the decade. There will also be rapid growth for the places that make optical, ophthalmic, and photographic supplies, including photocopying equipment. (Have you noticed that the copying machine has taken the place of the water cooler as a good place to exchange office gossip?) The electronic components industry (transistors, special purpose vacuum tubes) will continue to prosper. So will the communications industry (telephone and telegraph apparatus, radio and TV transmitting, signaling and de-

* Source for all charts: U. S. Department of Labor.

CHART 4

STATE AND LOCAL GOVERNMENT AND SERVICE INDUSTRIES
WILL HAVE ESPECIALLY RAPID EMPLOYMENT GAINS

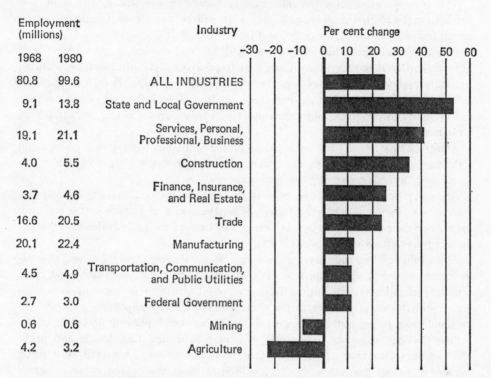

Employment (millions) 1968	1980	Industry	Per cent change
80.8	99.6	ALL INDUSTRIES	
9.1	13.8	State and Local Government	
19.1	21.1	Services, Personal, Professional, Business	
4.0	5.5	Construction	
3.7	4.6	Finance, Insurance, and Real Estate	
16.6	20.5	Trade	
20.1	22.4	Manufacturing	
4.5	4.9	Transportation, Communication, and Public Utilities	
2.7	3.0	Federal Government	
0.6	0.6	Mining	
4.2	3.2	Agriculture	

Source: Bureau of Labor Statistics (*The Manpower Posture of the Seventies*, November 1970).

tection equipment and apparatus) and the makers of plastics and synthetics. Of course, this is going to be accompanied by growth in the industries that service other industries: electric, gas, water, and sanitary services, for instance. And restaurant equipment and cleaning equipment and air conditioners—and all the people who service them.

Business services are expected to expand rapidly. So will the mining of chemicals, and fertilizers. These have had consistently high growth rates in the recent past, and are expected to keep up their good track record in the future.

Some industries are expected to show a change in their growth rate in the seventies that will be different from their recent rates, either up or down. Note that the coal industry is recovering somewhat from the chronic anemia that has afflicted it in recent years. Orders from abroad have been a tonic to the growth rate—but the invalid may have a relapse after about 1975, when nuclear energy takes over some of the market. The oil-supply/price change will surely affect this.

New construction is expected to increase with demand for houses, apartment buildings, buildings to house government offices, and commercial and office buildings. Naturally all the industries that supply material for the construction industry, particularly fabricated structural products, stone and clay building materials, construction machinery, and, to some extent, metals and lumber, are expected to grow more rapidly through the 1970s than in the recent past. Another, and related, winner will be the miscellaneous electrical machinery and supplies industry, destined to grow because of the increasing use of batteries for a wide range of industrial and consumer applications.

And since we are one of the most mobile nations in the world, with a built-in market for the many things we produce, there will be more need for the industries connected with air travel, air cargo, and land trucking.

We are also a nation that likes to eat—and the food service industries have been growing so fast that they actually suffered from a personnel shortage even during the early part of the seventies, when unemployment was high. Besides restaurants, colleges, schools, nursing homes, hospitals, hotels, motels, industrial plants, and office buildings in congested downtown areas and in suburbs short of restaurants all serve meals.

And since man doesn't live by bread alone the amusement industry is going to go right on expanding—including the movie industry, where, the Bureau of Labor Statistics says, "a modest recovery has been underway."

Not everything is onward and upward at the same pace, however. Some industries, *though they will continue to grow,* will have a rate of growth in the seventies lower than their rate in the 1957–65 period, one of the base periods the BLS used in assessing the outlook up to 1980.

The synthetic fibers industry, for instance, will grow more slowly, but will still advance at an estimated annual rate of 7 per cent. The radio, television, and communications industry will decline from its 1957–65 rate of 9 per cent to a projected growth rate of just over 6 per cent. The electronic components industry will decline from a 15 per cent annual growth rate to between 8 per cent and 9 per cent.

Now that we know the major categories of jobs during this decade and probably the next, let's take a look at educational requirements. There will be a rising number of college graduates, about 10 million of them, during the 1970s—a figure bound to have an effect on the job market. Large segments of the working population will be educationally upgraded, and this will probably mean that the general scarcity of professional personnel and the great demand for college graduates experienced in the 1960s have probably ended barring some national emergency, for a long time to come. But the availability of more college-trained people will make it increasingly difficult for people without degrees to advance in the professions or to be promoted to higher-level positions in other fields.

To have some idea of where jobs will be for the college-educated, take a look at Chart 5.

Even for the college-trained the situation isn't wholly optimistic. So let's be pessimistic and point out where the outlook *isn't good.*

The largest of all professions, and one that has been a major source of jobs for young women—elementary and secondary school teaching—has changed drastically, from shortage to surplus. Gone is the parental advice to "get a teacher's license because no matter what happens you can *always* get a job teaching." Demand will be, in general, restricted to replacing those who drop out. The reason lies partly with the population—there just aren't enough children around to create a growing demand for people to teach them, and partly with a decline in federal, state, and local aid to education. Would-be teachers should look to areas where there may be spotty shortages; the industrial arts, vocational skills, mathematics, remedial reading, and speech correction. Or they might consider serving in areas that still have short-

CHART 5

EMPLOYMENT REQUIREMENTS WILL RISE MUCH FASTER IN SOME PROFESSIONS THAN IN OTHERS

Per cent growth in selected occupation groups, 1970-80

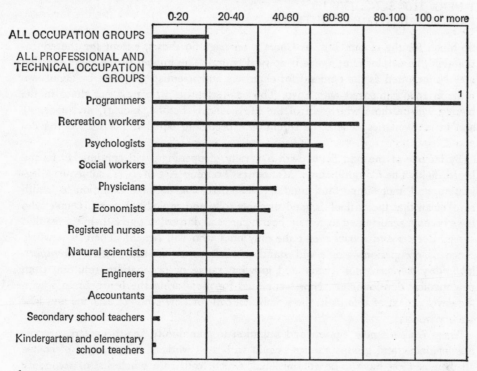

¹Increase in employment requirements projected at 150 per cent.
Source: Department of Labor.

ages: urban ghetto schools, rural areas, or schools that pay less than salaries in other professional fields. Or they should acquire the special skills needed to serve the handicapped child.

One of the shocks of the 1969–70 recession was the comparatively high unemployment rate among many, but not all, engineers and scientists: about 3 per cent for engineers and about 2.6 per cent for scientists. Although this was well below the 6 per cent unemployment rate for the remainder of the nation it was still about four and a half times the 1968 rate for engineers and somewhat less for scientists.

Engineers with the highest unemployment rate, 6.3 per cent, were, not surprisingly, those who had previously been in space activities; engineers in defense-related work also had a relatively high jobless rate, 4.8 per cent. However, civil engineers had an unemployment rate of only 0.2 per cent and petroleum engineers 0.7 per cent. Among natural and social scientists more than half of the unemployed were chemists, 3 per cent, and physicists, 3.9 per cent, up sharply from prior years. Scientists and engineers with doctorates had much lower unemployment rates than those with bachelor's degrees. But a master's degree proved of little help—in fact the M.A.'s or M.S.'s had slightly higher unemployment rates than the B.A.'s and B.S.'s, probably because the advanced degree made employers feel they were overqualified for some lower-level jobs.

WHERE THE SUNSHINE IS:
BRIGHT EMPLOYMENT OUTLOOK

So much for the gloom. But, as Chart 5 on page 69 shows, except for the education field the employment figure is upward bound. The impact of the mini-recession may be forgotten as the demand for engineers and scientists increases by about two fifths in 1980 compared with 1970. The only scientists who may not share in the bounty will be those who train in the life sciences (botany, biology, and zoology) and in mathematics, where the supply is expected to equal if not exceed the demand.

By far one of the best fields, with a variety of openings, will continue to be the health field. The Comprehensive Manpower Training Act of 1971, subsequent legislation, and, more important, funding, plus increasing national attention to health care, mean that the outlook is good through 1980 and probably beyond. People who have become accustomed to certain health care standards don't give them up readily.

And *doctors and nurses* aren't the only ones who will benefit. There is a whole range of occupations—some old standbys such as *dietitians, physical therapists, laboratory workers,* plus a new and growing range of occupations resulting from new medical developments. New techniques for monitoring the heart, brain waves, the development of infants in the womb will call for new kinds of analysts and laboratory workers.

There is also a new interest and attention to community health centers, preventive medicine, and group practice—again with new workers needed. And of course all these services have to be administered, which leads to a whole list of secondary occupations: *administrative staffs* for hospitals and health centers plus public relations people, social workers, medical records librarians, and others.

A related field is counseling—again with a bright future. The outlook is best for *rehabilitation counselors,* with a current and a future shortage, especially for those with graduate degrees. There will also be good jobs for *college and career counselors* and for *employment counselors,* especially for those with master's degrees or experience in hiring. B.A.'s with some postgraduate work in counseling courses will find a welcome at state and local government offices.

Engineering, as noted before, will be a profession that will grow. The outlook is excellent for biomedical engineers, as increased research and development in applications of computer systems to medicine, instrumentation systems, and environmental pollution leads to new opportunities. There is also an anticipated demand for *civil engineers* as more attention goes to such urban problems as housing, mass transportation systems, and environmental pollution.

Natural scientists will be in demand, with favorable prospects for geologists, geophysicists, meteorologists, and oceanographers. These are fields in which advanced degrees are almost a necessity. The same is true of the physical sciences, where the Ph.D. is the academic equivalent of the union card. The one exception to the need for the Ph.D. may be in the food sciences, where Ph.D.'s aren't necessary to serve the expanding market for convenience foods.

Among the *social scientists, economists* are the favored sons and daughters. The best jobs will go to those with advanced degrees, but B.A.'s too will find opportunities. However, political scientists and sociologists without the Ph.D. will find the going rough, while their better-educated brothers and sisters are getting jobs. The *political scientists* will find most openings in the groves (and concrete mazes) of academe, but *sociologists* will find opportunities in the implementation of legislation aimed at developing human resources.

Whiz kids with figures—*actuaries and statisticians*—will continue to be in demand from industry and government. *Accountants* will also enjoy being sought after in the future as they have been in the past and present.

Lawyers have bright prospects. There is a growing need for their services as business expands, new government agencies spring up, new laws that need interpretations are passed, and there are efforts to expand the use of legal services available to low- and middle-income groups. Consumer law is becoming a new specialty—both advocacy consumer law, representing consumer rights, and, conversely, helping corporations defend their interests against consumer groups and government regulations.

Psychologists with Ph.D.'s will find increasing call for their services in mental hospitals, correctional institutions, mental hygiene clinics, and community health centers.

The outlook for *managers, officials, and proprietors* is mixed, but good. Changes in the size and type of business organization have affected this group in different and divergent ways. The development of chains and supermarkets has eliminated many small retail businesses and the self-employment of their owner-proprietors. On the other hand, the openings for salaried managers and officials have increased. Although the net results of these opposing trends will probably result in a slower rate of growth for this segment of white-collar jobs, the demand for *salaried managers and officials* is still expected to increase rapidly. Business, government, and service institutions are becoming increasingly dependent on trained management specialists. And technological development adds jobs—for instance, an increasing number of *technical managers* is needed to plan research and development programs and make decisions on the installation and use of automated machinery and automatic data-processing systems.

Such managers will look for and rely on *purchasing agents,* especially those who have a degree in business administration, plus some background in engineering or science so they can do the purchasing for companies that deal in complex products involving knowledge of machinery, machine processes, or chemistry.

And *systems managers* will continue to be sought as electronic data processing continues to spread in industry and government.

A *policeman*'s lot may never be a happy one but there will be an increasing demand for an increasingly well-trained police force. Men and women who have training in electronic data processing, engineering, sociology, and social work will find their lot more rewarding, if not happier.

So much for the skills needed—or not needed. Those of you who want to get a much more detailed and specific look at job prospects might consult the eight hundred-page, biennial *Occupational Outlook Handbook,* which describes eight hundred occupations and thirty major industries, and covers training needed, range of earnings, and entry requirements. It also describes, in some detail, the employment changes expected in the decade of the seventies. The format is easy to read and logical, which may account for its record as an all-time best seller among government publications. Available from any regional office of the Bureau of Labor Statistics, U. S. Department of Labor. Price for the 1974–75 issue, $6.85. It also should be available at your public library, along with a quarterly, *Occupational Outlook Quarterly,* which keeps the *Handbook* up-to-date.

Another source for job and industry outlooks is the *College Placement Annual* —a survey of employment needs anticipated by about two thousand corporate and governmental employers who hire college graduates. Copies available to alumni from most college placement offices or by mail ($5) from the College Placement Council, P. O. Box 2263, Bethlehem, Pa. 18001.

Scientific, Engineering, Technical Manpower Comments, a monthly magazine, summarizes current developments affecting the recruitment, education, and utilization of scientists and engineers, and has a special section on the technological job market. Subscriptions are $7 per year from the Scientific Manpower Commission, 2101 Constitution Avenue, N.W., Washington, D.C. 20418.

Another source is the trade association of the industry you are interested in. Check your classified telephone directory for local offices or the *Encyclopedia of Associations* at your library for descriptions of the associations and their headquarters address. The *Encyclopedia* should be available from your library.

Of course you not only want to know what skills and education will be needed, you also want to know what parts of the country will grow. For that, please continue on to Chapter 11.

Boom Towns, U.S.A.

"As long as the real action is in hell, heaven has a poor chance."
—Ernest Dichter, founder,
The Institute for Motivational Research

Just as one man's meat may be another man's poison so one man's idea of a heavenly place to live may be another man's idea of a place to stay the hell away from. There's no denying, however, that growing areas are areas of opportunity, not only for jobs but also for starting the service businesses that spring up when people are working. You don't have to be an urban planner to know that when a new industry starts the people who work in it need places to eat lunch, have their hair done, their shoes repaired, their torn stocking replaced, pick up some eggs for breakfast, buy birthday cards, etc. And the new industry itself often needs auxiliary services —lawyers, accountants, public relations firms, auto repair shops, doctors, motels with meeting rooms, sometimes even airfields and marinas.

On a broader scale a developing part of the country needs what the planners call the infrastructure: roads, utilities, transportation, perhaps even a certain level of skills and talents to be drawn on, such as a pool of good office help, or a university where people can get advanced training and professors can be called on to undertake research projects.

Whether your interest is to find a job, start a business or simply move to a part of the country where things are happening, you'll be interested in some projections developed by the prestigious National Planning Association (NPA), a non-profit, non-political research organization that regularly issues regional economic projections.

First, let's define the regions as the National Planning Association uses them.

New England: Maine, New Hampshire, Vermont, Massachusetts, Rhode Island, Connecticut.

Middle Atlantic: New York, New Jersey, Pennsylvania, Delaware, Maryland, the District of Columbia.

Great Lakes: Ohio, Indiana, Illinois, Michigan, Wisconsin.

Southeast: Virginia, West Virginia, Kentucky, Tennessee, North Carolina, South Carolina, Georgia, Florida, Mississippi, Louisiana, Arkansas.

Southwest: Oklahoma, Texas, Arizona, New Mexico.

Plains: Minnesota, Iowa, Missouri, North Dakota, South Dakota, Nebraska, Kansas.

Mountain: Montana, Idaho, Wyoming, Utah, Colorado.

Far West: Washington, Oregon, California, Nevada, Alaska, Hawaii.

Jobs first. Where has employment been rising fastest? In the Southeast, Southwest, and Far West, with the Mountain states just a shade behind. These are the areas that grew rapidly during the 1960s and have continued to expand during the seventies, though at a slower rate in the early part of the decade. They are expected to continue to grow at a faster pace than the remainder of the country. The growth rate of the Southeast will decline a bit more than the other three regions, however.

Why the faster rate? In the Southeast, despite the drop in farm employment, trade, service, and non-durable manufacturing grew faster than elsewhere. (Economists define non-durables as consumer items that last less than three years, such as clothing, shoes, and drugs. Durable goods for consumers are the automobiles, appliances, furniture, jewelry, and books that last—or at least are supposed to last —more than three years.) The availability of low-wage, unskilled labor and the faster growth of incomes helped make the Southeast a southern belle in trade, service, and manufacturing industries.

There were different reasons in the Southwest. There, manufacturing was the leader in supporting a rapidly growing economy. In a sort of chicken and egg arrangement there was a strong demand for electrical components and instruments that gave jobs to an increasing number of women willing to leave their kitchens for a factory bench. They were joined by men leaving the farm, and this combined work force made it possible for the instruments to be produced, which brought more workers, which encouraged more industry, etc. In addition, as the Far West grew the Southwest provided the transportation and distribution links between the Southeast and Far West, with more jobs all around.

This happy situation, for those who live there, is projected to continue throughout the seventies, right up to 1980, and probably beyond. In fact, says the NPA, "the growth of employment in the Southwest and Far West regions is likely to continue to be substantially faster than the national average."

This doesn't mean that a graph of the economic growth of these regions would just be one upward line. There was a great deal of unemployment in California and the state of Washington during the 1969–70 recession. Nor does it mean that every city, town, and hamlet prospered equally or that everyone was dropping into Neiman-Marcus to order his and hers planes for Christmas. But the trend, despite zigs and zags, is heading up.

In other areas the zigs and zags are part of a downward trend. The New England, Middle Atlantic, and Great Lakes regions have had a relatively slow growth of employment, and this trend too is likely to continue. These are older parts of the country, from which textile and other manufacturers moved when they could get cheaper non-unionized labor and more modern plants in the South. However, these regions, partly because they were older and had educational institutions and skills to draw on, developed some high technology industries—the computing industry was born in Philadelphia and nurtured in New York and Boston—that offset some of the loss of manufacturing. Without this advantage the regions would have suffered more than they did.

The Plains states, with their heavy dependence on agriculture and weak competitive position in just about all industries except transportation equipment and non-electrical machinery, have had an unemployment rate well above average.

Unfortunately, these things feed on themselves. When industries close or cut back, the services that depend on the industries and their employees as markets also close or cut back. And then the people in the community who can leave—particularly the young and the people with salable skills, who represent much of the real wealth of the community—often go looking for better opportunities elsewhere.

Does this mean that you should pack your bags immediately and head for the Southwest or the Far West? Not until you look at the whole picture: job opportunities and regional growth aren't necessarily equated with more money around, despite those stories about Texas millionaires lighting their cigars with hundred-dollar bills. Statistics can be misleading if they illustrate just one part of a story. And in this case part of the whole story is in the fact that there is still a lot of money lying around in places outside of Texas—in fact, outside of the faster-growing regions.

WHERE THE MONEY WAS—
AND STILL IS

If income is the whipped cream on top of the nation's economic pie—though it is expected to be spread more evenly by the 1980s—much of it is going to stay right where it is and has been for quite some time. To be specific, in 1968* the Middle Atlantic and Great Lakes regions together accounted for about 45 per cent of the total income all of us got in the form of wages, salaries, dividends, rents, interest payments, Social Security, unemployment compensation, and Christmas present from Aunt Minnie. People who lived in California, New York, Illinois, Pennsylvania, and Ohio alone accounted for about 40 per cent of the total income in the United States.

Here's how the National Planning Association evaluates the situation:

Between 1968 and 1980 total personal income of U.S. residents is projected to rise from $684 billion to $1,160 billion (in 1968 dollars) or by 4.5 per cent per year. As in the past, the largest dollar gain in personal income in the decade of the seventies is likely to take place in the Middle Atlantic region, and the smallest increase in the Mountain states.

In relative terms the Southeast, Far West and Southwest regions will continue to experience above average growth in personal income for the same reasons they have done in the past—continued high gains in employment and in average employee compensation. However, our projections also imply a significant increase in the rate of growth in the Mountain region.

Note that these are over-all figures. But what we are interested in is how the pie is cut, how big our individual slices might be—in other words, what are the projections for per capita earnings? And here's what NPA foresees on that score.

In the past the highest per capita income has been in the New England, Middle Atlantic, Great Lakes, and Far West regions, where it has been above the national average. Why? Because the industries that pay more—the manufacturing and serv-

* 1968 is chosen as a base year because it was before the deep U.S. involvement in the Vietnam war, and therefore is considered a more typical year than the years that followed.

ice industries—are located in these regions. In the Southeast, Plains, Southwest, and Mountain regions, where more people earned their living from the mines and the farms—industries that are not only declining but also becoming more automated—per capita income has been below the national average. These trends will continue but the gap will get smaller as manufacturing spreads and the regions become more homogeneous.

Now let's narrow the picture a bit more. Within regions both number of jobs and income have tended to be higher in metropolitan regions (that's why you can't keep them down on the farm) and this pattern too will continue during the seventies. However, just as the gap between the wealth and poverty of regions is narrowing, so is the gap between metropolitan and non-metropolitan areas, though not by very much. In 1968 the per capita average income was 10 per cent higher in metropolitan areas than in non-metropolitan areas; by 1980 the gap is projected to drop 1 percentage point to 9 per cent. But there's a catch—the difference in the two areas in hard cash, dollars, has been widening in the sixties and seventies and this trend too will continue right up to 1980.

In 1960, for instance, a city mouse had $1,000 more to spend than a country mouse. By 1968 the city mouse had picked up another $100, making $1,100 more; by 1980 poor country mouse might be gnashing his teeth as his city cousin gets $1,600 more a year than he does.

Then again, he might not be. No discussion of where the jobs will be or where the money will be is complete without considering *what the money will buy*. Who gets more for his dollar, city mouse or country mouse, in the supermarket, the apartment house, the suburban house, the auto repair shop, Joe's Bar and Grill? Who pays more to have his children's teeth fixed, his hair cut, or some clothes drycleaned—and who gets a better job with less hassle?

Here comparisons are not so simple. How people allocate their money depends on so many variables: how much they have to start with, since the percentage spent on food usually declines as income rises; what part of the country they live in, since New Englanders spend more for housing than Plains-men, but less for transportation; how much they want to get around, since Southeasterners spend less than Far Westerners for travel and recreation. Comparisons are made more difficult because they can't allow for differences in life-styles and backgrounds of culture. (The NPA didn't allow for differences in the cost of living in preparing its charts.)

And there are other intangibles. The highest-paying job you've ever been offered isn't going to really "pay" if it's in an area of the country that you dislike, or far from family and friends whose closeness is very important to your happiness. And the high salary isn't much good if it's all eaten up by higher housing, transportation, and food costs. And the most exciting and challenging job offer may have one enormous flaw if you're a two-career family and there is no comparable job offer, or even the possibility of a good job, for one of you.

Knowing where the action is is only a start. Then comes the really difficult part —evaluating the information in terms of your own financial, physical, and psychological needs. In the last analysis the most difficult part of the decision is weighing all the factors and making the choice that's best for you.

But if you do decide you want to make a change, knowing how to write a good résumé is one of the first prerequisites. If you want to know more about this art, proceed to the next chapter.

· 12 ·

Résumés, Or: The Art of Packaging YOU

"A well-written life is almost as rare as a well-spent one."
—Thomas Carlyle

Have you ever had a suppressed desire to be a copywriter? Have you ever thought you could write an advertisement that would sell a product? If so, suppress yourself no more. Writing a résumé is your chance to turn out sparkling copy that is going to sell a product you know well and believe in—yourself.

For that's what a good résumé is, a selling piece. Its purpose is to show that a sterling product, *you*, is so appealing that a prospective employer won't be able to resist taking that first and all-important step in the buying process: calling you for a personal interview.

Consider what you look for in a product you are considering buying. The product has to fill a need, offer some durability, be proven in use, and look well. And that's exactly how your résumé should present you—in an attractive package that some employer will feel is worth investigating and perhaps buying.

Remember that a résumé is important not only because it makes the first impression but also because it may be read again and again as the choice narrows. The résumé may be passed around among several departments or forwarded to several individuals, or even put away and taken out at another time when another opening becomes available. *So the résumé has to keep on selling for you*, perhaps through several readings and discussions.

The résumé—the package that promotes you—has several components which can be varied, placed in different order, or given special emphasis. In general, however, for a job in business or industry, academe or the social services, all the components should be there. (Government is a somewhat different case which we discuss on page 80.)

Of course your name, address, home and business phone, if you're willing to be called at your office. (Don't forget to include the area codes.)

Then, for a general-purpose résumé, i.e., one that is not addressed to a specific individual or for a specific job, your objective should be stated. You might want to say something like, executive assistant to president, or marketing manager with responsibilities for consumer products, or research director. If you are interested in several related positions, all of which you might qualify for on the basis of your experience, state them all. If your experience is light, or if you would like to change fields, your objective will have to be stated in more general terms, such as, "a position of responsibility where I can use my training and have an opportunity to take on more responsibility," etc.

Your aim in this paragraph on objectives is to project yourself as a strong, resourceful, organized person who knows where he is going. It's a mistake therefore to imply that you will take anything that's in your field, which is the impression you can give if your objective is too general. You will risk losing out on some jobs, perhaps, because you have guessed wrong on the particular talents being sought, but better to risk that than appear as a person who lacks focus. A fine line to draw, I admit, but it has to be drawn.

Next, a brief paragraph describing the experience and background, including education, that qualifies you for the job you're after. This paragraph should summarize not only your experience but also your abilities. You are a skilled researcher, or an experienced administrator, or an effective expediter, or a proven salesman. (You'll prove these statements in your chronological listing of the jobs you've had and your accomplishments in them.)

Next a chronological listing of your positions, starting with the most recent and working backward. This too is part of the selling package, so you cheat yourself if you only list years employed and duties, e.g., 1970–present, assistant to the head of the public information department. This is no time for false modesty. Drop the "I", which gets to be repetitious, and then consider all the aspects of your various jobs that might appeal to your next employer.

Did you supervise any employees? Supervisory experience is always a plus. Did you help in dealing with the community? Public relations is also a plus. Were you a liaison with other departments? Sometimes getting along with other departments can go a long way toward smoothing the work flow, and can be a real asset. Were you effective in dealing with personnel at a different level or in a different age group, either higher or lower than your own? This ability to get along with others is a real asset.

Your description of the work you did should detail not so much your precise duties, which may be similar but can never be identical to those in a new job, but rather your accomplishments. Did you save money on the job, improve an existing system or introduce a new one, generate new business, cut turnover? Details like these should be described, something like: Responsible for getting out a weekly price list to all drugstores in the Midwest region. With no increase in staff managed, after studying the work flow, to increase the size of the mailing and get it into the mails two days earlier.

Next, your education, with degrees and honors, if any. This might be followed by any articles you have had published in trade magazines, or any honors you have received for civic responsibilities. You might also include volunteer work you have done if it's pertinent, either because of skills you have learned, such as public speaking or community relations, or because it adds a new dimension to your personality. This is particularly true if you are a woman who has been out of the job market for several years because of domestic responsibilities.

Finally, personal data including age, marital status, dependents, health (including any physical limitations, if pertinent), willingness to travel or relocate, army service.

SOME OPTIONALS YOU
MIGHT OPT FOR

Should you include your *hobbies?* Some career advisers recommend it—my own honest opinion is that it's a mistake unless the hobbies directly relate to the job. If you're applying for a job as an editor, for instance, and your hobby is photography, that would obviously be a plus. But my own reaction, as a consultant to a new firm hiring office personnel at a secretarial and middle-management level, was that hobbies intruded on the businesslike approach of the résumé. I could readily see a man developing a paunch and letting his membership in his expensive health club go to waste being turned off by someone who listed his hobbies as skiing, horseback riding, and tennis.

Club affiliations also may or may not be an asset. They should be included only if they add significantly to your desirability; otherwise there is the danger that they may, for obscure or even subconscious reasons, turn someone off.

Should you include your *references?* Unless they are asked for specifically, or unless they include someone prominent, such as someone in government, probably not. Employers take it for granted that you aren't going to give the name of anyone who thought you were a medium let alone a total loss, so glowing letters saying what a real doll you are aren't that impressive. Most employers do want to check, however, when they are seriously considering hiring you, so a simple "References available on request" can serve your purpose very well.

How about *salary?* This is always a sensitive question. If not asked for specifically, say nothing. If you set too high a figure you may automatically disqualify yourself. If too low you are not only cheating yourself out of future income, you are also minimizing your talents by putting a low price tag on them. If there is a requirement to state salary try to hedge by saying something like "low" or "medium five-figure range." Then at least you have some bargaining power.

THE SPECIAL-PURPOSE RÉSUMÉ:
FOCUS AND FUNCTION

So much for the essential parts of an all-purpose résumé. Like many all-purpose things, however, just because it's designed to cover many markets it may not be effective in selling to a particular market, for instance, a specific advertised job.

If you are answering an ad there is a great temptation just to pop your all-purpose résumé in the mail. If you are really serious and interested in the job, resist the temptation. Answering an ad in a hurry isn't really necessary—in fact, some executive counselors say that chances of your résumé standing out are better if you send it later in the week, after the first flurry has subsided. Your résumé should be re-written somewhat, with a slant toward the job opening you're after.

One major change will be in the first paragraph, where you'll substitute the open-ing advertised for your more general objective. But you should also redo the body of your résumé, if your experience can be *legitimately* angled to the job that's adver-tised. Don't stretch it too far—even if your résumé doesn't show the gap your ig-norance of a given area or your lack of skill may show up during a personal inter-view. Better to be honest or even use your general résumé almost unchanged, and state in a covering letter that your previous experience includes skills and responsi-bilities that you think are transferable.

The academic world is something quite different: the résumé becomes your *curriculum vitae* or "CV" and its emphasis is soft-sell. Since scholarship is the name of the game the first entry is your academic credentials, undergraduate and graduate, followed by awards and then publications, if any. Since the academic tradition is that most jobs are filled through faculty recommendation, the CV is usually sent to someone who has a specific job opening. Your objective should in-clude naming the particular position you are after plus your general field of interest.

After educational qualifications and publications comes the job history, again soft-sell and quite specific. If you've had administrative experience or such extra-curricular activities as work with students in advising on academic matters, or guiding students through their Ph.D. theses, or counseling them with their per-sonal problems, or sponsoring student activities such as athletics, dramatics, news-papers, etc. these should be noted since they are a strong plus.

References are always listed. If letters of recommendation aren't enclosed there should be a statement that these letters will be forwarded on request.

The world of *government jobs* also has its own special requirements. Most jobs are filled through Civil Service, which means you fill out a long and detailed ap-plication blank, the famous Standard Form 171, "Personal Qualifications State-ment." Space in the SF 171 is limited in the places where you have a chance to show your true talents and do the necessary bit of personal promotion: the sections for describing your "duties, responsibilities and accomplishments" and "special qualifications and skills." *Your chances are much better* if you attach a separate sheet listing your job experience and accomplishments, noting "see at-tached sheet" in the skimpy, squeezed-tight SF 171 space.

HOW TO ADMIT
YOU'RE NOT PERFECT

Now that you know what the standards are, here are the exceptions that prove the rule. Variations on the standard format can often help you minimize your liabili-ties. For instance, suppose you've had very little actual work or business experience because of age, a long academic career, or army service. Then forget about putting your work experience first and emphasize your strong academic background or your career objectives or your army experience. Your youth and lack of experience could be a plus factor, since you will bring a fresh, youthful approach to your job. Your army experience, if it included learning to get along with all kinds of people, showing your leadership qualities, even adapting to unpleasant situations, would be a real asset. Volunteer work, extracurricular activities, part-time jobs all add depth to you as a person and show your *potential;* this is something that employers look for.

Suppose you've held some interesting jobs, but didn't stay on them for reasons that could be credibly explained in an interview, but would look like job-hopping on a résumé. Then, though it's customary under "Experience" to put the dates first and then the job description, it would be better to reverse the order, putting the title and description first and the dates at the end. If you really did quite a bit of job-hopping but then settled into one spot for a reasonable length of time you might list the short-run jobs under "miscellaneous experience" and give duties and accomplishments without stressing dates, except some inclusive dates—1968–70.

If you don't have an academic degree you'll be tempted to omit the educational background entirely. Don't. Your omission will stick out like a big red arrow. Instead, state your formal education as simply as possible, mention any non-credit courses you have taken for self-improvement, and *stress the experience* you've had on the job. This experience could be more valuable than formal courses. Some corporate offices, in fact, prefer people with B.A.'s or less, feeling that they are much less likely to be looking for better jobs elsewhere, more content to stay with one company and look for from-the-ranks advancement, and, perhaps most important, more willing to take either low-prestige jobs or jobs that involve getting on the plant floor and working with blue-collar employees.

THE BOOK IS JUDGED
BY ITS COVER

Your résumé can be perfectly worded, in the best conceivable order for the job you are looking for, and your qualifications can be just right. But, and it's a big BUT, if the typing is sloppy, if there are smudges, crossed-out words or dates, handwritten corrections or additions, misspellings or grammatical errors, forget it. You're wasting your stamps. *Neatness counts,* whether it's in industry, business, government, or academe.

You can understand why. Think of yourself when you go to a store, a supermarket for instance, to pick a package off the shelf. Do you take the package that looks battered or do you take the one that's fresh and crisp-looking? Or watch people take newspapers from a pile at a newsstand. They usually reach for the paper underneath the top copy, though the news is identical, because they want something that isn't mussed. The psychology of the résumé is the same. And there's a subtle bit of flattery in a résumé that looks as if it was done just for that particular employer.

And in the eyes of the employer your attitude toward your résumé or CV indicates your attitude toward your work. If it's careless, sloppy, badly done, you give the impression that that's the kind of job you do.

(One of the biggest gripes of academicians who go to the seminars, meetings, and conventions that are also hiring halls is the state of the résumés they find in their boxes. They are sometimes badly typed or full of errors, or, worst of all, poorly collated so that pages are in the wrong order or some are missing altogether. Needless to say the careless scholar doesn't get a job offer.)

Furthermore, in the eyes of an employer your attitude toward your résumé also shows your attitude toward the job being offered. If you change dates or make additions in ink, you may think all you're doing is updating your résumé—but the employer doesn't look at it that way. To him you are showing that you thought so little of the job that it wasn't worth your while to spend any time retyping. Your "what the heck, I'll throw this old résumé in the mail" feeling shows that you have a "what the heck, I'm not really serious about this" feeling about the job being offered. It's the wastebasket for your halfhearted efforts.

Should you go in for elaborate designs, fancy folds, unusual typefaces? Unless you are applying for a job in one of the creative fields, such as advertising, where the résumé is a sample of your work, the consensus is no (though one consulting firm differs and says yes). These extras may look frivolous, especially to the more conservative employers, and work against rather than for you. Fancy folds and odd-size paper don't fit into standard file folders and may be a nuisance.

However, if you are planning a mass mailing, your résumé should be typed on an electric typewriter in the most legible type available, assuming you're having it done by a professional typing or résumé service. If you're typing it yourself be sure you have a new ribbon and that you are using a good quality bond. If you're planning to have the résumé duplicated from your original, remember that a pale original will result in pale duplicates. If you use a corrasable bond and/or cover up your errors with chalk, as long as the corrected mistake is as dark as the rest of the copy the chalk and the erasure won't show up in the duplicated copies.

Distinctive paper shouldn't be ruled out. Bright pink isn't going to endear you to the personnel officer of a tool and die plant, or to a female executive who is a devout Women's Libber; bright yellow can be hard to read in the glare of office lighting. But a distinctive gray or off-white may make your résumé stand out from the others and give you a competitive edge.

Think about the layout of the page when you see the résumé all typed. How does it look? Is it attractive, easy to read? Are the various categories distinctive, so the reader can tell at a glance what your objectives are, where your experience has been, your training? Even with your own typewriter you can get these effects with capital letters and underlines, and lots of white space between categories.

AN ABSOLUTE MUST:
THE COVERING LETTER

Your résumé shouldn't go out unescorted—it should be accompanied with a *brief* covering letter that gives you the chance to stress some things that couldn't be handled easily in your résumé, to wit:

If you have a particularly strong selling point for the job you're after, the covering letter gives you a chance to mention it. "I was responsible for cutting costs 15 per cent in the products I was buying. I believe I could effect comparable or better savings for your company since my technical background makes me completely familiar with much of the materials you buy."

If you are changing fields you can explain why you want to make the change and what qualifies you in the new field. "While teaching mathematics at the junior high school level during the past five years I have been taking courses in the evening in various aspects of electronic data processing. My aim was to change my career from the teaching field to one which offers more opportunity for advancement. I believe that I am now sufficiently prepared to make the change."

If you are changing jobs because you would like to move to a different area of the country you can state this reason without interfering at all with your regular all-purpose résumé.

Your résumé should always include, quite specifically, what ad you are answering. It should state the position you are applying for, where you saw the ad, the dateline of the ad, and the section in which it appeared, if it was in a newspaper that has several sections. For instance: "In response to your ad for a personnel supervisor which appeared in the business section of the . . . *Times* on May . . ." This is necessary because an employer or personnel department may have placed several ads, or may have placed the same or similar ads in several newspapers, or in different sections of the same paper—or even the same ad in the same paper but on different dates. Employers not only want to know what ad you are answering but also which medium has the best drawing power.

Finally, the covering letter gives you the opportunity to offer to come in for a personal interview at a mutually convenient time. Or, if a phone call isn't out of place, you can suggest that you will call at a certain time so that you can discuss the job possibility further, and perhaps set up a personal interview.

And, as with the résumé, *style and neatness count.*

Have someone who knows you and whose judgment you respect check your résumé and your letter copy before you either have it typed or type it yourself in final form. Have a bit of role playing—let the person try to put himself behind the desk of the employer, with phones ringing perhaps and a pile of résumés to be gone through. Then let him judge if you've said what you wanted to say and made the package as attractive as possible.

If you are having a service type the résumé for you (try to find one that can do the job so that each copy looks individually typed—not absolutely essential but nice work if you can get it) insist on seeing a proof sheet before giving the final go-ahead. Examine it carefully for layout, typographical errors, clean copy. After all, it's not only your money but also your future at stake.

Finally, having done the best you could, relax, get ready for the interview, and don't worry about how you'll spend the extra money you envision getting. Love will find a way.

How to Keep Your White Collar from Getting Frayed: Is a Union the Answer?

"When a fellow says it hain't the money but the principle o' the thing, it's th' money."

—Frank McKinney Hubbard

They're all doing it: engineers, legal secretaries, file clerks, stockbrokers, bank tellers, social workers, even Harvard University teaching assistants. Learning the latest dance, eating organically grown vegetables, flying kites? No. Joining unions.

There was a time when toilers in the white-collar vineyards didn't have to look around very much to know that the grass was greener on their side of the fence. They came to work later and left earlier. They were paid more. They got higher fringe benefits. They had more job security. Their work was usually more interesting and they had better working conditions.

And there were also some intangibles. The white-collar job meant middle-class status and some social standing.

This didn't mean that white-collar workers and professional people didn't appreciate the advantages of doing things collectively. They were often members of groups like the National Education Association, the American Library Association, or the Songwriters' Protective Association—venerable institutions which sometimes dealt with management, or sponsored benefits like health insurance, or organized campaigns to influence legislation. But for a long time professional organizations and white-collar associations either shunned affiliation with blue-collar unions or shunned the ultimate tactic of a union—the strike.

Times have changed and so has the status and the outlook of the professional and white-collar worker. Some of the offices themselves became more like factories —the noise of a factory production line wasn't too different from the noise of a room full of key-punch operators. Automation in the office eliminated some white-collar jobs (though the total demand for white-collar workers didn't diminish). Engineers who had often been a small elite group within a company worked in huge hangar-like rooms, with desks jammed next to each other—for all the world like a production line.

In many offices unorganized white-collar workers watched their blue-collar neighbors in the adjoining factory floor win higher wages, better working conditions, better health and insurance benefits, longer vacations, and better pension plans through the power of collective bargaining. And their blue-collar dollars, thanks to union-sponsored buying plans, often brought them discount buying privileges that were rightfully envied.

Then the successful organizing campaigns of teachers' unions around the country, especially during the decade of the sixties, gave a new impetus to the organization of professionals. And the advances won by teachers, plus the fact that they were willing to use strikes or the threat of strikes, helped dispel the feeling that only people who worked with their hands joined unions. The feeling of course was nurtured by the fact that some of the teachers belonged to unions that were affiliated with the blue-collar AFL-CIO (the merged American Federation of Labor and the Congress of Industrial Organizations).

Another big push to unionism came at the very end of the sixties when cutbacks in defense and space programs, and in support for universities through government-sponsored research and development grants, cut a wide and grim swath through the ranks of scientists, engineers, college teachers, and some of their supporting personnel. Aerospace engineers in particular began to reconsider their feelings about unions. When they were laid off because of the decline in the aerospace program their life and health insurance benefits were no longer paid for by their employers. Usually they had to be back on the job for at least thirty days before the company again picked up the tab for their coverage. In contrast their fellow production workers, members of the United Automobile Workers, continued to have their life and health insurance paid for by the company, since that was part of their union contract.

And so white-collar workers and professionals—who used to think joining a union meant resigning from the middle class—have been thinking second thoughts and doing something about it. The list of people who are exploring the possibility of setting up a union, or preparing for collective bargaining, or getting ready to hold elections is surprising in its variety. It includes, among others, chemists, hospital interns and staff doctors, lawyers, museum curators, the foreign service section of the U. S. State Department, and stockbrokers. Sometimes the organization they propose or actually sign up for isn't called a union and isn't affiliated with any national group—but it bargains like a union and upholds the principle of collective bargaining, a new approach for many who had previously counted on their own efforts to win the things they wanted from a job.

What are the advantages these union-come-lately members hope to gain? The list is long, and not too different in principle from the aims that their predecessors in blue-collar unions united for. But there is a major difference—some of the groups, just because they perform professional or specialized services, are asking for a policy-making voice in *how* they do their jobs. Teachers' unions want a say in how schools are run, social workers want a say in how their applicants are handled, nurses want to help set patient care standards. Some white-collar union leaders say these demands are as important to their members as are the hours of a working shift, for instance, or blue-collar members. But except for this new slant on union

membership white-collar workers in general have the same demands as their production workers and craftsmen friends.

First and foremost is the right to collective bargaining, evening the balance between the employers' economic power and resources and that of employees. The
weight of the employers' resources is matched by the weight of the union's ability to
close classrooms or stop planes from flying or cut municipal services.

But there's more to collective bargaining than the threat of striking. Most labor
agreements take place without a strike, but none take place without negotiations,
very often tedious and protracted on both sides. These negotiations aren't simple affairs—they involve facts and figures, government regulations, local customs, and
sheer staying power. Who supplies the facts and figures and how they are interpreted are a crucial part of the negotiations. Unions are able to hire their own economists, researchers, and lawyers or draw on the talents of outside economists, lawyers, and other specialists. With the advent of TV the press conference and the
union leader making his case on the nightly news roundup have become part of the
who-wins-what-from-whom settlement.

In among the major negotiating sessions when contracts come up for renewal
are the mini-sessions that take place from disputes that arise on the job. Instead of
dealing with an employer on a one-to-one basis, with the implicit threat of job
loss, the union supplies a buffer who goes under such names as shop steward, union
representative, business agent, or member of the grievance committee.

Second are the tangible benefits unions say they win for their members. They
point to higher salaries, better working conditions, better sick pay, more holidays,
longer vacations, improved fringe benefits such as health, insurance, and pension
plans. The health plans often offer services or coverage not only to the union member but also to his dependents.

Third there is job security. Union members frequently have clauses in their contracts that say they can't be fired unless employers can prove some kind of gross negligence. Laying off employees because there is no work is a different matter—but
even there union contracts often specify the conditions and order under which employees are to be rehired if business improves.

Fourth, unions point to the clout their members have just from being part of the
labor movement and being able to count on union solidarity in cases of labor disputes. Fellow union members can, if they want, refuse to make deliveries, or refuse to
cross picket lines, or boycott a company's products unofficially if not officially. In
cases of prolonged strikes they can even offer financial support to striking union
members. A concomitant to this is the extra clout provided by the "extended union," the union members' families, friends, and sympathizers. (In New York City,
for instance, it's been estimated that at least 15 per cent of the electorate is com-
prised of this extended union group—a fact never forgotten by the city's politicians.)

Fifth, there are the services that union members get from their unions—and in
the white-collar field some of these can be quite unusual. The New York local of
the American Federation of Television and Radio Artists (AFL-CIO) had an
"open door" week during which paid-up members got interviews with casting directors from twenty major advertising agencies in New York City that produced
commercials for TV. The Air Line Pilots Association (AFL-CIO) got several colleges and universities to set up educational programs that enabled pilots to take

classes in various cities, depending on their home base and layover or turnaround base. Office workers who are in District 65 of the Distributive Workers of America get doctor's prescriptions for 75 cents, a free pair of glasses every two years, and free counseling service from a trained staff on everything from landlord/tenant problems to how to pursue a hobby to how to get an abortion.

One of the little-publicized benefits of unionism to white-collar employees is information on a most fascinating topic—someone else's salary. Since blue-collar workers are usually paid at a given rate for a given job they know pretty well, sometimes in fact to the penny, what their fellow workers earn. Not so for white-collar workers—they are famous for their reticence about how much they make. This genteel shyness has made it possible at times for employers to pay less than the going rate, or to pay two individuals doing essentially the same work different salaries, depending on each employee's bargaining power. (Women, in particular, were victims.)

Consider Miss Jane Doe, legal secretary, who works for a senior partner in a law firm. She knows every quarrel and every torrid reconciliation of her girl friend's romance with a law clerk in a small firm next door, but she doesn't know how much the same girl friend earns working for a junior partner. Then Miss Doe gets a union newspaper and reads about a newly won contract for legal secretaries, and finds that she is earning less than the other secretaries. She shows the paper to her friend and the other secretaries, and everyone makes comparisons, mentally if not verbally.

The white-collar unions naturally enough make a strong case for the benefits of belonging to their unions. But in 1970 (the latest date for which figures are available) approximatley 16.2 per cent of all union members were in white-collar jobs—a little more than 3 million persons. Out of a white-collar labor force of about 38 million in 1970 this was a small number. Of course, many of these were individuals not eligible for union membership because they held supervisory or managerial jobs. Still, even allowing for this special group, it's a fact of life that unionism hasn't been an overwhelming success among American white-collar workers.

Why not? A variety of reasons are advanced, if not necessarily proven. Some are historical, some emotional, some dollars and cents.

Historically white-collar workers have felt they had more in common with the manager on the other side of the desk than the worker on the other side of the building. They believed, and they were right, that there was more status in being a manager than a worker, to say nothing of the things that went with the status, such as more money, pleasant offices, more job security, more holidays, longer vacations, etc. And there was also the pride in doing a job, a feeling that the job was important and so was the individual, not just one of the crowd. Joining a union meant losing some of that feeling that might be defined as professionalism and giving up some of that individuality.

Another reason has been that old-fashioned law of supply and demand. For many white-collar workers it's been a seller's market. Who needed a union when you could quit your job today and walk across the street and get a comparable or even better job tomorrow? Or when employers were looking for you and coaxing you to join their engineering staff, or help write their computer programs, or take dictation from their executive vice-presidents. (And in some major metropolitan areas even at the height of the mini-recession executive secretaries were still being sought after.)

Most of the nation's offices are "manned" by women and women have never been considered good union material. Because they are susceptible to blandishments like wedding rings and babies they are in and out of the labor market. And while their children are growing they often can't take full-time permanent jobs, and therefore aren't as concerned about the security and benefits that union membership promises, especially since these benefits usually don't cover part-timers.

But there are drawbacks to union membership as well, and they have nothing to do with attitudes or historical background.

When you become part of the group you gain from the group's strength, but you also have to abide by the group's decision. And the most painful decision you may have to abide by is the decision to strike. It may come at a time that is difficult for you financially. It may come at a time that you think is wrong strategically. It may even be a decision that you think will hurt rather than help your cause—but if the decision is to strike you have no alternative if you're a good union member.

And if you do go on strike you may find yourself very unpopular among your white-collar neighbors, particularly if their services are cut because you aren't working.

And even if you agree with the union decision, and even if you don't lose any popularity contests, you may find that the money lost by striking isn't made up by the increased salary or fringe benefits that you won. So you may be no better off than before.

Consider too the question of promotion. You may work very hard at your job and do it superbly, but if union rules and the union contract say that promotion is by seniority, you've got to stand in line.

Since competence is a relative judgment you may find that people who in your judgment (and perhaps in the judgment of their superiors as well) do only a mediocre job are protected by their union membership or the hiring and firing rules established by union contract. This means that not only are their jobs protected, but also their viewpoint on how these jobs should be done. And this in turn affects how a department is run. If the department has a mediocre showing you are, willy-nilly, caught in the web of mediocrity, which may hurt *your* chances for advancement.

Furthermore, outside the direct scope of your job the union may take a stand on your profession that you consider detrimental. A teachers' union, for instance, might endorse or promote teaching methods that you find absolutely inimical to your viewpoint, but as a card-carrying union member you would be obliged to uphold the union position.

An extension of this could be the requirement that you uphold the decisions of other unions. If you expect solidarity from your union "sisters and brothers" you've got to give in return. Part of your dues could go for supporting other people's strikes. Fine if you approve, but pretty irritating if you don't, and maddening if you actively disapprove. You might, for instance, oppose strikes by policemen, or firemen, or hospital workers, or bridge tenders, but be part of a labor council that includes these unions under a blanket of co-operation among municipal unions. Then your union's treasury might give help to such unions if they strike. (It isn't only politics that makes strange bedfellows.)

And speaking of politics, your union might, without your approval, donate money to support political candidates that you disagree with.

Which brings up the question of the standards of union leadership. Although no leaders of white-collar unions have been tainted with scandal there have been enough revelations about other union leaders to fill several volumes of congressional testimony. They have been found guilty of everything from filching from the union treasury to mismanaging union pension funds for personal aggrandizement to extreme violence against rival union slates attempting to elect new officers. (Joseph A. Yablonski, a United Mine Workers candidate for presidency of that union, was murdered by men hired by some old-guard UMW leaders, to cite the most extreme example.)

How can you decide whether you should join a white-collar union? The only good basis for a decision is *enlightened self-interest.* Are you in a field where the odds favor your succeeding in gaining the advancement, job security, working conditions, and fringe benefits that you think should be part of your career? Or are you in a field where circumstances you just can't control such as legislative acts, governmental fund appropriations or decisions by boards of trustees, are going to decide these things for you? When you look ahead do the odds favor your being able to provide security through your own efforts for yourself or your family as you get older? (A good question to ponder in view of the seemingly inevitable rise in the cost of living.)

If you can't answer yes to these questions then you may personally benefit from the collective strength that an organization offers, whether it's called an association or a union. You may find that the drawbacks are outweighed by the advantages, and you may even be able to overcome some of the objections—such as policies that you are opposed to—by seeing that you have a voice in your union's decisions. In some fields, as white-collar unions gain in strength, you may not have to or be able to make this decision. The closed shop, sometimes called the agency shop, may become a reality and you may have to join as a condition of employment. In other fields you may still be able to make a choice, and then you can only examine the whole question rationally—putting aside for the moment any prejudices you have—and play the odds.

You might just win.

· 14 ·

What to Do If You Lose Your Job, Or: Keeping the Wolf at Arm's Length

"If you're working it's a recession.
If you were fired, it's a depression."
Folklore, during the mini-recession of 1969–70

There was a time, and not so long ago, when it seemed impossible that white collars would ever get frayed. Education was the password, and the future for anyone with some college, to say nothing of a degree or even two, seemed made up of personal choices, not impersonal throws of the employment dice.

Then during the mini-recession all kinds of people—engineers, teachers, stockbrokers, copywriters, physicists, government employees—found that the future they thought was so secure wasn't unconditionally guaranteed after all. For many the paycheck stopped—but the apartment lease, the car payments, the loan and the mortgage payments didn't.

If it happened once it can happen again. (For more on the occupational outlook see Chapter 10, p. 70.) If it does happen to you, what's the best way to proceed? Your first reaction, when you find the pink slip or the yellow notice, or you're told that you're "surplused" (a phrase popular in the aerospace field), is to want to crawl into one half of a large clamshell and close the other half on top of you. Resist this temptation. It's probably the worst course you could pursue. Your best bet is to restore your sagging morale so that you have the strength to carry you through what may be a difficult period. And one way to do this—which will also make the difficult period a little easier—is to plan a course of action. The feeling of doing something concrete can reassure you that you still have resources and can spread some confidence to the other mouths you're feeding.

First step should be to arrange to collect your unemployment compensation. Find out all the benefits you're entitled to and be sure you know how to collect them. You may not need them all, but knowing they're there can be a relief.

Next, of course, a brief appraisal of your immediate assets: money in checking and savings accounts, stocks and bonds, insurance policies that you can borrow against, plus an appraisal of your less tangible assets, particularly skills that can bring in income. Some of the things that you have done as a hobby, or because you couldn't find anyone to do them for you, might be income producers. Carpentry, patio building, children's party-giving, minor repairs—list them all. Your first choice, of course, is to get back to a full-time job in your own field, but making a list of possibilities can give you a psychological boost; you are not completely without alternatives or choices.

(For suggestions on job hunting see Chapter 12 on how to write résumés.)

Before you start your hunt, however, and even though you may dread doing it, *you* should get in touch with all your creditors. Don't wait until you've missed payments or until they've heard from other sources that you've lost your job. In this day of corporate shake-ups and changing population trends and shifting government policies, losing a job is neither rare nor synonymous with personal failure. And how you react can influence how people react to you. The fact that you are coming to them shows that you are not only acting in good faith, but also that you have faith in yourself and in your abilities. And since you have worked out a tentative plan on how you will manage you are now in a better position to talk, with some confidence, to your creditors. Remember that it's to *their* interest to help you pay off your obligations. If you don't pay they will be stuck with a loss that they'll have to absorb. If you do pay, although very slowly, you are still an asset, not a liability.

So get on the telephone and make appointments to see whoever should be seen. If possible get to a department head who makes decisions and has some authority, rather than someone lower in the organization chart who will be afraid to take a risk. (And who may be more unsympathetic because your bad luck reminds him that he too could get a frown from Lady Luck.)

Dress carefully for the appointment and look well turned out—important for you, psychologically, and also for the effect it will have. Your appearance shows that you're in temporary difficulty but you're not beaten. Among other things, you are meeting people who are in the business community and who may be in a position to help you, or who may be asked their opinion of you during your job search.

Your first priority should be your automobile loan, for two reasons: (1) the car is constantly depreciating in value, so the longer you hold on to it, the less it's worth; (2) the terms of your loan agreement probably say the car can be repossessed if you don't meet your payments.

Then work on your other loans. The bank or savings and loan institution that holds your mortgage will help you work out a plan—it may be to pay only the interest on your mortgage until you are solvent again. Home improvement loans or other loans may be extended over a longer period of time, or you may even be granted a moratorium for a short period of time. Much depends on the circumstances, your plan for getting another job, your relationship with the bank and with your other creditors.

You should remember to check your life insurance policy either on your own or with your agent. Many cash value policies have a provision for the automatic premium loan. If you can't pay your premium before the end of the grace period—the time after the premium's due date during which your policy still holds good—the company may pay the premium for you, and charge it as a loan against your cash reserve. All provisions of your policy remain in effect until you can pay again yourself, and you receive any dividends that are due. But the benefits due in case of death are reduced by the amount of the premium payments that the company made for you.

The fact that you are going to your creditors, instead of waiting until they come to you, shows your responsibility. You'll get more than a gold star on your report card—you'll maintain a good credit record that will be useful in the future and you'll also be getting yourself off the hook in the present.

Nobody Can Tell You When to Drop Dead, Or: The Outlook for Being Your Own Boss

"Don't settle for a 1930 income in 1972—you can earn $25,000 a year—part time income."

—An advertisement for a franchise to sell household-cleaning equipment

It's a day like many others, only worse. The train is thirty-five minutes late; there's a major traffic tie-up; the subway crush is so bad you feel you've been in a steam bath with your clothes on.

Your fellow workers are unusually unco-operative, the boss doesn't even thank you for staying overtime on Friday night, and the idea you presented to the company's executive committee is rejected with a curt note that shows they didn't understand at all what you were trying to accomplish.

"What am I doing here?" you ask yourself. "Why am I knocking myself out for these *schlemiels* who don't appreciate my talents, that bastard who wouldn't thank me if I spent all weekend here, and those miserable neurotic executives who wouldn't know a good idea if it came up and bit them?"

You indulge yourself for a few minutes in that lovely daydream you've had before. You're working close to home and commuting at odd hours to avoid the rush; you have the freedom to try your ideas—most of which turn out to be profitable; you work with a pleasant group who treat you with respect and genuine affection because you're really a good boss.

As you recline in your easy chair, sipping a drink and surveying the beautiful view from your patio or penthouse, it's not clear whether you've come from the business you started yourself or the business you bought into as a franchisee. But it doesn't really matter since either way you're so delightfully prosperous.

Now, fasten your seat belt because Cloud No. 9 is about to run into a lot of turbulence. First, get up off that easy chair and take a good look at it—because you're not going to get much chance to sit in it. As David B. Slater, former president of the Mister Donut chain, said in discussing a restaurant franchise, "It sometimes shocks applicants visiting the headquarters to hear us tell them that for their $25,-

ooo investment and the eighty hours of hard work a week we expect they'll be putting in the first year, all they can *expect* is a fair reward for their labor and a reasonable return on their capital investment. No more—without a great deal of
luck."

And speaking to a group of engineers interested in starting their own business,
Robert J. O'Brian, a management consultant with Booz, Allen & Hamilton Inc.,
said, "You'll work harder than you ever thought you could. Commitment is the
glue that holds the whole thing together. Unless there is total commitment to make
it go it won't work."

What is "total commitment"? It could be eighty hours a week at the office, store,
or factory—plus more hours nights and weekends. It could mean several years or
more of hamburgers for dinner, no new clothes, an old car, a shabby apartment or
house. When your friends are off at the swim club or music festival or sports arena
you're minding the store or paying the bills or out talking to customers. You may
become a stranger to your spouse, your lovers, your relatives, your children. Mar-
riages have been known to get bumped apart riding along the nerve-racking, energy-consuming entrepreneurial road to success.

Well, you say, I don't think I'd let that happen. I realize there are personal hazards, but since I know about them I'll deal with them—and it's worth overcoming
them for the opportunity of being your own boss.

Here comes a big air pocket, from A. L. Tunick, charter president of the International Franchise Association, in a booklet written for the Small Business Administration:

The principal disadvantage of franchising is the subjugation of your personal identity to
that of the parent company, which has tremendous sums of money invested in building and
maintaining its identity for your use. If you enjoy having your business known by your name
a franchise may not be for you . . . Deeper than the loss of personal identity is the fact that
in a franchise operation you cannot make all the rules.

Contrary to the many "be your own boss" lures in franchise advertisements, you may not
truly be your own boss . . . You may have no effective voice in deciding your own future or
the products you want to sell. Your hours and days of business may be specified in the contract.

This view is echoed by Al Lapin, Jr., head of one of the most successful franchising businesses, International Industries. Mr. Lapin, who got his start franchising
the International House of Pancakes restaurants, told *Fortune* magazine he thought
the notion of independence for the franchisee has been oversold.

"That independent businessman idea is misunderstood," he said. "Maybe in
Samoa you can find one. A man becomes a franchisee because he wants to belong.
If he tells me he wants a Pancake House because he doesn't like to take orders, I
don't care if he's President Nixon's brother in Whittier, I won't sign him on."

THE "INDEPENDENT" BUSINESSMAN—
IS HE REALLY?

Is the situation any better for the independent businessman? Is *he* really his own
boss? Consider a typical week in the life of Alvin W., who is in the process of setting up a service business in the health field. On Monday he has to meet with his

banker, who wants to be informed about the status of the business before he contin-ues to approve the company's line of credit. On Tuesday he has to meet with his ac-countant to set up tax records for the employees he's begun to hire. He must comply with myriad government regulations concerning the hours they can work, the mini-mum wage they can be paid, the amounts that must be withheld from their salaries for tax purposes, the kinds of records he must keep, and new regulations that keep coming up as wage controls are introduced or changed or dropped. And he has to keep records of just about everything.

On Wednesday he must meet with some doctors that will work for him as con-sultants and answer all their objections about the contracts they are asked to sign. On Thursday he has an all-day session with an equipment manufacturer who has been reluctant to live up to the service arrangement he guaranteed before the equipment was leased. The manufacturer claims he can't get enough servicemen and therefore the malfunction of the equipment is beyond his control, so it may be a difficult session.

On Friday he has to explain to his stockholders where the company is heading, how the money they've invested so far has been spent, and when they can expect to get some return on their investment. He'll spend the whole day writing and rewrit-ing his statement, and since he can't afford to pay overtime he'll spend part of the weekend, with his wife's help, getting out a mailing to the stockholders. On Sunday morning he'll think back longingly to the day when he was only accountable to the vice-president in charge of new developments, instead of to his banker, Uncle Sam, and the stockholders.

All of these headaches, whether from the problems of being in business inde-pendently, with partners, or as a franchisee, require tremendous outlays of physical and psychic energy. (That easy chair is going to last a long time because it will get very little use.) But energy and motivation and will don't buy stock, rent space, pay salaries; for these cash is needed—capital to enable the business to get started and keep going until it begins to make a profit. Remember the old saying about starting a business on a shoestring? Shoestrings that are worth anything come very high these days.

Checklist for Evaluating a Franchise Offer

Prudent would-be entrepreneurs considering a franchise offer will investigate be-fore investing. The following checklist offered by the Bank of America should prove useful.

The Company
1. How long has the firm been in business?
2. What is its financial strength?
3. What are its plans for future development?
4. How does it rate with the Better Business Bureau?
5. How selective is it in choosing franchisees?

The Product
6. What is the product's quality?
7. Is it a staple, a fad, a luxury item?
8. Is it seasonal?
9. How well is it selling?
10. Would the franchise buy it on its merits?
11. Is it priced competitively?
12. Is it packaged attractively?

13. How long has it been on the market?
14. Where is it sold?

The Sales Area

15. Is the territory well defined?
16. Is it large enough to offer good sales potential?
17. What are its growth possibilities?
18. What is its income level?
19. Are there fluctuations in income?
20. What is the competition in this area?
21. How are nearby franchisees doing?

The Contract

22. Does the contract cover all aspects of the agreement?
23. Does it benefit both parties?
24. Can it be renewed, terminated, transferred?
25. What are the conditions for obtaining a franchise?
26. Under what conditions will the franchise be lost?
27. Is a certain size and type of operation specified?
28. Is there an additional fixed payment each year?
29. Is there a percent of gross sales payment?
30. Must a certain amount of merchandise be purchased?
31. Is there an annual sales quota?
32. Can the franchisee return merchandise for credit?
33. Can the franchisee engage in other business activities?

Continuing Assistance

34. Does the franchisor provide continuing assistance?
35. Is there training for franchisees and key employees?
36. Are manuals, sales kits, accounting system supplied?
37. Does the franchisor select store locations?
38. Does he handle lease arrangements?
39. Does he design store layout and displays?
40. Does he select opening inventory?
41. Does he provide inventory control methods?
42. Does he provide market surveys?
43. Does he help analyze financial statements?
44. Does he provide purchasing guides?
45. Does he help finance equipment?
46. Does he make direct loans to qualified individuals?
47. Does he actively promote the product or service?
48. How and where is the product being advertised?
49. What advertising aids does he provide?
50. What is the franchisee's share of advertising costs?

Consider the approximate price of some franchises, for instance. A Carvel ice cream center is $10,000, a Baskin-Robbins ice cream franchise, $12,000 minimum plus an additional $7,500 that can be financed. An Orange Julius quick drink and hot dog snack bar, $17,500.

An automotive supply store, Firestone Tire & Rubber Company, $25,000 or more; a Goodyear Tire & Rubber, $35,000 or more (the variables in both cases depend on location, equipment, inventory).

A Player's Cinema Systems (films for hotels, motels, cocktail lounges), minimum initial investment, $12,500.

A Kopy Kat duplicating center, $12,500.

Or how about some fairly typical businesses. A beauty shop, $10,000 to $18,000; a coffee shop, $23,000 to $46,000; a coin-operated self-service combination laundry and dry cleaner, $50,000 to $75,000. (Again the variables depend on location, equipment, supplies, etc.)

A day nursery with moderate but good standards, for twenty children, about $50,000.

And what do you get for investing this kind of money? Trouble, sometimes. Many franchisees have been very unhappy about their benefits from becoming part of a franchising arrangement—some to the point of taking their cases to court. Among the complaints have been arbitrary cancellation of the franchise contract for infringement of any one of hundreds of rules in the operations manual, at a loss to the franchisee; requiring that a franchisee buy his supplies from Big Daddy and then grossly overcharging for these supplies; promoting sales through expensive games, stamps, and other gimmicks and making the franchisee pay for them; through national advertising setting prices at unreasonably low levels in order to raise total volume, but leaving the franchisee with very low profits.

The independent businessman doesn't face these problems, but he has plenty of his own. In addition to all problems inherent in any business today's would-be entrepreneur has to face some of the problems of the times we live in. Inner-city areas, which traditionally have been the spawning place for new businesses, because cheap rents were possible, are deteriorating and have difficulty in attracting labor because they are dangerous (mothers won't let their daughters work there as office staff); they are also subject to vandalism and theft, or have sometimes been razed altogether to make way for expensive urban renewal projects.

Retail stores and small service organizations have always been a traditional way to get started—but now many of us don't want to shop in stores in blighted downtown sections, or we don't want to travel from one shop to another when we can get everything more quickly under one roof.

Interest rates have been high, making it more expensive to get started with borrowed funds or to keep going by asking your friendly banker to continue his friendship. He may be willing, but the price is still high.

And of course while Big Daddy, as franchisor, isn't laying down the rules as to how you have to run your business, he isn't around to give advice about advertising, and financing, and purchasing, and employee and customer relations either. So some of these things you have to learn the hard way, by trial and error: how to prepare a five-year projection for a banker, how to keep employee compensation records, how to be out of the office selling and in the office running the place, how to handle temperaments tactfully, and how to sweep floors efficiently.

THE NEW BUSINESS
FAILURE RATE—OUCH!

With all these obstacles would you guess the rate of new business failures is high? If you say yes, you're absolutely right. According to Dun & Bradstreet, Inc., the business-reporting firm that's been keeping records on such matters for many years,* the

* D&B excludes the professions, farmers, and many small, one-man services from its tabulations.

record for new ventures' success is not exactly what you would call rousing or even cheery.

Though most firms manage to make it through the first year the rate of failures begins to accelerate after that, reaching a peak in the third year, but heading downward after that. By the end of five years, however, in a pattern that's been fairly typical for the decade of the sixties and into 1971, the cumulative rate for new business flops reaches about 55 per cent. For businesses that have endured six to ten years the annual failure rate has been about 22 per cent; above ten years the comparable figure is also 22 per cent.

Why does it happen? Dun & Bradstreet, on the basis of its reports and on information from knowledgeable creditors, says that fraud, neglect, disaster, and "reasons unknown" account for about 8 per cent of the flops—and the remaining 92 per cent is attributed to general mismanagement, composed of about 50 per cent incompetence, and then almost equal parts of lack of experience in the line of business, lack of managerial experience, and lack of balanced experience, i.e., "experience not well rounded in sales, finance, purchasing and production on the part of the individual in case of a proprietorship, or of two or more partners or officers constituting a management unit."

Discouraging, isn't it? And yet, when so much is at stake, why not know the odds? They're certainly not totally stacked in your favor.

BUT SOME MAKE IT;
AND HELP IS AVAILABLE

But they're not totally against you either. It depends on whether you're an optimist or a pessimist. The pessimist would say that more than half the new businesses failed. The optimist would say that almost half succeeded.

If you're a pessimist, stop right here. You can make such a convincing argument for your outlook that there's no point in reading further. There are certainly enough ways to achieve what you want out of life within the existing structure, with time left for politics, hobbies, contributions to society, large or small, or just plain cultivation of a garden of the mind or of flowers, without bothering with this kind of hassle.

If you're an optimist you can play the odds to win. Dun & Bradstreet also points out in recent years more than 400,000 new firms are started each year; obviously some succeed. Yours might just be among the 22 per cent or so that do. What will you need to push the odds in your favor? A winning combination of money, place, timing, motivation, personality, a willingness to work incredibly hard, and just plain luck. (To cheer you on, keep in mind that the Necchi sewing machine company, the Sam Goody record chain, the D'Agostino grocery chain, and the Lewyt vacuum cleaner company, among others, were all started by penniless young men who ended up millionaires.)

To start, take the following quiz, prepared by the Small Business Administration. See what rating you would give yourself on the personal characteristics needed to get a business started. Under each question, check the answer that says what you feel or comes closest to it. Be honest with yourself.

Are you a self-starter?

    I do things on my own. Nobody has to tell me
      to get going.

    If someone gets me started, I keep going all right.   ———

    Easy does it, man. I don't put myself out until
      I have to.   ———

How do you feel about other people?

    I like people. I can get along with just about
      anybody.

    I have plenty of friends—I don't need anyone else.   ———

    Most people bug me.   ———

Can you lead others?

    I can get most people to go along when I start
      something.

    I can give the orders if someone tells me what
      we should do.   ———

    I let someone else get things moving. Then I
      go along if I feel like it.   ———

Can you take responsibility?

    I like to take charge of things and see them through.

    I'll take over if I have to, but I'd rather let
      someone else be responsible.   ———

    There's always some eager beaver around wanting
      to show how smart he is. I say let him.   ———

How good an organizer are you?

    I like to have a plan before I start. I'm usually
      the one to get things lined up when the gang
      wants to do something.

    I do all right unless things get too goofed up.
      Then I cop out.   ———

    You get all set and then something comes along
      and blows the whole bag. So I just take things
      as they come.   ———

How good a worker are you?

    I can keep going as long as I need to. I don't
      mind working hard for something I want.

    I'll work hard for a while, but when I've had
      enough, that's it, man!   ———

    I can't see that hard work gets you anywhere.   ———

Can you make decisions?

    I can make up my mind in a hurry if I have to.
      It usually turns out OK, too.

    I can if I have plenty of time. If I have to
      make up my mind fast, I think later I should
      have decided the other way.   ———

    I don't like to be the one who has to decide
      things. I'd probably blow it.   ———

Can people trust what you say?

    You bet they can. I don't say things I don't mean.   ———

I try to be on the level most of the time, but
   sometimes I just say what's easiest.   _____
What's the sweat if the other fellow doesn't
   know the difference?   _____
Can you stick with it?
   If I make up my mind to do something, I don't
   let *anything* stop me.   _____
   I usually finish what I start—if it doesn't
   get fouled up.   _____
   If it doesn't go right away, I turn off. Why
   beat your brains out?   _____
How good is your health?
   Man, I never run down!   _____
   I have enough energy for most things I want to do.   _____
   I run out of juice sooner than most of my friends
   seem to.   _____
Now count the checks you made.
   How many checks are there beside the *first* answer
to each question? _____
   How many checks are there beside the *second* answer
to each question?_____
   How many checks are there beside the *third* answer
to each question? _____

If most of your checks are beside the first answers, you probably have what it takes to run a business. If not, you're likely to have more trouble than you can handle by yourself. Better find a partner who is strong on the points you're weak on. If many checks are beside the third answer, not even a good partner will be able to shore you up.

If you're still, or perhaps even more, convinced that you have the makings of a future millionaire, the next step is to prepare yourself for the difficult times ahead. You're going to need all the help you can get—and there are lots of sources available to you. Let's talk about printed sources first—and first a word of caution about them. Don't assume, just because it's in print, that it's the last or the only word. Always check the dates of any publication, whether it's put out by a private organization or by the government, to be sure the advice applies to the current scene, or at least isn't too outdated. Look for the copyright or first printing date, usually in the front of the book or pamphlet; if the book or pamphlet has been revised the revision date is given.

SOURCES FOR READING MATTER
THAT WILL GET YOU STARTED

Now for some sources. The U. S. Government publishes many pamphlets specifically designed to help the beginning businessman. For a list of free publications from the Small Business Administration covering everything from "Handicrafts and Home Businesses" (No. 1) to "Selecting Employee Benefit Plans" (No. 213) ask for *SBA 115 A* at your nearest Small Business Administration office. (You'll find the address in your telephone directory under the U. S. Government listing.) For a list of publications that are for sale, at minimal cost, get a copy of *SBA 115 B*, which includes many individual publications on topics such as material handling, advertising, cost accounting, etc., plus a series on starting and managing various types of small businesses (bookkeeping, restaurant, dry cleaning, camera, flower, music store), plus annual management aid series for small manufacturers, research series, etc. Note that the publications on this list are not available by mail from the SBA, but rather from the Superintendent of Documents, Government Printing Office, Washington, D.C. 20402. However, you may be able at least to get a look at them at your local SBA office.

Many of the publications on these lists are quite current, and usually brief, clear, and authoritative. Some, however, because they cover a broad topic, such as advertising, aren't too much help, except in a very general way. A few were quite outdated when I looked at them, though there may be new or updated versions by the time you read this.

The Bank of America publishes the *Small Business Reporter* ten times a year, both on current topics, such as "Health Food Stores," and on topics of continuing interest such as "Business Management, Advice from Consultants." They're very well written, authoritative, and, if the topic warrants it, contain recommended additional reading. Although they're addressed to a California audience, and therefore often include California legislation or equipment prices, they are still broad enough to be worthwhile reading for anyone interested in small-business problems. A subscription to the *Reporter* is $8.50 for ten issues. You can also get back issues on specific business topics at $1 each. For a subscription or an index to the material write to Bank of America, *Small Business Reporter*, Dept. 3120, Box 37000, San Francisco, Calif. 94137.

Another good source of information is Dun & Bradstreet, Inc., mentioned before, which specializes in material for business and industry. They publish weekly, monthly, and quarterly bulletins on such topics as new business incorporations, failures (by size, volume, area of the country, etc.), trade reviews, businessmen's expectations, plus booklets and pamphlets on other topics of interest to businessmen. For a copy of their publications list write to Dun & Bradstreet, Inc., 99 Church Street, N.Y., N.Y. 10007. Here too be sure to check the publication or revision date on the material, or ask about it in advance—some of their publications, when I looked at them, were five years old or older. On some topics this may not be too important; for instance, generalities about maintaining good customer relations. On other topics, particularly where figures or ratios are involved, older data may be of questionable value.

One of the best sources of published information in any field is the trade magazine or magazines serving that field. Here's where the people in the field gripe about their problems, worry in print, and discuss the future. Certainly you'll want to look at and probably subscribe to such magazines while you're considering a business.

Trade associations, which sometimes publish such magazines, often have additional information available. So do Chambers of Commerce, and city and state Departments of Commerce or of Development. Obviously, the better informed you are, the better equipped you are to understand what you're getting into—or should stay out of. Your local library and particularly your local librarian can be very helpful in getting material for you; what's not on hand can be obtained through interlibrary loan. A librarian is a person to be carefully cultivated—one who takes an interest in you and has time to give you can be worth his weight in bound volumes.

What Form Should Your Business Take?

Once you've made the decision to become your own boss you want to organize your business in the most profitable way. You'll be limited somewhat by how much money you have to start with, the nature of the business itself, and your own strengths and weaknesses. But you should be familiar with the following possibilities. They are general guidelines only; before you make any decisions you will, of course, discuss the question with an accountant and a lawyer.

Individual ownership. If you're an independent spirit with lots of drive this form, the simplest and least expensive to set up, will appeal to you. As the sole owner you're in complete control. You make the decisions, you answer only to yourself, when things go well you can—within the limits of good business practice—give yourself a big fat raise and/or a big fat bonus. Naturally, there's a big fat drawback. If there are only losses, not benefits, they're all yours too. And it's not just a question of weeping into the crying towel you keep in the bottom desk drawer. You are *legally* responsible for all the obligations or debts incurred while you are in business. Furthermore, and worse luck, your liability is not limited by the amount of money you put into the business. Any assets in your name—your car, bank account, stocks, or bonds—can be claimed by your creditors. Lawyers have a name for it: unlimited liability.

The partnership. Now things get a bit more complicated. There are no legal upper limits on how many persons can be in a partnership, but the required minimum is two. If there are just two they unite as co-owners; they can invest equal or different amounts of money, training, talent, or services and receive the same or different shares of the profits, depending on their initial agreement. And, unless they agree otherwise, each partner has an equal right to share in managing the business and making the decisions. A partnership can be so informal as to be nothing more than a verbal commitment, which is usually not a good idea, nor sound business. No matter how much each of you loves, honors, and trusts the other, it's better and avoids future trouble to have a formal written agreement drawn up with the advice of an attorney. Such an agreement should specify the size of each partner's investment, how much time each partner will spend in the business, how profits and losses will be divided, what the responsibilities and powers of each will be, especially when it comes to buying goods and services and spending the partnership's money. Love affairs have a way of withering on the vine when an unexpected or ill wind blows.

The partnership has some of the advantages of individual ownership and some of the disadvantages, plus some advantages and disadvantages of its own. It is less expensive than a corporation, the partners have control and can share in the business profits. Because they draw on each other's capital and talents they may have more chance for success. They may be able to get more credit, both because they have more capital and personal resources, and because the business doesn't depend solely on one person. Furthermore, since they share the work the individual burden isn't as great. But, of course, there's the other side of the coin. They also share the separate mistakes each makes and any losses. And, like the individual owners, partners have unlimited liability.

Actually, there are two kinds of partnerships, general and limited. The most common form is the general partnership. A limited partner has limited liability. He's responsible only up to the amount of his original investment, and doesn't have joint responsibility as do the general partners. He is entitled to a share in the profits, but doesn't share in management. Limited partnerships are often set up by a business when it wants more money; an individual cannot become a limited partner by contributing services only.

The corporation. This is the most important of the three forms, and the most expensive and complicated to set up. The corporation can be an individual or a group of individuals who join to do business by incorporating. The government grants them a charter which gives the corporate unit some of the legal rights and powers of an individual; in effect, the law considers the corporation as a person. And as a person or legal unit the corporation can buy, sell, incur debts, own property, etc. But—and it's a big but—the individuals in the corporation have no personal liability. Corporations can get the money they need for the business by selling stock in the corporation, i.e., shares in the ownership of the company. If the business succeeds and the board of directors decides to do so, the profits are distributed to the stockholders as dividends.

GETTING PERSONAL HELP
FROM PEOPLE WITH KNOW-HOW

Even more important are the personal contacts you make. And here too there are people available to help you. The Small Business Administration was specifically set up to foster new companies or help struggling young companies get better established. To quote from a pamphlet of theirs, "SBA, what it is, what it does" (sic): "Small Businesses make up more than 95 per cent of our business population,† more than 40 per cent of our business activity and provide work for more than 35 million of our people. Therefore, it is obviously vital to our national welfare to encourage, assist and protect this sector if we are to insure a highly competitive free enterprise system as the basis of the American way of life. This is the mission given to the Small Business Administration by the Congress."

Part of the work of the SBA is a free counseling service through SCORE, Service Corps of Retired Executives. More than three thousand retired business executives, in almost two hundred chapters throughout the country, help small-business men and *prospective* small-business men (including franchisees) with their problems. They're on hand, in the local SBA office, for counseling to would-be entrepreneurs. They are men who enjoy their work because it gives them the feeling, though they've been retired, voluntarily or involuntarily, from the active business world, that someone still needs their expertise and finds them useful. You can take advantage of what they have to offer without committing yourself in any way. (With apologies to Women's Lib, it's usually men since it was the very rare woman who was in the business world as an executive enough years ago to be retired.) If they get interested in your project they can and do stay with you all the way. Many of the offices around the country can report success stories of businesses started on an SBA-furnished shoestring flourishing to the great satisfaction of the counselor involved and, of course, of the businessman himself.

† [Author's note: Don't get your hopes too high because of this figure. Though small businesses do comprise "more than 95 per cent of our business population," you'll note that the bulk of business, about 60 per cent, is handled by larger companies. Furthermore, though they've not been quite as profitable lately, the five hundred largest industrial companies—listed by rank in *Fortune* magazine every year—traditionally have higher profit margins (return on sales or money invested) than smaller companies.]

However, there are ways and ways of utilizing the talents available. Like many other things in life, the more you put into it, the more you get out of it. You have to do your homework first. Before you make an appointment with a counselor make an appointment with yourself, or with your partner or partners. Then state clearly —you might even want to write out—the information the SBA counselor will need from you, as follows:

1. Your training and experience in the field you're interested in, plus additional related experience you have. For instance, you may be a mechanical engineer by training, but also know accounting from courses you took while in college. Or you may be a trained nursery school teacher who worked in a public relations agency summers and knows something about public relations.

2. Your financial status, money you have available or that could become available if you were starting a business, such as loans from relatives and friends or credit from suppliers.

3. Any preliminary work you've done—locations you've scouted that look promising; people you know in the field who might help you; sources of supply that could be very advantageous.

4. Your own estimates about how much money (capital) you need to get started and keep you going until the business is self-sustaining, how many people you think will be needed, how much time you can devote to the business, and, if you are thinking of trying to hold onto your job at the beginning, who in your family will help—wife, husband, mother-in-law.

5. How much salary you're going to have to pay yourself from the business in order to survive, if it will be your only source of income. (Notice I said "survive," not live in the style to which you'd like to become accustomed. That will come later, but in the beginning you may have to cut your standard of living in order to have money for the business.)

The counselor is going to ask you these things anyway; you will be doing both of you a favor if you think them through ahead of time. (Some counselors have told me they are amazed by the vague ideas and lack of preparation of many of the would-be businessmen who come in.)

Now let's consider the men available to help you. Obviously, if you have in mind starting a small business manufacturing left-handed widgets you would get the best advice from a retired manufacturer of left-handed widgets, or if you want to open a boutique for imported blouses it would be lovely to be referred to someone who had just sold a blouse boutique after thirty-five years of successful operation. Your chances of hitting the jackpot like this aren't good. However, they are good that you can be referred to someone who has had some kind of manufacturing business or who has run a small shop or had experience importing merchandise. Naturally, if you know exactly what you're looking for it's much easier to get it, which is, of course, the great advantage of doing your homework.

This brings up some of the drawbacks of the SCORE chapters. Naturally, they draw on the pool of talent in the area they're in, and this pool reflects the businesses of the area. In the New York City chapter of SCORE, for instance, most of the men on hand have had experience in businesses related to clothing and fashion, since New York is still the center of the garment trade and the fashion industry. If you wanted to open a florist shop such men wouldn't be able to give you very specific advice; they lack not only specific knowledge but also a "feel" for the florist business and how it operates. Another general drawback is that the men draw on past knowledge, and history doesn't necessarily repeat itself. Times have changed since they were in business and they may really not be in touch with to-day's market.

You also have to count on a certain amount of waste motion until you get to meet the person, or persons, who can be of most help. In theory, since you have done your homework and know exactly what you are looking for, it should be possible to call and make an appointment to speak to someone who would be just right for what you have in mind. In practice it doesn't work that way. The men are a bit skeptical about phone inquiries, since they've had a surfeit of callers who have no more than a vague idea that they'd like to be their own boss. They are also quite busy with people they've already begun to counsel. And, since they are volunteers, they don't always hold themselves to a rigid schedule, so that though the office is always covered a man who is scheduled to be on duty at 10 A.M. may not, unless he's made the appointment himself, come in until after lunch.

Let's say you have done your homework, made your appointment, and come in to the SCORE office for an interview. (It is also possible, if appropriate, to have the counselor come to your home, or for you to go to his office, if he maintains one, or even to his home.) The two of you begin to discuss your problem and he begins to use words and initials you don't understand—like "P&L statement" (profit and loss —a summary of the revenues and expenses of a business for a given period of time, a year, for instance) or "fair trade" (a statute in many states that says a manufacturer can set the retail price for certain goods and that everyone selling the goods must charge the set price. It's being contested in many states.) You may be embarrassed about revealing your ignorance, but it will be even more embarrassing to fail. So forget your tender ego—it's got to get toughened anyway and you might as well start—and say quite frankly that you don't understand. You will not be demeaning yourself in the slightest—you will simply be showing that you are smart enough to ask questions so you can learn.

Another person who can be a big help is your banker. You don't have a banker? Do you have a checking account in good order? If you do, you have a banker, and if you are thinking of going into business he can be your best friend. He can help you arrange a loan, supply information about the community, give credit references on suppliers and customers, and sometimes help your customers get financing so they can afford to buy from you. If he can't do this himself because he handles only personal accounts, he can introduce you to the person in the bank who can—and it's merit points for him for bringing new business to the bank. Lots of other people can help you too—manufacturers, suppliers, advertising agencies, the policemen on the beat perhaps, and the sanitation man, as long as you are willing to listen and to learn, to ask questions without worrying about appearing foolish.

You have, of course, to maintain a healthy skepticism even as you're listening. You will always find some experts who assure you something can't be done—and on the basis of their experience they may be right in saying it. But your case may be the exception that proves the rule: your timing may be better, you may have a better idea, you may be willing to work harder, you just may be luckier. Listen and learn, but in the final analysis, you've got to make the decisions yourself. To maximize your luck get as good a lawyer as you can afford, preferably one who knows something about the businesses you're interested in. He will be one of the best investments you can make.

IT CAN BE DONE;
SOME WHO ARE DOING IT

To cheer you on your way, consider two success stories that show it can be and is being done. And just to overcome what may seem a masculine bias I've chosen two feminist stories as reported in the June 1973 issue of the feminist magazine *Ms.* Dilys Winn, an advertising copywriter, was asked by a friend what she was going to do for the rest of her life. "Without really thinking about it, Ms. Winn said, 'I'm going to open a New York bookstore called Murder Ink.'"

Six weeks after she said this she opened her bookstore's doors for business on Manhattan's West Side, an astonishingly diverse neighborhood of many races, creeds, academic and financial levels. In the interim she had conferred with her accountant, gone to several well-established bookstores on Fifth Avenue, noted all their mystery book titles, and found out from publishers all she could learn about costs, delivery schedules, and credit. As pluses Ms. Winn had a $10,000 bank account, keen marketing judgment as to what mystery books readers would like to read, a colorful personality—and a real stroke of luck. The day she opened Murder Ink a New York *Times* reporter, new in the neighborhood, wandered by her shop while looking for a laundromat and wrote a feature story for the *Times*. She got a rash of publicity in all the media—the kind of publicity that money usually can't buy—at absolutely no cost. As a result Ms. Winn has developed an extensive mail-order business, has plans to franchise the Murder Ink concept to would-be mystery bookstore owners in other cities, and is "well above" her break-even point.

A more typical profit and loss picture is Liberation Enterprises, started by two free-lance commercial artists, Rose Fontanella and Stephanie Marchus. The two women formed a partnership to buy products wholesale mainly from women and then to retail the items by direct mail. They also sell products that they develop themselves. The two began in February 1972 with about $5,000 they "borrowed" from their own savings. Even more than Ms. Winn the two partners spent untold hours doing their homework: reading about mail-order businesses, looking at mail-order catalogues to get some idea of the competition, shopping stores to learn about pricing and marketing, and visiting manufacturers. Each continued to work as a commercial artist so they could put all Liberation Enterprises' income back into the business.

After about a year the two were able to pay back to themselves some of the money they'd invested, but they chose instead to reinvest it in their business. They have since been able to pay all the business expenses out of sales, while building the business and a good credit rating. By 1975 they expect to reach the break-even point and, of course, go on to being profitable.

No overnight millionaires in this be-your-own-boss race. Unbelievably long hours, hard work, frustration, self-doubts. But also help from those who are in business, advice and encouragement, and—despite all the obstacles—still people who achieve the American dream. You may be one of them.

Good luck!

· 16 ·

Danger Ahead:
The Questionable Practices
of Some Employment Agencies,
Job Counselors, and
Executive Consultants

"I've made my fortune—and I'm going to retire."
—J. Paul Getty, age twenty-four,
to his parents, after he'd made
his first million dollars as an
independent oil operator

Money may mean nothing in your young life—but unfortunately the butcher, the baker, the bank, and the finance company don't share your view. So the time comes when you decide you need more money and a new job to provide it. Or, in this day of technological change, mergers, and shifting employment trends, you may find yourself looking for a job through chance, not choice.

Job hunting is hard work. It's also time-consuming, energy-consuming, and on occasion ego-threatening. Knowing this, a whole industry has grown up that tries to overcome or offset all these factors and, not incidentally, to keep its owners, managers, and employees from being on the job market themselves.

This is not to say that the whole industry is bad, immoral, or fattening on the gullibility of its clients. In fact, if you are career-minded and develop a good relationship with an executive of a knowledgeable, well-run personnel agency who keeps in touch with you he can often hold the ladder for you and maybe even give you a gentle shove upward. Ethical firms in the industry serve a useful function for their clients, both employers and employees. But the ones that operate just on the fringe of legality or permit their employees to engage in some dubious tactics can actually be a hindrance when you're looking for a job. And if you bite into the one rotten apple in the barrel it's no consolation to know that all the other apples in the barrel are good.

First, let's take a look at the several levels that comprise the employment industry field. At the narrow and exclusive pinnacle are the executive search firms, also known as executive recruiters or "headhunters." It's their job to find executives for their clients, companies who pay a fee, or sometimes a yearly retainer, to the search firm that will find the right person for quite a high-level job. They come looking for you when you're already in a delightful salary bracket and a responsible position (and probably don't need them). If this is your present cheery situation, read no further.

But if this is not your happy state of affairs you'll be interested in the next level— the executive job-hunting counselors also known as career consultants, advisers, placement specialists, and other variations on the same theme. Most are not employment agencies and don't offer jobs. What they do offer is *packaging*—to help you in your job search by showing you how to emphasize your strengths and minimize your weaknesses, and in the process sell yourself to a new employer or even upgrade your status with your present employer. They usually deal with middle management personnel in the $14,000 and up job market.

Their package to you may include help in preparing a résumé and then circulating it: aptitude testing; psychological testing; counseling, including both a general discussion of the job market you're in or trying to get into and suggestions along the way as you look for opportunity. And variations in between, depending on the background, expertise, training, and inclinations of the person or group who started the agency.

And that's an interesting point. Because there are no qualifications required, no licensing needed, no standards set for becoming a career consultant, you too, if you had the will (some would say the nerve or *chutzpah*), the rent money, and the letterhead, could set yourself up as an executive placement counselor. You would then be entitled to a fee for your packaging and counseling services, which could vary from very good to very poor, and from honest and helpful to less than honest and perhaps even damaging or fraudulent.

This is *not* to say that all such agencies are cheats or frauds or even incompetent. Some do offer real services to individuals who aren't sure where their talents lie, or whether they can make any further progress in their own field. Or even how to put their best foot forward without tripping over it. Sometimes they provide psychological support when someone feels he has exhausted his own resources and needs to turn to outside help.

Yet it's this very need for psychological support that turns off the executive recruiters or headhunters. They make a practice of *not* hiring anyone whose résumé comes to them via a counseling firm. How do they know the résumé comes from a counseling firm? Some have imprinted stationery, but more generally they send out the résumés on unmarked stationery, so it seems as if they came directly from an individual. However, the style of the résumé is so conventional and the covering letter so uniform that experienced headhunters claim they can not only tell that the résumé was prepared by a counseling service, but also by which counseling service!

As one headhunter put it, "I look for men who are leaders. These agencies provide a useful service to someone who needs them. They do offer a psychological crutch—but if a man needs such a crutch he's not my man."

Another criticism of such counseling firms is their carelessness. They have been known to send résumés haphazardly to executives of companies by title, e.g., president, chief of operating division, or director of sales and marketing, instead of by name. This of course aims résumés right for the wastebasket.

(Such practices, of course, reflect carelessness on the part of management—something I have personally observed. In the course of writing this chapter I became an "applicant" at one of the counseling firms. In their prime brochure, which listed the company's staff, complete with pictures and background, I found seven errors, including incorrect spelling of company names and ordinary spelling errors that a junior proofreader would be ashamed to admit to.)

More serious than these drawbacks are enough proven charges of misrepresentation or fraud to lead to cease and desist orders from the New York City Department of Consumer Affairs, and from the Federal Trade Commission. Here is a list of the sins of omission and commission brought against various counseling firms:

1. Advertising or stating in promotional material that the counseling firm was an employment agency and could get jobs for clients, or making such claims orally.

2. Not telling clients the fees for the program, or the least and the most expensive program available, before they signed a contract, or urging them to switch to more expensive programs after they'd signed and started.

3. Persuading clients to contract for vocational and psychological tests with independent testing organizations without disclosing that the counseling agency receives a rebate from the testing organization. Or using information derived from psychological testing of the client to persuade the client not to cancel his contract. Or suggesting that the individual's qualifications would probably lead to success in placing him or her in a better job—when in fact the agency was willing to accept anyone who was willing to sign up and pay a deposit.

4. Stating there was no financial risk to the client, when in fact there was such a risk. Clients with some agencies had to deposit from $500 to $2,500 and often didn't get this deposit refunded if they decided to withdraw.

If you understand the limitations of such firms—they don't have jobs unless they say so in writing, they're not well regarded by headhunters—they might be helpful. There are certainly times in anyone's career when he may need advice, a psychological boost, or even the impetus that comes from paying for a service. If you decide to go ahead check the Better Business Bureau and/or your local or state consumer protection agencies before signing a contract.

A better alternative, if it's career direction that you're seeking, is to investigate the psychological and aptitude testing services that may be available from colleges and universities in your area. They usually offer such services at a much lower fee than comparable tests administered by or through a counseling firm.

PERSONNEL AGENCIES—
SOME RAGGED EDGES

In contrast to the executive counseling services, which exist primarily to serve job seekers, personnel agencies exist to serve the employers who not only provide their basic commodity, jobs, but also usually pay the fee. Naturally enough, therefore, their operations are geared to please employers. In addition, most agencies' interviewers, or "placement counselors," as they prefer to be called, draw at least part of their salaries from commission. So it's up to them to be, as the ads say, "sales-motivated"—and that means continually on the lookout for new business.

Part of these efforts to please include being able to anticipate openings and/or always having a ready supply of good applicants on hand so the agency can give prompt service. Furthermore, having a variety of applicants in the file gives an agency a better competitive position in a highly competitive field which, though it may require licensing, is open to anyone with enough capital to pay for some office space and some newspaper advertising.

Add on to these factors just one more: a somewhat uncertain market for professional people or for some white-collar jobs, and what do you get? Situations like this:

The come-on ads. They're general enough to fit the description of several possible jobs in a particular category, though there may be only one job opening on record with the agency. Many qualified people call and come in to register, thinking there is a bona fide job opening. Then, after an interview, they're told that the job has been filled.

Sometimes the agency sets one of its employees to work calling employers and mentioning that a person with qualifications they may be looking for is now on file. For the employer this is great. If he's been thinking of expanding, or replacing poor old Joe who hasn't been doing too well lately, he now knows he'd have no difficulty. For the agency it's great: they've shown the president or personnel manager of Outer Space Inc. that they know his problems, are thinking of him every minute, and can always find him someone he needs quickly.

But how about the poor applicant, who gulped down a cold hamburger in a phone booth so he could dash over on his lunch hour. Who stayed up late the night before typing a résumé slanted to the job opening advertised. Or spent train fare to come into the city to apply. He's wasted time, money, psychic and physical energy for a non-existent job.

The "elastic" salary range. Most jobs have a salary range within which the interviewer can maneuver, depending on the qualifications of the applicant. This is usually true even for jobs that say "salary open." The person doing the hiring is interested in getting the best person at the lowest possible figure, but he can offer somewhat more, perhaps to a midpoint in the range for the job, if he finds an exceptional candidate.

The personnel agency asks for the salary range, of course, and will often ask how high the company will go to get *exactly* the right person—which may include a combination of requirements that cover everything from total dedication to smoking the same brand of cigarettes as the boss.

Guess which end of the salary scale appears in the newspaper ad.

And finally there is the case of the *job "possibility."* An agency hears that there may be openings at a particular company. The counselor who handles the account and knows the company has a pretty good idea of the kind of person needed for the job. He calls up his friend in the department concerned and says he thinks he can find Mr. or Ms. Right should the job become available. He gets a tentative go-ahead, something like—"Well, when the manager of the new international division arrives a few weeks from now he's certainly going to need an assistant, so if you have somebody good lined up he'll want a look." The counselor promptly advertises the job as if it did indeed exist.

Then people like Eve N. answer the ad. Eve is a *cum laude* graduate of one of the most prestigious of women's colleges. Her father was a diplomat when she was a child and in addition to being well traveled she speaks fluent French and does fairly well in several Eastern European languages. Her background fitted well with the job as advertised—in addition she is well spoken and attractive. She spent several hours preparing a good résumé, came in for the interview with the agency, was sent to the company and interviewed there too by one of their personnel department interviewers. He was quite impressed both with her *and* with the kind of applicant the employment agency sent.

But of course Eve never heard from the agency again. She thought she had flunked, spent many an unhappy hour searching her soul wondering where she had gone wrong—dress too short or too long? Did she talk too much or not enough? Was her résumé poorly written?—all of which lowered her morale by several big notches. But the fact was that the job never materialized, since the manager brought his own assistant with him. However, the employment agency got several job orders later for other jobs in the company.

Unfortunately, even in states where employment agencies are licensed and/or operate under some kind of regulation, such abuses exist. And they continue to exist despite laws or statutes specifying fines or loss of licenses, forcing an agency to close, if violations are proven.

(I have discussed these practices plus some outright illegal actions, such as accepting job orders that discriminate on the basis of race, creed, religion, or age, with the president of one of the largest and most ethical agencies in the New York metropolitan area—where there are strong consumer protection laws at both the city and state level. He acknowledged that these abuses exist, despite efforts not only of the city and state officials but also of officials of the Association of Personnel Agencies of New York State. Though these practices are continuous they are somewhat more prevalent in bad times. The problem, he said, lies partially with those employers who are perfectly happy to go along with such abuses because "they don't want to get involved" or because the agencies "get me people.")

How can you protect yourself against such agency practices? It's just about impossible to screen out some of the abuses, short of asking point blank if there is actually that specific job available at that specific company, which—with its implication that the personnel counselor is telling less than the truth—isn't usually feasible. But you can follow a general line of action:

1. Try to get an evaluation of agencies from friends or business acquaintances.

2. Check on the agencies used by companies that you are familiar with and respect; if you can do it discreetly find out the agencies that your present employer deals with.

3. If you're in a strange city check with the local Better Business Bureau or consumer protection agency, if there is one.

4. If there is a local association of employment agencies consult their membership list. These are the more established, better-financed agencies who have a stake in maintaining the ethics and professional practices not only of their members but also of all the employment agencies in their metropolitan area.

5. If you're at the start of your career and you get help from an agency keep in touch with the counselor who helped you, as well as with the company. There's a very high turnover in the placement field and you may want to follow the job-

hopping of your counselor. Then, when you're in the market again and you note an opening through this counselor you can discuss it with some assurance that you're getting, if not the whole story, at least most of it.

6. Finally, on the question of salary range, you have more leeway. People expect other people to be probing when it comes to money. No harm in asking whether the advertised salary is the high figure or the low, and showing that you are knowledgeable.

Of course, if you think you've been given the run-around report it to the association of agencies or the Better Business Bureau or consumer protection agencies. You may save yourself grief in the future.

Job hunting is never easy, but there's no need for it to be disreputable or fraudulent.

· 17 ·

How to Counteract Some Bad Advice to Wives—Plus Some Good Advice Geared to Your New Outlook

"Biology is destiny."
—Sigmund Freud
"***!!! to you, Dr. Freud."
—A Women's Libber

It used to be either/or. Either you got married or you worked. Then came Women's Lib and some far-out advocates who said marriage is a form of legalized prostitution and work is something male chauvinist pigs get women to do while they are out having a marvelous time with challenging careers. In between are the vast majority of young wives caught in a world of multiple choices, very often with no "right" answers.

The big change is that women do have choices; no more either/or. They can stay single without losing status. They can marry early or late, have large families, small families, or none at all. They can (though fewer and fewer do) follow the traditional pattern and devote their lives to their husbands and their children. They can combine marriage and a career and children simultaneously or in a variety of sequences. Or they can marry, have children, and work; there is a difference between working and having a career and that too is a choice that must be made.

Each of these options has its own special problems—as what in life doesn't?—but some have more problems than others. Assuming the choice is voluntary, probably the least problematical, from a psychological if not a financial standpoint, is the one-career family, usually the male career. He brings home the wolf pelts, she cooks the meat and makes a snappy car coat from the fur. And probably the most difficult to juggle is the two-career family.

Thanks to the new life-style, Women's Lib, a generation of boys raised by working mothers, or who-knows-what, it's no longer considered just woman's work to attend to the nitty-gritty: shopping, putting out the garbage, seeing that the clothes get cleaned and the windows get washed. In theory, if not thoroughly in practice, these chores have become anyone's work—to be divided equally, depending on who has the time and the talents to do the chore efficiently.

The real problem of two careers comes when the careers begin to diverge—when the husband gets an irresistible job offer in a different city and the wife has an immovable job she cherishes that can't be duplicated elsewhere. It used to be taken for granted that the wife would move. This is no longer necessarily true, particularly if there are no children. Sometimes the husband says no thank you. Sometimes it's possible to manage to maintain two households. Sometimes it's the first step toward a divorce.

Some couples forestall this problem by becoming a "package deal," a solution that may be possible for husbands and wives just out of graduate school with similar credentials. Here too things are changing. Companies that used to frown on keeping Miss Jones, research, if she married Mr. Smith, operations, are now not only accepting executive couples, but even finding them an asset. The companies reason that there's small chance they'll lose either partner because the other one is transferred to a different location. It isn't always easy, or even possible, to be part of a package like this and then to "sell" it. However, for those who have been successful it's been a happy and lucrative experiment.

These new life-styles are still the exception rather than the rule. Undeniably children complicate any marriage, and when the wife has an interest in being more than wife and mother, the complications are even greater. In theory the new life-style says that if both parents are working they split the chores. In practice it often doesn't work that way—and male chauvinist pigdom isn't always the reason. There are other causes, including economic ones.

Women are still not earning as much as men. It's true that in the professional fields what the U. S. Department of Labor calls the "earnings gap" between salaries offered to male and female college grads has narrowed considerably in recent years, particularly in accounting, chemistry, economics and finance, engineering, liberal arts, mathematics, and statistics. At its lowest point the gap was under $100 annually, a big improvement over previous years. But in other fields the gap still exists. There are several reasons. Men are paid more for similar work, though the difference may be justified by giving the man's job a different job title. Men have the higher-paying jobs in a given field: they are the executives, school principals, doctors, and administrators; women are the secretaries, teachers, nurses, and assistants. More women work part-time, have less education and therefore more of the less-skilled, lower-paying jobs in the less-skilled, lower-paying fields. But even allowing for all these factors women still earn about 20 per cent less than men.

This earnings gap affects who does what, when, and for whom (the economists call it division of labor, and assume that it's done on the basis of efficiency, not sex). The sad truth is that the doctor, the dentist, and the shoe store man couldn't care less about who empties the garbage. All they want to know is who fills the bank account. So if Daddy gets paid more, at least while the children are young Mommy is more likely to have to accommodate her schedule to Daddy's, unless everyone agrees to a lower standard of living. (Since I don't want to be blackballed by any present or future Women's Liberation, feminist, or women's equality group, many of whose aims I agree with, let me say right here that I am neither espousing nor condemning this accommodation. I am simply "telling it like it is" at the moment.)

When the two-career family is faced with a choice that involves moving and Daddy's career pays more, the odds favor Daddy, even if Mommy's career is set back. Not fair, maybe—no, not fair definitely—but fairness is not one of the things that make the world go round. With this perspective, it's no wonder that many young wives find it difficult even to consider giving careers the same devotion that men do. Add to this the undeniable pleasure that comes from hearing baby's first "coo," watching him turn over for the first time or take his first tentative step without holding on—and many young wives choose to defer their return or commitment to the working world until their children are at least partially self-sufficient.

If you think you are, or will be, in this group you will probably get either no advice or poor advice about how to handle this period of postponement.

And postponement it usually is—rather than farewell. The woman who works before she gets married or until the children are born and then never goes back is getting to be more and more of a rarity—as you've probably noted by looking around at who cashes your checks at the bank, waits on you at the store, greets you when you open a charge account, or ushers you into your doctor's office. (If you're interested in facts and figures, in 1972 women were, according to the Bureau of Labor Statistics, two out of every five American workers. Most of them were married and half were over thirty-nine years of age.)

Now what happens when you kiss your youngest child goodbye at the school bus stop and suddenly realize you're not a full-time mother any more? Your reaction can vary from "Thank the lord, at last! Thought I'd never make it" to an acute attack of suddenly feeling middle age tapping you on the shoulder. But at this point you usually begin planning on what you're going to do with your newfound little bit of freedom—and *at this point it's very, very late*. The time to start planning, if you want to have at the very least a job you enjoy, and at the most a career, is when you are looking for your beginning, though not necessarily your first, jobs. And your attitude should be the same as men's, i.e., a belief that they are going to work most of their lives and therefore jobs are steps—if not always upward at least sideways, and certainly never backward.

Several things operate against such female attitudes, even in this day of Women's Liberation. There is still some of the "it doesn't matter it's only for a short time" syndrome. It's exhibited by advice such as this, from a popular magazine, to the job-hunting wife:

"Like, does it really have to be something in the front office? A job in the stockroom may not be as chic, but the lesser need for classy couture can have a happy effect on both personal and household expenses—fewer new clothes, less money for the hairdresser, little or no addition to the dry-cleaning bill; you can even brownbag lunches and snacks without losing face."

My answer is YES, it *does* have to be something in the front office. Because when you, as a housewife returning to work, or looking for part-time work, or even planning to do volunteer work, are asked, "What experience have you had?" and you say you worked in the stockroom that's where you're going to have to start again—and probably in the basement stockroom at that. Nobody cares how much you saved on cleaning bills or fancy clothes or hairdresser charges; what they care about is what kind of work you did so they know where to place you.

You also have to watch out for your husband's unconscious attitude that it doesn't matter, even if *you* decide that it does. He too has to take the long-range viewpoint and think of your careers in terms of how it will go five or even ten years from now. Among other things this will make him more aware of the importance of equal pay for equal work, because an unequal paycheck is going to short-change your joint income.

Beware too of his unconscious transference of his frustration at not being able to tell off his boss onto your boss—a feeling that someone in the family ought to be free to quit. And since he, the mainstay of the family income, can't do it, you should. Both of you have to think in terms of investing your time now for a future payoff —your job is a deposit that you're going to draw against someday, so you want to make it count for something.

This in fact has to be the idea that always simmers in the back of your head, governing your thoughts and actions on the conscious and subconscious level. Such an approach means that you look at the work you're doing and think of the possibilities of doing it part-time, or of doing some of it at home on a free-lance basis. If your job can't be done on such a basis keep an open eye and mind for other jobs in your department, section, or company, that might be done part-time or free-lance. And get to know the personnel manager so that you can someday suggest such possibilities to him, or so that he will both think in these terms and think of you when part-time openings become available.

This doesn't mean that you are going to look at any old part-time job as an opportunity. Coming in to clean offices at night is probably always available, but that's not exactly what you have in mind. You want something that's related to your ultimate career, and that will, as first choice, develop the skills you have. You want a job that will keep you in touch with the people of influence within the company, so they can remember what a real doll you are, what an asset, someone they don't want to lose contact with. You may have to plan how the work can be done and then convince your employer that it's feasible.

Take heart in the fact that companies are much more open-minded than they used to be about such possibilities, thanks to some women and even a few men who have proved that it works. Catalyst, an organization that pioneered in encouraging college-trained women to continue their education, or to use their talents in part-time jobs, has much written material and a wealth of experience to draw on. Their newest series of publications is geared more than ever before to the combination wife-mother-working woman, and how to become one. They have a series of pamphlets, divided into three general classifications: self-guidance, educational opportunities, and career opportunities. The guidance pamphlets give practical advice in preparing for work and planning a job campaign; the educational series gives information on requirements, curricula, etc. in ten fields of study; the career opportunities pamphlets cover twenty-seven separate fields for jobs. All of the pamphlets are aimed at women, all are well researched and authoritative; all suggest practical things to do and part-time and/or full-time opportunities. To get information about their publications write to Catalyst, 6 East 82nd Street, New York, N.Y. 10028.

The question of salary is always interesting. When you're a full-time employee you usually cost the company a great deal more than your own salary; some companies add on 100 per cent additional expenditures under the general heading of overhead. Included in this catchall phrase are the space you occupy, the furniture you use, the services you call on, such as lounges, cafeteria, maybe medical care, plus—often a big item—company contributions to a pension plan, profit sharing, or group health insurance.

When you are a part-timer some of these expenses—depending on how the company's employee benefit and accounting systems are set up—are either reduced or eliminated. So your employer is getting someone with experience who knows the company, who will be on call for peak loads or emergencies, and who may cost less than a full-time employee because of lower overhead. When you think of or discuss salary, keep this in mind. Admittedly you're not in the best bargaining position, since part-time jobs aren't always easy to find. But you can at least be aware of the fact that you are offering skills and know-how at a good price, considering the reduced overhead. The advantage in hiring you therefore is not just yours, but mutual.

As Chart 6 shows, there is a growing trend toward part-time work, so you will be swimming with the tide. Whether you use a paddle or a surfboard to stay in the mainstream doesn't matter. It's getting in there and swimming that counts.

CHART 6

The proportion of workers employed part-time by choice increased rapidly in the past decade. The service-producing industries provided most of the part-time opportunities. If the trend continues, by 1980 one out of every seven persons will be a part-time worker.

Per cent of non-agricultural employees voluntarily working part-time

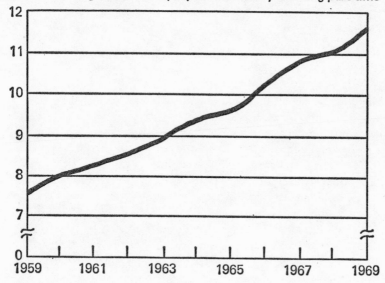

As a group, those who most frequently want part-time work—16-24-year-olds, married women aged 25-64, and older workers—will increase substantially.

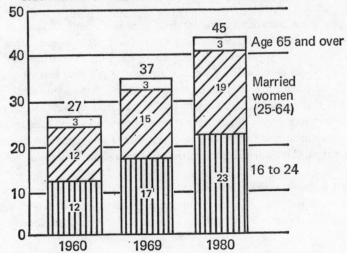

16-24-year-olds, married women,
older workers in civilian labor force (in millions)

The growth of part-time work opportunities will help meet the part-time work needs of students, married women, and older workers.

Source: Bureau of Labor Statistics (*The Manpower Posture of the Seventies*, November 1970).

· 18 ·

How to Do Well While Doing Good —A Purposeful Approach for Wives

"The secret of success is constancy to purpose."
—Benjamin Disraeli

You're planning to have a baby, or you're lucky enough to have one already. You're not interested in working until the baby's ensconced in nursery school or kindergarten. But eventually you know you would like to "do something," preferably something interesting, valuable, and lucrative (and not necessarily in that order).

When should you start preparing? Yesterday. The day you think about having a baby isn't a moment too soon. Why? Because the best-laid plans of wives and mothers are usually feasible only if there are options—and you may have to take a hand to be sure the options are there.

For instance: You want to have a part-time job when your first child is old enough for nursery school. You don't want to, or cannot, pay the tuition for a private nursery school. Perhaps you were smart enough to rent an apartment in a development that has a nursery school on the site, or you still have the chance to do so. If not, the answer obviously is a do-it-yourself project, getting together with other mothers and fathers who share your viewpoint and ambition.

If what you want is an informal, you-mind-my-dumpling-and-I'll-mind-yours arrangement, little formal organization is needed, but that's not what you should be after. What you need is something more formal, more structured, and above all more reliable. You will need space, equipment, probably even one paid professional person. This goal takes time, effort, information, research, money, patience, true grit, and selfishness—selfishness, so you start it and count on its being flourishing in time to benefit *your* child.

My friend Susan K., for instance, had this very much in mind when she moved from an apartment in Brooklyn, New York, to a brand-new suburban development on Long Island. While she and Stuart were busy seeding their lawn Susan was busy getting together with neighbors to form a co-operative nursery. And by the time her oldest daughter was ready for the nursery, there it was, doing fine. More than that, there were new volunteers on hand to take over some of the work of managing the co-op, so that Susan could think of her next step—enrolling in the local college so she could begin to get her master's degree in preparation for the day she would go back to work.

But private nurseries aren't the only answer, though they may be the most likely one for some time to come. Some apartment complexes, as I've already mentioned, include nurseries. Colleges and universities have long had such centers as a boon to students studying childhood development, to say nothing of the boon to the faculty wives whose children seemed to thrive on a combination of developmental study and plain old-fashioned tender loving care. Churches and synagogues have also sponsored play groups and/or nursery school and even after-school centers for children of their congregations.

An interesting development (and an idea that has been widely accepted in Europe and Scandinavia) is the nursery on the premises for working mothers, and who knows, perhaps someday for working fathers. (Who is to say that it has to be Mother who brings Johnny with her and picks him up after the day's work? Maybe Daddy would like to take Johnny and bring him home while Mother stops off after work to run errands, or shop, or get dinner started.) As of 1970 there were eleven U.S. companies with day care centers for their employees' children. They were sponsored by unions or hospitals or government agencies, and proving their worth to the children, the employees, and the employers.

So why not think of forming co-operative nurseries on the job? And local industries, particularly those short of womanpower, might be approached with the idea— especially if it could be shown that the cost was minimal considered against the cost of turnover and absenteeism. (For a full description of the programs already in existence write for "Day Care Services: Industry's Involvement," Bulletin 296, 25 cents, Women's Bureau, Workplace [sic] Standards Administration, U. S. Dept. of Labor, Washington, D.C. 20210. And for an excellent book on starting day care centers I recommend *Day Care* by E. Belle Evan, Beth Shub, and Marlene Weinstein. Beacon Press, Boston, Mass., $6.95. The book gives practical information on how to start low-budget centers, how to evaluate and define good day care, what equipment is needed, what the legal requirements are, and much more.)

No matter how you solve the problem of getting away from your domestic and child-care chores for a few hours (even the most adorable, lovable, wonderful baby in the world lacks a certain something when it comes to inspiring conversational sparkle), you want to use some of your time off productively. And productively means not only taking care of some immediate psychological needs today but also thinking of tomorrow. Volunteer work has frequently been the answer for the present—but with good planning it can also be the answer if you'd like to see a tall, handsome job in your future.

Take my friend Sophie C., for instance. She had majored in French literature in college, but chose marriage instead of her senior year and the diploma. When she began reading stories to her son at bedtime she decided that children's books were more interesting than French literature and that someday she'd like to do some kind of work with children's books. She went to the local library and offered to do volunteer work. The only help they needed at that point was clerical—and so she spent her precious few hours of "leisure" typing catalogue cards and filing reservations for best sellers. Her husband and friends thought she was out of her mind.

But she got to know the people in the library and they got to know her. And she began to learn about how the library worked and who did what. Soon she was helping out in the children's rooms and becoming a good friend of the children's librarian. She learned how children's books were selected, what the children liked, and what their parents looked for. After a while she was, still as a volunteer, helping to promote the children's library services and later lobbying for more money for children's books.

When a poorly paid position doing public relations work for the library came up, it was only natural that the librarian thought of Sophie. And Sophie was happy to get paid for what she enjoyed doing, and might even have done as a volunteer. Today, her children on their own, she has a fine job as director of public relations and promotion of children's books for a major publisher.

So volunteer work can be a great time to do well for yourself while doing good for others—if you look for volunteer work that gives you a chance to learn skills that can someday be salable. It can also be a great time to experiment in fields you think you might be interested in—without having to adhere to the inflexible schedule of a paid job.

It's also possible either to maintain skills you already have or to extend them. Florence S. is an elementary school teacher who doesn't want to work while her two girls are still toddlers. Florence has been helping out one afternoon a week at a home for neglected and abandoned children with severe emotional problems. She finds that she has a special empathy with these children. And, knowing that the market for elementary school teachers has just about dried up (see Chapter 10), she is planning to take some evening courses in the psychology of dealing with "special" children. She's convinced that she'll be able to find a job in this field when she wants it, though she doubts if she could find a position as an elementary school teacher. Furthermore, she thinks she may be able to get academic credit for her volunteer work—which will save money in future tuition costs and in the time needed for academic work before she's eligible for a job.

Volunteer work has also proved useful to two divorcées I know. Hilary M., who organized volunteers for various affairs, fashion shows, and cake bakes—to raise money for the local hospital—went on to a good job doing very similar work for a fund-raising organization after her divorce. And Betty D., who helped book lecturers for a junior museum, took a job doing the same work for her suburban community after her divorce.

I'm not saying that all volunteer work should be looked on as a steppingstone to paying jobs. But I am saying that it doesn't hurt to keep your own aims and goals in mind while signing to do volunteer work. The work will be more meaningful because it will be part of your larger plan. And just because you do feel the work serves a dual purpose you will probably be better at it, which will be a pleasure for the people you are working with, will add to the very real contribution you are making to the public good, and will certainly work to your advantage should you need references in the future.

It's only fair to point out that in recent years, particularly since the rise of the feminist movement, the validity of doing volunteer work for the public good has been questioned—and very critically. Members of the National Organization for Women (N.O.W.) have taken a very strong stand in their national platform against the concept—"Women, don't fall into the compassion trap. Volunteer instead for social change . . ." Here's how they look at the question:

. . . Most volunteering that women do is actually of the kind that most properly can be called SERVICE VOLUNTEERING. [Their capitals.] It is simply public services which are performed by non-paid personnel. Or it is charity which is dispensed as a service to the public service sector. For women it is also often memberships in auxiliaries or clubs which serve to aid their husbands' careers.

The service volunteer helps to maintain and support a system which does not work equally well for everybody. The efforts of the volunteer to cure society's ills is an attention to symptoms rather than to causes. It is a band-aid approach to massive social problems..

N.O.W., because it feels this way, says that volunteerism

is an ideology which conceals from our view the truth that service volunteerism is yet another form of activity

which serves to reinforce the second-class status of women;

which is one more instance of the ongoing exploitation of women;

which takes jobs from the labor market, and therefore divides middle-class from poor and working women;

which buttresses the structures which are keeping women in a subordinate role;

which is antithetical to the goals of the feminist movement and thus detrimental to the liberation of women.

In contrast to this viewpoint is the stand of Mrs. Ellen Straus, who originated the "Volunteer Professional" concept and founded a very successful citizen complaint service, Call to Action, manned by volunteers who answer complaints phoned to about fifty radio stations. Mrs. Straus feels that status doesn't have to be equated with pay, and that it's very difficult to draw a line between service-oriented and change-oriented volunteer work. Many volunteer activities connected with the schools or prisons, for instance, may very well be effecting social changes by doing what N.O.W. would call "service-oriented" work. She does feel, however, that the status of all volunteers should be upgraded (including male volunteers, of course) so that they have "professional" status. As part of the upgrading she has suggested the following program:

1. written job agreements with agencies using volunteers, outlining mutual responsibilities;

2. reimbursement for expenses;

3. on-the-job insurance;

4. child-care facilities at work;

5. federal income-tax deductions for volunteer hours;*

6. inclusion in the Social Security system;

7. written evaluation of job performance for future employers;

8. placing volunteers who enter the paid-job market on the basis of their volunteer experience.

Certainly each side can make a good case for its viewpoint. However, both viewpoints work to your advantage. Since the whole question of volunteering is being discussed, social work agencies are probably more anxious than ever before to give

---

* The Internal Revenue Service allows volunteers to deduct some expenses incurred during volunteer work. N.O.W. raises the very interesting question—at what rate of pay should these deductions be listed? Their view is that it should be at the going commercial rate for comparable services, ranging from "$3.50 per hour for typists to $20 and up for women executives."

volunteers more choice of jobs, to treat volunteers with respect, to make their working conditions as pleasant and personally profitable as possible. (Good agencies have always tried to do these things, of course, but a new awareness has made them even more sensitive to the value of the free labor they are getting.) And, in keeping with your very personalized approach you might consider not only the usual agencies—churches, hospitals, settlement house, united charity appeal groups, and so on—but also consumer groups, ecology groups, lawyers organized to help indigent prisoners, Vietnam veterans groups.

Regardless of your basic, long-run philosophy about volunteer work, or the group you choose to work with, in the short run you may find yourself in the enviable position of doing well for yourself while doing good for others.

19

The Substitute Parent: How to Find and Keep a Good One

"With one foot firmly planted in the business world and the other foot sliding around on a loose marble or a waxed floor in the home, the working wife and mother, a multipurpose female, is a stranger to boredom."

  —Letty Cottin Pogrebin, author of the best seller *How to Make It in a Man's World,* editor of *Ms.* magazine, and columnist, "The Working Woman," for *McCalls Magazine*

The key to holding a job and having a career is often held in the hand of a lady who comes to your home every morning to take care of your pre-school child. You would like her to be a paragon of virtue: warm and outgoing, so she can give your baby love and understanding; intelligent, so she can offer some guidance; quick-witted and coolheaded so she can respond well in emergencies; reliable, so you're sure of getting to work; unencumbered, so she can adapt to your hours; efficient, to do all the chores—and not too expensive.

Where will you find such a paragon? You won't. You'll aim for that but along the way you'll settle for someone less than perfect, compromising on the least important things such as no encumbrances in order to get the most important things, warmth, intelligence, reliability. You may be shocked at the salary you'll have to pay and if you're not shocked your older relatives and non-working friends will be, saying, "After all, you're just hiring a baby-sitter." And that, I think, is exactly where people go wrong—the "just a baby-sitter" approach. (I base my opinion on my years as a working wife and mother who was blessed with very satisfactory mother substitutes.)

You are not hiring "just a sitter." You are filling a very important position—taking care of and influencing a very important person, your child. You need to give the job all the accouterments of an important position: dignity and a touch of prestige, fair pay, reasonable hours, good working conditions. Let me discuss these one by one, so you'll see what I mean.

Dignity and prestige: The person is treated with dignity from the very beginning. She has a title, "housekeeper" or "nursemaid," or, if she's young and likes the title, "mother's helper." I rather like "assistant," as a good, general, all-purpose designation. She is not called "my girl," or "the girl," which to me has no dignity at all. If she will be dealing with grocers, cleaners, deliverymen she should be introduced by name and title—"This is Mrs. or Ms. Smith, my assistant, who will be giving you the dry cleaning from now on, etc." If you bring home a colleague or friend the housekeeper is always introduced. If you or your husband is connected with a well-known local institution, such as an engineering company, a bank, or a school, the assistant likes to know. It lends some prestige to her job to know (and to be able to tell her friends and neighbors) that she is, in an indirect way, connected with the same institution, just by helping you.

Fair pay: The salary is equal to or a little better than the going rate in your community. If it's customary to pay carfare as well, you pay that. You explain that under the provisions of the Social Security law you are bound to pay half of her Social Security tax, and that this is important to her because it will pay benefits and provide her with income when she reaches retirement age. If she works out well and becomes a regular employee she gets paid holidays and a paid vacation—say one week the first year and two weeks the next and following years. If she works on holidays (so *you* can have a holiday) she gets time and a half. If her vacation doesn't coincide with yours (she may have family obligations that prevent it) it hurts, but you pay her while you're gone. (You may ease the pain somewhat by having her do things that there isn't time for ordinarily, polishing the furniture, cleaning out little-used closets, dusting the books.) Since she has to eat and pay her bills while you're gone if you don't do this you may find yourself without an assistant when you return, which costs much more than two weeks' salary.

Reasonable hours: Your assistant is a working woman like you, and like you she wants to be able to plan her time. You have to specify the hours and then abide by them faithfully, barring emergencies. She should start early enough to allow for a little overlap so you don't have to rush out before you have a chance to tell her that your child had a bad night and may be cranky, or that you promised he could have an ice cream cone in the afternoon. If you're due home at five-thirty you don't stop off to shop, no matter how tempting an unadvertised sale may be. You take it for granted that she only wants to work Monday through Friday, and if you ever need her on a weekend you pay time and a half or double time, depending on the standard in your community.

Good working conditions: She is told precisely what is expected of her—complete care of the baby, of course, plus whatever other duties the two of you agree on. There is a temptation to avoid doing this, based on the secret hope, I suspect, that the person, with no definite guidelines, will then manage to do everything and do it well. This is unfair, unrealistic, and unworkable. Your assistant, not knowing what's expected, will be under tension, which won't do the baby any good. You won't be satisfied and may go from one extreme to the other; some days feeling you've been taken advantage of because your house is a mess when you expected it to be clean, other days accepting slovenliness when it could have been prevented. *You* will be upset, which won't do the baby any good. Far better to decide on the limits of responsibility—how much, if any, housework, laundry, shopping, food preparation—and abide by these limits.

A word of caution here. Though you want to manage your domestic affairs in a businesslike way, the relationship between you and your assistant is not quite analogous to the relationship between a boss and his assistant in industry. If the gold-plated plastic hangers don't get shipped on time or the letter to the Wee-Do-It-All! Company doesn't go out on Friday that's bad but not crucial. But if the baby's diaper isn't changed on time, or he's not picked up promptly at nursery school, it is crucial. If the boss screams at his assistant that he's a stupid idiot for goofing his assignment the assistant can scream back, throw paper clips, or get psychic relief by spending his lunch hour griping to sympathetic colleagues. Not so your assistant. The nearest target is the baby—but you certainly don't want frustrations vented on him. So the relationship is three-way and very delicate. It has to be built on a solid foundation of mutual trust and respect. One of the best ways to achieve this is to lay down the ground rules and abide by them.

Therefore you specify how much, if any, cooking, shopping, errand running. You say how you feel about use of your telephone for making or receiving personal calls, or visits from friends and relatives while you're at work. You specify how many meals are included in the job. You arrange always to have in the house ample food and beverages that your assistant likes. You say you will either pay extra for over-time or give compensating time off.

THE RIGHT PERSON—AND
HOW AND WHERE TO FIND HER

What characteristics will you be looking for? Someone who is kind, with a feeling for children, particularly infants and young children. Someone who is flexible, since children's moods, physical well-being, and even digestive systems are very volatile and require sensitivity from adults. Someone with a gentle voice and manner, and without annoying mannerisms or tics.

Almost as important is reliability; you need someone who will come every day, on time, and stay on the job for a reasonable length of time. People's lives change, and no one can commit himself forever—but you should hire someone you estimate will stay a minimum of a year, and preferably much longer. Your child needs this stability, so he doesn't have to adjust continually to a stranger—and so do you! There are few things more upsetting to a working wife or couple than having the minutes tick by as you wait, sometimes in vain, for your housekeeper to show up.

Preferably you want someone who has a minimum of responsibilities herself. The ideal answer is a grandmother whose children are grown, or a mother whose children are at least of junior high school age so they can fend for themselves until she gets home. Night school students are a possibility, and are usually very good for as long as they last—which may not be too long. Though they say, and mean it when they say it, that they are looking for a permanent job until they get their degree, too often they either change their minds or the curriculum is changed so they have no choice but to take daytime courses.

You want someone intelligent, which doesn't necessarily mean well educated. (You've probably noticed that the two characteristics don't always go together.) Your assistant does have to, or at least should be able to, read instructions or follow written notes. She has to be able to cope with minor or—though you hope this won't occur—major emergencies, and this requires intelligence. So you have to be a bit cautious about someone who has difficulty with English, unless she has no problem making herself understood.

Where do you find your gem? It's not easy and it's not something that can be rushed. Your best chance for getting someone recommended is to ask your friends and neighbors, though there are several minor hazards to this. Neighbors may suggest themselves or relatives whom you would find unsuitable. Friends who are working and have a good assistant are often fine sources, though you have to be sure that their concept of a suitable person is the same as yours. Drawing on all your tactfulness, therefore, you have to make it very clear that the final choice is yours and there are to be no ruffled feathers if it doesn't work out.

If you have no luck, and your local newspaper has a "Situations Wanted" column, scan it. Even if you don't find anyone this way (and I never have, though I've tried it) you will get a "feel" for the situation, i.e., going salaries, what employees are looking for on jobs (near transportation? no heavy cleaning? no cooking?), and what fringe benefits are being offered. You may find that many of the ads are actually placed by employment agencies trying to place their applicants, but this too is informative, since you learn what agencies specialize in household workers. Depending on the agency fee, your cost in time, trouble, and money, and the price of an advertisement that you place, you may find that using an employment agency is the best method of hiring someone.

If you do plan to use agencies check them carefully—unless they come very well recommended—through your local Better Business Bureau, consumer protection service, or state employment office. You have to be sure they are reputable and have no history of supplying unsatisfactory individuals or exploiting their applicants, since in either case you will be the one to suffer. Ask the agencies if they can give you the names of several satisfied customers, and also ask how they check their applicants' references, i.e., do they accept letters from previous employers or do they call them? And in either case do your own calling as well. I've doublechecked on both private and public employment agencies and found their methods of looking into references casual, to say the least. I would never rely on them.

The method I've found most successful is running an ad myself, and this is what I would recommend if you don't get someone through a friend or neighbor. The very fact that someone can read the ad, has the initiative to look for a job on her own (as compared to letting an agency find a job for her), and then follows up on the ad brings you a certain caliber of person right away. The ad should be full of specifics:

Hours: days of the week, e.g., Monday through Friday, 8 A.M. to 6 P.M.; occasional overtime on Friday nights if possible.

Duties: Care of year-and-a-half girl plus light housekeeping. You might, depending on the ad's cost, even want to get into some details, such as "no heavy cleaning," or "light housework including ironing."

Benefits: Five-day week, no weekends (which is why many people like to work for a working mother!); paid holidays and vacation.

You might want to be just a bit cagey about the salary, since someone who is making more than you are offering but is very unhappy might turn up in your net, and be happy to take your job because the hours and working conditions are better and you're a pleasure to work for compared to the misanthrope who is her current boss. However, you should say "good salary," so you don't turn away applicants.

You should also, since you're "buying" in a market where the supply is dwindling and the demand is great, state some of the other things that make your job desirable—a one-story house or apartment; any appliances you have, such as washer-dryer or dishwasher; what transportation is near.

Then, and very, very necessary, RECENT REFERENCES REQUIRED.

With your phone number you might put down the hours you prefer to be called, such as evenings after 8 P.M. or whenever you are free to discuss the job with few interruptions. You want to get impressions over the phone so you can save both time and effort by eliminating some of the callers. You'll be able to tell, by their voices, the kind of questions they ask, and the kind of experience they've had, that some applicants are quite unsuitable.

The next step, of course, is to set interviews with those who sound like good prospects. (Take it for granted that everyone will say she loves children—only a fool would say otherwise.) How do you judge individuals at an interview? It's a combination of things you observe plus your intuition—the emotional reaction you have to a person. You listen to the voice and the speech—would a child find it soothing? You can tell something by the clothes—not by their quality but by how well put together, how neat or how sloppy the person is. I am almost instantly and entirely biased against someone with food spots on her clothes, not because I'm a neatness freak, but because this kind of carelessness could mean that the person might not measure exactly how much cough syrup the baby should get. On the other hand, I'm leery of people who indicate they are compulsively clean, because they're apt to be bothered—and show it—when the child soils his diapers or discovers that fingers and strained spinach can trace a wonderful pattern on freshly washed overalls.

Barring a major snowstorm, a ten-car accident on the freeway, or the fact that you live in such an out-of-the-way place that no one can find it the first time, the person should arrive on time for the interview. If she can't manage to get there on time the first time she may cause you all kinds of headaches when you are dependent on her in order to get to your job promptly. You have to take the time to have a fairly leisurely interview with someone you're seriously considering, so you can have your antenna out—trying to judge qualities of friendliness, warmth, and common sense. And you have to back your impressions with a reference check. A written letter from someone out of town is very little use, except to get the name of the person and place a long-distance call if it seems warranted. For local references check the phone book to be sure the person you're talking to actually lives at the address given, and is really a former employer, not just a friend.

When you do get a previous employer on the phone don't be embarrassed to ask what salary the applicant was paid, how long she was employed, why she was fired or quit. Was there a good reason—family moved, a relative took over the job of child care, or the children got older and some other arrangement was made for their supervision? (It's also entirely possible that the people were difficult employers and that your applicant would have been out of her mind to stay on that job if she could change.) If the person hasn't worked before or hasn't worked in the years her children were growing up, ask for and check references from ministers, shopkeepers, or landlords, who can at least give a character reference.

Once you have the right person you'll want to invest some time (and money) getting your child accustomed to the stranger. She should go around the house with you for several days, not doing much perhaps, but observing, until she is accepted by the baby as a friend and until you feel confident you've covered all the situations that need to be covered.

Following this course of action I had exactly two assistants while our children were growing up. (My husband, because of the demands of his job, wasn't able to help at all.) The first assistant stayed with us for three years and left, by mutual consent, when she was offered a much better-paying, live-in job with a friend of ours. The second worked full-time while our children were young, and still works part-time for us. She has matched what I think was fair treatment with many "extras" that money can't buy: stopping on her way in the morning to pick up tomatoes that are cheaper in her neighborhood than in ours, reminding me it's time to send the sweaters to the cleaners before they are nibbled on by moths, checking the grocery bill to be sure we haven't been overcharged. As two working women we have a mutual respect and admiration. I can only wish you similar good fortune. I've also recommended this course of action to several young mothers going back to work and they've had good success with it. I think you can try it and get out of the kitchen with few qualms.

I wish I could say with *no* qualms, but in all honesty I can't. Despite the brave new world of Women's Lib, and more and more mothers of young children out working, I think there is still a strong residue of the old feeling that mothers should be home with their young children. If you choose to be a working mother, for whatever the reason, you are going to run into some of this feeling. And it's going to make you feel guilty, especially if the baby cries and clings to you as you leave in the morning. There will be days when you are going to decide to go to work when the baby is a little bit sick, and that's going to make you feel even guiltier. And then there will be days when the baby is quite sick and you will have to stay home from work—usually when it's important that you be there—and then you'll feel guilty about your job. And, again despite Women's Lib, it's not yet generally accepted that a husband can call up and say he can't come into work because the baby is sick, though it's acceptable for a mother.

To complicate your life even further there always seem to be articles popping up in magazines demonstrating the psychological harm done to children when their mothers work. (As a working mother allow me to let my biases show through and say I have yet to read articles about the psychological harm done to children when their mothers are out playing bridge, golfing, going to fashion shows or cocktail parties, though they may actually spend less time with their offspring than working mothers.)

Since convincing arguments and evidence have been presented by psychologists, psychiatrists, and others both for and against working mothers I leave it to them to have the last word. Yet, if I may put in a small but firm voice for the working mother, I haven't noticed any marvelously adjusted children in past generations of non-working mothers. The children, now grown, seem to have their share of hang-ups, even if someone was home to greet them at lunchtime and after school. My own sons are nice, self-supporting, self-sufficient young men, with no more than the normal complement of garden-variety neuroses. They are also very much *un*-male chauvinist pigs, with no compunctions about changing diapers, cooking a good dinner, and helping their female colleagues get fair treatment on their jobs.

I suspect that *the* final word on working vs. non-working mothers will never be written; much depends on the individuals involved and the circumstances they're in. In the meantime I do believe it would be impossible to take a group of adults sitting around at a party, pick out the ones who are "maladjusted" and say of course they had working mothers. Think of your friends. Would you say that was a fair comment?

So until the last word is written you'll be right in doing what is best for all of you—remembering that happy parents, particularly happy mothers, make happy children.

20

The Work-Study Game Plan
for Wives

"I think women should be trained to believe they will always have to be economically independent. In fact, I think it should be a requirement for a marriage license that women have a marketable skill or profession before they get married."

Law professor Judith T. Younger

Would you believe that back in 1963 people in Washington were talking about, thinking about, and even worrying about wives and mothers?

What are they going to do, they wondered, when the pile of diapers begins to shrink, they put the high chair away, and they suddenly realize all over again that there's a big world out there that they'd like to get back into? One of the major recommendations of the worriers, the President's Commission on the Status of Women, was a comprehensive program of continuing education geared to the needs of the individual woman.

So, since 1963, there have been commissions on the status of women established in the fifty states, the District of Columbia, Puerto Rico, the Virgin Islands, and about ten cities. And there have also been study groups, federal funding of research projects, new programs at two- and four-year colleges, universities, and in adult education programs. Most important, perhaps, has been the rescheduling of courses to hours that make it possible for mothers with young children to manage home, husband, children, and still bite into the educational pie.

If you are wondering what kind of resources are available in your community your first step might be to send for a useful pamphlet, "Continuing Education Programs and Services for Women," Stock ⚹2902-0042, available from the Superintendent of Documents, U. S. Government Printing Office, Washington, D.C. 20402, 70 cents. In addition to giving background on this question of education and employment of women wanting to return to work there are some very useful appendices, including schools with special programs for adult women, by state; related services or programs for adult women, by state; and a report on federal funds appropriated for continuing education programs.

Courses in many different fields from community counseling to computer science are available, and there is a wide range of offerings around the country. Further-more, the more flexible approach is illustrated by the Central Florida Junior College, Ocala, which says it will "arrange any course of interest to women pro-vided there is a minimum enrollment of fifteen students." Out in Nebraska the Chadron State College offers, through its Continuing and Occupational Education Program, a variety of short non-credit courses, including training for nurse's aides, geriatric aides, and food service supervisors. The University of North Carolina, Chapel Hill, schedules a weekly non-credit course, "Expanding Opportunities for Women," that is open to women over twenty-five years of age who want to explore local opportunities in education, employment, and volunteer activities; testing and counseling services are also available.

Another example of this trend toward flexibility, and this may be one of the most flexible programs around, is the "Weekend College" at the C. W. Post Center of Long Island University in Greenvale, New York. Students need only a high school diploma to enter, tuition can be charged to credit cards, husbands as well as wives can enroll (with a bargain rate for two), and children age five or older can be enrolled on Saturdays in an arts and crafts "creative experience" from 9 to 3.

The success of many of these new programs has encouraged other colleges to consider them. So it's entirely possible that if the course, study program, or coun-seling you want isn't available locally there's nothing to stop you from suggesting such a program to a college administration, or the director of adult education or continuing education or whoever else is responsible for innovation.

You'll note that many of these courses are for fun and/or profit but not for credit. In the beginning, when you're just getting your academic feet wet, that's fine. You may very well feel unsure of yourself—Will you really be able to get out of the house or will the roof fall in and the baby break out with chicken pox just as you're about to walk out the door? Will you really be able to get down to studying again? Will you find the time to read? Will you like it?

Cheer up. Once you've made the adjustment you'll find—if you're like most of the other women who've enrolled—that you do not only as well but usually *better* than when you were a teen-ager the first time around the academic circuit. You're older, you're more mature, you're self-motivated instead of being compelled by others. You will probably surprise and delight yourself.

Once you've made the adjustment, found that the roof doesn't even wobble as you walk out the door and that your husband has some hidden talents for cooking or shopping, you ought at least to think about taking courses for credit—even if you're not immediately sure what your goal will be. Admittedly it will cost more and it will be more of a commitment, but the payoff is correspondingly greater. True, learning and doing have their own reward—but frequently this reward is not recog-nized in the coin of the realm. For many jobs the degree is the union card, whether it's called that or not, and the better jobs go to the degree holders—and especially to the holders of the better degrees.

If you decide you don't want a job, you haven't lost much. But if you have the opportunity to get the credits, and you don't use that opportunity, you may regret it later. You or your circumstances may change, and you may decide you are in-terested in a degree—only to find that you are short of credits that you could have had if you had arranged for them. This is above all true when you have had a career that you might want to go back to someday. Then you should make every effort to take courses, for credit, that are going to help you keep up with your field—even if it means going to a college that is farther away instead of within ten minutes' drive.

You may encounter some difficulties in doing this, Women's Lib, federal funding, and new programs notwithstanding. There are still faculties and administrations that haven't accepted flexibility and insist that some programs can only be pursued full-time, or only by regular students. But you may also find some allies on the faculty, either because they are in sympathy with these new approaches or because they have wives or daughters who are or who will be in exactly the same position.

(I, for instance, was one of the very first, if not the first, mother with two children to attend the Columbia University Graduate School of Journalism. The fact that I was able to complete satisfactorily the one-year, grueling nine-to-five daily course plus weekend assignments encouraged the faculty to admit other women with school-age children in following years. My friend Lou H., dean of a business school, enlisted faculty support when the wife of a faculty member was denied admission to a graduate school because she was a woman, and also because she had to adjust her schedule somewhat to make it possible to meet her home responsibilities. The rules were bent, the woman graduated later with honors.)

Now for some words of caution. If you are undecided about a career consult Chapter 10, which tells you where some of the shortages and some of the surpluses exist. If you are preparing for a career by enrolling in a particular program that is reasonably new, particularly one of the two-year programs, try to check out the placement or prospects of graduates. Not all of the programs have been well conceived, and not all of them have been accepted. Take the health care field, for instance. Since 1965 there have been several congressional acts providing for training programs for workers in the allied health professions, the name given to health personnel who are not doctors, nurses, or dentists. Thousands of training programs have been established in hospitals, medical centers, universities, and community colleges. (In a field that began, well before 1965, with laboratory technicians and nurses' aides, there are now more than 125 job titles.)

Furthermore, no one denies that hospitals and other institutions are understaffed, and that, theoretically, every one of the graduates of all these courses should be able to find a job. Yet, many of them haven't, or at least haven't found the jobs they trained for, not because the need didn't exist, but because the institutions had no funds for hiring or buying equipment.

In addition, because so far there are no standardized training, no proficiency testing, no established criteria for issuing credentials, certificates and diplomas that are acceptable at one place aren't necessarily acceptable at another. This means that some people have had trouble getting their first job because their training wasn't recognized; others have had trouble changing jobs for the same reason. If at all possible then, canvass your area's institutions, if that is where you are aiming, to find out who recognizes what in the way of training.

Finally, keep in mind that investments in academic credits for a would-be working wife are governed by accounting rules that would make any certified public accountant blanch and groan. There are no neat balance sheets, no income here and outgo there and a proven profit at the end. In the beginning, in fact, you may very well find that your outgo—when you add up baby-sitter costs, extra clothes, possible higher taxes, convenience foods, tuition—exceeds your income for quite some time. However, as your children get older your expenses for baby-sitters will go down and your income—as you get more experience and better jobs or raises or both—will go up. The day will come when you will break even and then, an even happier day, you'll begin to come out ahead. Eventually, depending on your ambition and opportunity, you'll find that you're making a substantial contribution to your family's standard of living. And you will have had fun along the way.

21

Are You a Born Renter
or a Born Homeowner?

"The only problem with this generation is that
I'm not a part of it."
—Policeman discussing the life-style
of young singles who've moved into
suburban apartment complexes

Apartment/house? House/apartment? Which is better, which is best?

Confirmed apartment dwellers say they wouldn't be bothered with a house if you gave it to them free and clear. "Mow that lawn? Tote that bale of fertilizer? Shovel that snow? No thank you."

Confirmed homeowners say, "Go back to an apartment and have to cook in a kitchen the size of a large table mat, while the kids upstairs roller-skate on my head? Never!"

The true answer, like most "true" answers, is somewhere in between. It depends not only on the merits of the case for each, but also on your psychology, temperament, and emotional state of mind, not to mention your financial state of affairs—which I will, in fact, mention immediately, since this is the most common and potent argument for home ownership.

You have, of course, heard the argument many times. You pay the landlord every month and at the end of twenty years what have you got to show for it? A pile of canceled checks or rent receipts that just add to general environmental pollution when you dispose of them. *Whereas,* if you own your home (there's a magical ring to those words—no one ever owns a "house," it's always a "home") at the end of twenty years you've paid off your mortgage and the home is yours, free and clear.

Well, there's some truth in that but some fallacies as well. First of all, that "free and clear" idea. It brings forth cheery visions of no more monthly payments—which just isn't so. There are still taxes, and they have a way of going up as communities ask for more and more services, many of which are paid for from property taxes. Furthermore, roofs continue to develop leaks, lawns still turn brown, and inside and outside walls still need painting. In other words, mortgage payments may be over, but taxes and maintenance costs are still with you, and may even go up as the house gets older and pipes and appliances begin to get weary.

Second, if you're the typical American, it's very unlikely that at the end of twenty years you'll be in the house for which (with sweaty palms and a sinking feeling that you were heading for bankruptcy) you signed your first mortgage contract. If you're fairly typical you will move about fourteen times during your lifetime, and during your homeowning days you may sell your house and move every seven years. (Don't even think of the packing and unpacking—it's too depressing.) So the decision, whichever it is, has to be viewed not as a lifetime commitment but as a choice made within a time span, and a span that can't necessarily be foreseen. However, just for the sake of argument, let's pick a time span and see what the dollars and cents differences might be between renting and owning.

Apartment Ideas, a quarterly magazine devoted to the interests of apartment dwellers, once worked out this problem in great detail, with some interesting conclusions. They started with a new, $25,000 split-level house that had three bedrooms, one and a half baths, carpeting, air conditioning, and kitchen appliances, in a good neighborhood with good schools. They assumed that the house would qualify for a Federal Housing Administration (FHA) loan with a down payment of 10 per cent and a twenty-five-year mortgage at an 8.5 per cent interest rate.

Then they matched this against a new, three-bedroom apartment with similar amenities in a similar neighborhood. They allowed ten years to elapse, while expenses added up for the homeowner, including the initial down payment, fees, operating costs, investment in such necessary items as lawn mowers and other maintenance equipment, less the tax savings open to homeowners. During the same ten years they estimated what would happen to the apartment dweller, who made no down payment, had lower operating costs and a smaller investment in maintenance, and was able to take the money he might have spent for a down payment and invest it in a savings account with a 5 per cent yield. However, the apartment dweller had no tax savings possible. When the two sums were compared *Apartment Ideas* found the total was a difference of only $740.

Of course, as the magazine points out, all kinds of things could have happened in those ten years that they didn't allow for. Rents could have gone up each time the apartment dweller renegotiated his lease. Homeowners' costs—fuel, repairs, lawn seed, all the things in the sieve known as "upkeep"—could also have gone up. (And, of course, you don't have to be told that, based on the experience of the past decade, the chances of this upward trend are, unfortunately, only too, too possible.)

However, in a more cheerful vein, there is also the possibility that the gods would have smiled on our test cases. The apartment dweller could have invested his little nest egg in some fabulous stock that quadrupled in value over the ten years. The homeowner's neighborhood could have improved and prices of houses in general could have risen, so that when he got ready to sell an eager buyer insisted on paying double the price the homeowner had paid.

All of which brings us back to the original thesis—financial reasons alone aren't enough to rule out either apartment living or homeowning. So let's take a look at some other considerations and see what effect they have. (They're not totally divorced from money talk, but they are not primarily dollars-and-cents considerations.)

BUYING A HOUSE:
LIFE-STYLE WITH THE SHINGLES

Buying a house is more than buying a piece of land, some bricks, boards, doors, closets, sinks, nails, light fixtures, and crab grass. It's also buying a certain life-style, a commitment to a geographical area and a community within that area. When you are a homeowner you acquire a new status and some new attitudes you may not have foreseen.

The process works like this. Before you move in you solemnly swear that you are going to get along just as you always have: your furniture has seen better days, you know, but replacing it will just have to wait. The house needs things done to it, but you're not going to do them, because your bank account is pitiful.

Then you move in. The rain you prayed for so you wouldn't have to sprinkle the lawn with the leaky hose pours forth—but after you smile and decide that somebody up there does like you after all you discover you have a leaky rainspout and several damp spots on the kitchen wall. And the dandelions sprout along with the grass.

Mowing a lawn doesn't compare with lying in bed on Sunday morning reading the paper, but you are now a part of a community and you don't want the neighbors to consider you a no-goodnik. Furthermore, you, too, have a stake in the neighborhood, so there you are, mowing the lawn, pulling up the dandelions, and noticing that one of the bushes is dying and will have to be replaced.

While mowing you worry about that leaky rainspout and the dampness on the kitchen wall. Your first reaction is "the hell with it," but suddenly you realize that it's your *property* and you have an investment to protect. You get on the phone and after many unanswered calls and busy signals you learn from the local rainspout expert's wife that he will do you a favor and come at 7:30 A.M. next Tuesday. You also learn that your hardware store man will advise you on how to repair dampness, since there is no local kitchen dampness expert even at 7:30 A.M.; and the money that you had put aside for a new winter coat is going to be spread—in the form of fertilizer—on your lawn, which now needs reseeding because of the flood-like rains. It's a sobering experience.

Then there are some more subtle pressures. Since the house belongs to you it is a reflection of you. People who couldn't have cared less about the layout of your apartment, which was, after all, pretty much like their apartments, want to see what you've "done" with your house. They want the guided tour—and suddenly what looked casual when it was in your apartment bedroom looks downright shabby when seen through a neighbor's eyes.

Next some parents get together and decide the kids in the neighborhood need a center with athletic facilities, a snack bar, maybe a swimming pool if they're not all going to grow up to be suburban delinquents. Every family will chip in a given amount (about what you had set aside for a washer and dryer) to get the center started. Of course you want to be able to use the facilities—can your child be left out of all the activities?—and so of course you say yes. The day you say yes the washer-dryer you've been coddling groans, whimpers, and then expires. So either

Daddy has to moonlight or Mother has to take a part-time job, not only to replace the washer-dryer, but also to keep up with the other expenses that the new community center is bound to bring with it. Gone is the time to enjoy the outdoors with the family together, which was why you moved into a suburban, homeowning community in the first place.

Just to make this picture as bleak as possible let's say the people who lived next door in your former apartment building had also been thinking of buying a house but had decided against it. They took the money they had saved for a down payment and invested it in some stock (against your advice). The stock was the Wall Street darling for the year, and they are just exhausted, absolutely exhausted, from all their meetings with brokers and lawyers and bankers and accountants, trying to decide how to invest their windfall.

Now, let's take a look at the other side. And in this case some of the arguments against homeowning can be just as potent *for* homeowning.

Let's start right back at the beginning, with the "comparable" three-bedroom house vs. the three-bedroom apartment. Let's say they offered the same amount of floor space (although usually a house will offer more, a basement, an attic, or storage space that few apartments can match). There is still one big item you buy when you buy a house that you don't get in an apartment—privacy. You don't have to shush your children, you can play your stereo at 2 A.M. or jog around the living room at 6 A.M. without worrying what the neighbors will say.

And though you pay for the utilities yourself, you can turn on the heat when you want to or turn off the air conditioner without depending on the decision of the landlord—which is not true in many apartment buildings.

It's true the house does reflect your taste, and correspondingly true that what you do with it becomes your property, not something left behind for the next tenant to enjoy at no cost to the landlord. You can arrange the kitchen to suit your fancy, tear down walls, add closets, plant tulip bulbs, or paint black cats on the ceiling with no one to ask and no one to please except yourself and your family.

Just because you have a new status as a homeowner you also have more clout as a property taxpayer, particularly if you live in a suburban community. You can vote on your local taxes, on zoning laws, and on issues affecting your schools. And it follows from this that there is a degree of permanency attached to home ownership that improves the likelihood that your neighborhood will remain stable. You and your children will have the security that this provides, including friendships. There's a lot to be said for that.

And there is always the delightful possibility that—should you have to move and give up this stability—you may give it up at a handsome profit, enabling you to buy an even nicer house somewhere else. House prices have been on the rise for the past decade and many young families are like my friends Nadine and Arthur H. They started out, with one baby, in a modest house in a suburb of Connecticut, which they improved with good planting, fresh paint, and lots of elbow grease. After a few years, with another baby and a promotion, they sold the house at a profit and used the profit as a down payment for another, larger house in a newly built development in Connecticut. When Arthur's company transferred him to New Jersey he was guaranteed a minimum price for the house if it couldn't be sold privately. But Nadine and Arthur did sell it, again at a profit, and bought an even nicer house in a new development in New Jersey.

Finally, there is the real psychological pleasure of ownership. Sure, you know the house is mostly the bank's and you also know all the things that are wrong with it. And maybe it isn't the house you had a mental picture of when you started out to buy. But it's still yours and some part of you responds happily and cozily to that fact.

(As for that couple who lived in the next apartment—too bad what happened to them. The stock they invested in was quite speculative and the stock market took a steep drop just after they bought in. They lost quite a bit and they're sorry they didn't listen to you and put the money into U. S. Savings Bonds.)

APARTMENT LIVING:
THE GOOD AND THE BAD

Still, when the four of you had been sitting around talking about owning vs. renting there were some pretty cogent arguments in favor of renting. Perhaps the most cogent was personal flexibility. Neighborhoods change or deteriorate; the apartment buildings themselves deteriorate; tenants change. You are bound by your lease, of course, but it's a comparatively short-term commitment. Or you have the freedom to sublet. (You hate the tuba player upstairs whom you've never met, but you sublet to a piccolo player who's been dying to play duets with a tuba player.) If worse comes to worst you can break your lease. (See Chapter 23 on some aspects of lease breaking.) In other words, in one way or another you can pick up and go, leaving the problems behind.

There are other, and in some ways more serious, reasons for cherishing this flexibility. Companies change, industries change, the whole economy changes. If you lose your job, if there is a slump, you aren't faced with a twenty-five-year mortgage, those inexorable monthly payments, and no, or not enough, income. And at just such a time houses are plentiful and buyers are scarce, since many people are shivering in the same ill wind. So you can't pay and you can't sell either. If you're lucky enough to find a buyer, you may have to sell at a loss.

Another aspect of this flexibility is your flexible psychology when you're renting. Because you don't think of your nest as a permanent one you're more open to possibilities for flying elsewhere. You're apt to be more adventuresome, more willing to try something new—a new career even, or at least a different community. Without the invisible ties that bind, the pride in ownership, you are more receptive to new ideas.

Furthermore, you have more time for new ideas. Time that might be spent cultivating a lawn can be spent cultivating new skills, learning new things, advancing your own career. And apartment living can offer these advantages to *both* partners, working husbands and working wives. *Apartment living can be particularly advantageous to working mothers,* assuming there is play space for the children. Unless the apartment complex is restricted to singles, apartment dwellers are likely to be varied in age and occupations. It can be easier to make all kinds of arrangements: for baby-sitting and after-school care; for swapping child care within the building, so that children don't have to be taken outside to a baby-sitter in bad weather; for getting taxicabs to come and pick up a group of children and transport them to and from a local nursery school.

And the money from two incomes can be invested, since it won't be tied up in a down payment, but will instead be earning money, even if it does nothing except sit in a savings bank and accumulate interest.

Finally, some of the newer apartment complexes offer luxuries that homeowners might envy—swimming pools, saunas, tennis courts, golf courses, recreation centers.

Again, wait, wait, wait before you run out to kiss the nearest landlord and sign a lease in blood to bind you forever. Some of the advantages are also some of the disadvantages. The lack of permanence makes for impermanent relationships, neighbors that live next door whose name you never know, whose children litter the hallways because they have no pride of ownership.

If you have an irresponsible landlord you can be without heat, without hot water, without plumbing—even in expensive, luxury buildings. People don't want to co-operate and start neighborhood projects because they don't believe they'll be around to see them completed.

Most of the little things you do to the apartment—the little comforts that complete the apartment—have to be left behind should you move on. If you do them you lose the time and money invested when you leave—and if you don't do them you spend two years having tennis rackets fall on your head or having to take every pot out of the oven when you want to bake two potatoes.

So what does it add up to? There is no right or best choice. Though your home-owning friends and perhaps your family will find it inconceivable that you should prefer renting, you may be a born apartment dweller, never happier than when you can call the maintenance department to change a light bulb. You may cherish your freedom and your freedom of choice more than having to adapt to group living.

On the other hand, if you want to put down a few roots, if you enjoy the pluses of home ownership, if your educated guess is that you're going to linger awhile in your present groove and you'd like to make it a deep one, you were meant to have a tryst with the First National Mortgage and Trust Company.

Whichever grass looks greener to you—yours or the landlord's—the nice thing about today's life-style is that nothing has to be forever. But in the meantime, whatever your choice, you'll want to know some of the problems you may face and how to handle them. If you're going to rent take a look at Chapter 23, to find out more about leases. If you're going to buy you'll want to get some insight into the business of selling, and the sales ploys of real estate agents, so have a look at Chapter 25. If you want to consider the possibility of having a foot in each door, i.e., the convenience of apartment living plus the tax advantages of owning, you'll want to look at co-operatives and condominiums, discussed in the next chapter.

22

Co-operatives and Condominiums: Advantages and Disadvantages

"Condominium owners . . . must deal with each other. We share the property; policy must be made and money spent. Friendships that survive the first three general meetings will last forever."
—Karen Sanders, self-described happy owner of a condominium in Westchester, New York

If you are a confirmed apartment dweller, co-operatives and condominiums seem an excellent way to avail yourself of some of the advantages of home ownership—tax deductions, control over costs, stability, choice of neighbors—without the maintenance chores. But there are also disadvantages, not usually pointed out by sellers, whether they are individuals or real estate agents. First, let's get our terms straight, since the two forms of ownership are different.

When you buy a co-operative apartment you buy shares in a corporation and become part owner of that corporation through your shares. It's the corporation that owns the apartment building plus facilities and grounds. The extent of your ownership is set by the number of shares you buy, which in turn is based on the size of your apartment. If you have a two-room cozy corner you own fewer shares and pay less than the owner of a three-bedroom, two-bath suite. Your monthly payment covers your share of the co-op's mortgage, taxes, and maintenance. You can of course use all the common facilities, from the laundry room to—if you're lucky—the swimming pool.

The corporation manages the building, either through a maintenance company that's been hired to do the job, through a hired manager, or through various committees elected by the tenants; the arrangements depend on the size of the building and the ambition or expertise of the tenants. There is usually a board of directors, elected by the tenants, who oversee the entire operation.

The condominum is different. Here, in effect, you are buying a house, except it's a house within an apartment building, rather than a house on a street (unless you buy a town house). Instead of buying shares in a corporation you buy your "house," the condominium, from either an individual or a builder. You can get your own mortgage; you are responsible for paying your own taxes on your apartment.

Your monthly payments go to pay off your mortgage. In addition you pay monthly for your share in the cost of maintaining the building and grounds, etc. (The two payments plus taxes may be lumped together if you've arranged for the financing through the building's developer.) Your building may be managed by an individual hired by your fellow owners, by some of the fellow owners themselves, or, much more common, by a management firm paid a fee for its services.

Which is the preferred form of ownership? Very often the question is quite academic—you choose the apartment you think you'll be happy in rather than choosing a co-op or a condominium. But there are differences. Because the condominium owner has his own mortgage he can, if he wants to, change his payments by refinancing the mortgage. He can sell his apartment more easily, since the new buyer can, in turn, arrange his own financing on terms that he prefers. More important, the condominium owner is liable only for his own mortgage; in contrast the tenant of a co-op shares in the liability of the co-op's mortgage. If some tenants default the other tenants must assume the defaulting tenants' share of the mortgage.

A more important question, for personal decision making, is the advantages of owning an apartment vs. renting one. Whether you rent or buy you still make monthly payments, but there is a difference. If you rent for ten years and then move you have nothing to show except a pile of canceled checks. If you own an apartment for the same ten years and move you can sell it, and you have the possibility of getting a nice fat check from the sale. True, there's no guarantee that you'll make a profit, but there is always that possibility. You could take a loss, too, but in view of recent real estate history the odds are in your favor.

Another advantage of owning is the stability and control that go with it. When you live in a co-op you have some choice as to your neighbors; no one can sell to a person the other tenants consider undesirable. In theory, in a condominium this is less true, since everyone owns his unit, but in practice the same rule pretty much applies.

Another aspect of control is costs. Though you have no guarantee that your maintenance costs won't go up if the cost of labor and supplies goes up, at least you have some say in the matter. You aren't unpleasantly surprised to receive in your mail a notice from a landlord that due to circumstances beyond his control rents are going to be increased by 15 per cent. People who live in a co-op have some pride of ownership, or at least a vested interest in their property, so they are more apt to take care of *their* building and grounds, and see that their children do likewise.

Do It Yourself Co-operatives

An alternative to privately developed co-operative housing is housing sponsored by membership groups, such as labor unions, credit unions, religious groups, or simply a group of individuals who've gotten together to form non-profit corporations that will build housing at a saving to members. Such groups have already built developments in New York City, California, Indiana, and elsewhere. Savings come from the advantages of buying land co-operatively, from lower mortgage rates (through federal and state mortgage plans), and from lower maintenance costs, since the owners take over some management duties and since families in co-ops tend to move less often and take better care of their apartments and the jointly owned facilities.

If you would like more information about this possibility write to the Publications Department, FCH Services, Inc. (a subsidiary of the Foundation for Cooperative Housing), 1012 Fourteenth Street, N.W., Washington, D.C. 20005.

Another plus: you are able to deduct the interest on your mortgage, or your share of the co-op's mortgage, from your income tax, and that saves you money. If you are in a high income bracket the savings is proportionately greater, but whatever savings you get are still greater than the zero tax saving possible to you as a renter. (This points up the fact, which you probably know already, that our present tax laws favor owners and discriminate against renters.)

So what's wrong with the arrangement? Several things, large and small. The very stability that is an asset is also a liability. The big advantage of renting is mobility. You get a better job, you have a yen to try living in New York or San Francisco, you unexpectedly have triplets—you sublet your apartment or you wait until your lease expires, and you're free. Not so when you own a co-op or condominium. Your fellow owners frown or prohibit subletting for any length of time. Or you have to move in a hurry and there are no buyers at the time, so you have to take a loss, sell through an agent at a large fee, or give up the idea of moving altogether.

Some of the cost savings may be more illusory than real. Your monthly carrying charges may be less than rent for a comparable apartment—if you don't count the interest your investment could be earning merely by being deposited in a savings account. You might actually lose money if your investment could have been invested in bonds with a high yield or in stocks that did very well.

Nor is it all as trouble-free as the ads say. Some buyers whose condominium purchase contracts also included contracts to accept a management service group for twenty-five years have not been all that pleased with the arrangement. Some in fact have been so unhappy they've sued the builders, claiming that maintenance costs were arbitrarily increased and tenants couldn't see the service group's books to find out if the increases were justified. Others have complained that finished condominiums didn't include some of the amenities shown in the advance plan, such as recreational halls, auditoriums, and even garage space. Still others have complained that the buildings were very poorly maintained.

Another problem is the advanced technology of heating plants, electronic elevator equipment, and air-conditioning mechanisms in big buildings. Management has to be able to judge and then hire men who will know what they're doing when they service such equipment—not always the case. (Elevator repair men almost live in the building I'm living in—but apparently they still don't understand the elevator control system or the system's been so badly designed that it can never be properly fixed.) As a co-op or condominium owner you may have to worry about this, to say nothing of the numerous craft unions you may have to negotiate with. You are also, incidentally, responsible for your own decorating and some repairs. All in all there may be occasions when you'll regret your role as owner-landlord as well as tenant.

Finally, everything is dandy as long as everyone remains prosperous. But what happens if there is a major recession and fellow tenants can't meet their payments and can't sell their apartments? If you're in a co-op you still have to make co-op mortgage payments, including shares of non-paying tenants. As a condominium owner you don't have to worry about any mortgage but your own, but you do have to worry about maintenance of common grounds and facilities. During the depression of the 1930s people did lose their investment in co-ops, which may have contributed to the decline of the co-op's popularity. It hasn't happened on any large scale in recent years—but there's nothing to say it couldn't happen again.

In other words, the perfect answer to the housing question hasn't yet been found. And there is no answer that's going to be perfect for everyone—and certainly no answer that's going to be perfect for you at all times and during all phases of your life. You have to make your choice on the basis of what's best for you at this time and this place—the mobility a rented apartment offers, or the stability of an apartment you own? Cash in the bank or an investment in housing that may appreciate in value and in the meantime offers tax advantages?

If your decision is to buy here are some questions to ask before you make some salesman happy by signing on the dotted line.

If you're buying from plans in a new building or a new complex of buildings you'll want to know:

a) Is the price firm or subject to change without notice?

b) What is included in the basic price? All appliances? Use of such facilities as swimming pool, tennis courts, gymnasium? If these aren't included, is there a fee, and if so how much and whom does it cover, individuals or a family?

c) If the entire complex or building isn't sold, who will pay the cost of the maintenance portion from the unsold apartments—the tenant-owners or the builder-developers? What, if any, maintenance contracts are you committed to?

d) If carpeting is one of your options, what grade of carpeting and at what cost? (Very often the cheapest is free, but if you want a better grade you have to pay extra.) If you do choose carpeting and there are concrete floors the concrete may be left as is. If you change your mind sometime in the future, you will have to spend your own money putting in the kind of flooring you want.

e) Who pays for the utilities, you, or are they included in the monthly payment? You may find, to your surprise if you are in an all-electric building, that you have an individual meter and the cost of heating/cooling your apartment goes onto this meter—which could add considerably to your cost, depending on how much you like air conditioning, use the lights, cook, etc. How considerably will depend also on the rates in your part of the country, so it's important to get some kind of dollars-and-cents estimate from the seller and add this figure to your monthly costs.

f) *Even after you've checked on all these questions you should get a lawyer to check further,* to be sure your interests are protected.

23

Leases, Or: Serfdom Updated

"The law is often unclear. And every case is different. So is every judge. Don't be annoyed when your lawyer says, 'I don't know what will happen.'"
—Emily Jane Goodman, lawyer and author of *The Tenant Survival Book*

Here's a foolproof way of falling asleep if you're ever troubled by insomnia. Take out your lease and start reading it. By the time you get to the third covenanted, demised, increments, as provided herein, whereas and aforesaid you will be in deep, deep slumber. And even if it were easy to read the tiny type, and it isn't, the lease is written in a form and a style of language guaranteed to confuse and conceal. (It's doubtful that even the well-informed rental agent could tell you what the various clauses *really* mean.)

If you do choose to try this new form of sleeping pill maybe it's just as well you don't concentrate on what the various clauses mean—because if you allowed this real meaning to penetrate you would unquestionably wake up screaming.

The fact is that the standard lease takes away some of your most elemental rights, guarantees you very little, and in cases of difficulty with your landlord sometimes states that you have to pay the costs of showing how naughty you've been!

Consider this clause in many leases, for instance:

It is mutually agreed by and between landlord and tenant that the respective parties hereto shall and they hereby do waive trial by jury in an action, proceeding or counterclaim brought by either of the parties hereto against the other on any matters whatsoever arising out of or in any way connected with this lease, the tenant's use or occupancy of said premises, and/or any claim of injury or damage.

Don't you recall learning in grade school that the American Constitution guarantees everyone a trial by jury?

There are other impingements on what we consider basic rights. Still, considering that the original basis of the landlord-tenant relationship goes back to the lord and his serf, with the lord owning not only the land on which the serf lived but also in effect the serf himself since he was not free to leave the land, it's not surprising that there are, to say the least, inequities.

Because leases and the laws that govern them vary from state to state it's impossible to say what particular obnoxious and unfair clause you will find when you get ready to rent. But there are many possibilities. It's very likely, for instance, that your lease will give you no rights beyond the right of possession. In most states the fact that a landlord isn't providing the services he is supposed to provide doesn't relieve you of the obligation to pay rent. If he violates local housing and/or health codes you can complain to the proper authority and then that authority becomes responsible for enforcing the code, i.e., getting the landlord to correct the violation. But while this process is going on—and it may go on and on and on—you must still pay the rent.

(We spent five years in a "luxury" building in Manhattan complaining to the landlord and, when that did no good, to the city Department of Air Pollution about a defective rooftop incinerator. While we lived in the apartment, on the top floor of a seventeen-story building, we put in screens, not to keep out insects—not too many at that height—but to keep out quarter-size pieces of soot and cinder drifting down from the incinerator. The building's management and the Department of Air Pollution were still fighting it out when we gave up and moved.)

Your lease might include a waiver of liability clause that says the landlord doesn't have to pay for any damages or injuries that occur in his building, *even if they're due to his negligence.* My friends Mickey and Sy had their apartment burglarized because a doorman allowed someone into the building while they were out to the movies. The landlord disclaimed all responsibility, though the doorman admitted that the robber had sneaked past him while he dozed. (Of course they paid a higher rent to live in a building with the security provided by a doorman.)

Your landlord may claim, under his right of free access, that he can enter your apartment several months before your lease expires in order to show it to prospective tenants—without your consent.

Why go on? The deck is stacked against you. The question is, what can you do about it?

Ideally, once you know that a situation presents problems that threaten you, you take steps to remove the threat. In this case you would read the lease carefully (with a ready supply of ice cubes to rub against your forehead whenever you begin to doze), underline what you consider offensive clauses, go see a lawyer, get his opinion, and have him rewrite the lease to your satisfaction. Then you'd meet with the landlord or his agent, hassle a bit, and arrive at a compromise that would be fair all around.

Hah! When you've got to move and all the apartments in the area are covered by the same type of lease, this is about as likely a possibility as finding your dream apartment, painted in your favorite colors, equipped with every conceivable appliance, at exactly the rent you can afford. When it comes to leases you usually sign what you have to sign because you have no alternative.

However, just because you're going to be shot at sunrise doesn't mean that you personally have to put on the blindfold. There are some things you can and should do.

(And, in all fairness, there are some tenants who take advantage of landlords. Pamela and Steve A. couldn't help but sympathize with the landlord who showed them an apartment whose living room and bedroom walls had been painted with several coats of thick black paint. They readily promised that they wouldn't change the colors of the walls, once the landlord had repainted in the colors they chose, without asking his permission.)

You should, if you can bear it, read the lease before signing, so you have some idea at least as to what you're being committed to. (If you're interested in a lawyer's "translation" of the clauses found in most so-called standard leases take a look at Chapter 5, "Leases," in Ms. Goodman's *The Tenant Survival Book*. The legal text gains considerably in the translation—you will be amazed and appalled.) It's a good idea to take the lease to a lawyer, preferably a local lawyer who is familiar with how various clauses are interpreted in the area. And this brings up a most interesting point—even though the landlord says, "This is a standard lease," there really is no such thing. The most the landlord can mean is that the lease is the standard one in general use by the real estate owners in the area. And this is true even if the lease says "Standard Form of Apartment Lease, the Real Estate Board of ———— City, Inc." and even if it's full of "Agreement of Lease" and "Witnesseth" in bold and beautiful black fancy English lettering.

It's nice to know too that lots of that fine print has never been tested in court. Even though you are, by signing, a party to a contract, *how* the terms of that contract are interpreted by the courts, if the situation should arise, would vary considerably. However, if you do get in trouble with your landlord and plan some action against him—consult a lawyer first. You might find that it would be poor consolation to be right and homeless.

You'll notice too that although most leases require a security deposit few spell out what that security deposit represents and the exact terms for returning the deposit to you. In some places it may be considered the last month's rent. In others it may be security against possible damages you might do. And if that's the case, what these damages are, in the landlord's view, and how he charges for them should be spelled out. In addition, his schedule for returning the security money should also be stated very specifically.

You should also pay strict attention to any typed-in additions to the lease, which are known as "riders." They are as much a part of the lease as the lease itself, and just as binding. For instance, a rider to your lease might say (as ours does) that if real estate taxes are raised tenants will be responsible for paying a certain portion of the increase—in effect raising the rent.

Finally, as in every transaction, to have faith is beautiful but to see it in writing is even more beautiful. Some overenthusiastic rental agent may promise that the unsightly closet installed by the previous tenants will be removed, or that the apartment will be painted, or that of course air conditioning is included in the rent. But these promises aren't binding on the landlord unless they're in writing and signed by someone in authority.

TILTING THE SCALES, OR: TENANT POWER

Since the law of the lease isn't on your side what can you do about correcting problems—in view of the fact that since you live in the building you are in some ways a hostage. It's not like buying a dress or suit that you don't like and returning it for

Lease

National Housing and Economic Development Law Project Standard Form Lease (California)

1. Parties

The parties to this agreement are _____

_____

_____

_____ , hereinafter called "Landlord,"

and _____

_____

_____ , hereinafter called "Tenant."

If Landlord is the agent of the owner of said property, the owner's name and address is _____

_____

2. Property

Landlord hereby lets the following property to Tenant for the term of this agreement: (a) the property located at _____

_____

and (b) the following furniture and appliances on said property: _____

_____

_____

3. Term

The term of this agreement shall be for _____ , beginning on _____ and ending on

_____

4. Rent

The monthly rental for said property shall be $_____ , due and payable on the first day of each month.

5. Utilities

Utilities shall be paid by the party indicated on the following chart:

	Landlord	Tenant
Electricity		
Gas		
Water		
Garbage collection		
Trash removal		
Other		

6. Use of Property

Tenant shall use the property only for residential purposes, except for incidental use in his trade or business (such as telephone solicitation of sales orders or arts and craft created for profit), so long as such incidental use does not violate local zoning laws or affect Landlord's ability to obtain fire or liability insurance.

7. Tenant's Duty to Maintain Premises

Tenant shall keep the dwelling unit in a clean and sanitary condition and shall otherwise comply with all state and local laws requiring tenants to maintain rented premises. If damage to the dwelling unit (other than normal wear and tear) is caused by acts or neglect of Tenant or others occupying the premises with his permission, Tenant may repair such damage at his own expense. Upon Tenant's failure to make such repairs, after reasonable notice by Landlord, Landlord may cause such repairs to be made and Tenant shall be liable to Landlord for any reasonable expense thereby incurred by Landlord.

8. Alterations

No substantial alteration, addition, or improvement shall be made by Tenant in or to the dwelling unit without the prior consent of Landlord in writing. Such consent shall not be unreasonably withheld, but may be conditioned upon tenant's agreeing to restore the dwelling unit to its prior condition upon moving out.

9. Noise

Tenant agrees not to allow on his premises any excessive noise or other activity which disturbs the peace and quiet of other tenants in the building. Landlord agrees to prevent other tenants and other persons in the building or common areas from similarly disturbing Tenant's peace and quiet.

10. Inspection by Landlord

Landlord or his agent may enter the dwelling unit only for the following purposes: to inspect to see if Tenant is complying with this Agreement, to make repairs, and to exhibit the unit to prospective purchasers, mortgagees, and tenants. Such entries shall not be so frequent as to seriously disturb Tenant's peaceful enjoyment of the premises. Such entries shall take place only with the consent of Tenant, which consent shall not be unreasonably withheld. If, however, Landlord or his agent reasonably believes that an emergency (such as a fire) exists which requires an immediate entry, such entry may be made without Tenant's consent. If such emergency entry occurs, Landlord shall, within two days thereafter, notify Tenant in writing of the date, time, and purpose of such entry.

11. Security Deposit

a) Tenant shall pay Landlord, upon execution of this agreement, a security deposit of $_____ . Said deposit may be applied by Landlord toward reimbursement for any cost incurred because of Tenant's violation of this Agreement, including nonpayment of rent.

b) Landlord shall place this security deposit in a bank savings account or savings and loan institution account bearing the prevailing rate of interest and shall credit such interest to the security deposit. Within 14 days of the date of this Agreement, Landlord shall notify tenant in writing of the location of such account and the account number.

c) Landlord shall inspect the premises within one week prior to termination of this Agreement and, before Tenant vacates, shall give Tenant a written statement of needed repairs and the estimated cost thereof.

d) Within two weeks after Tenant vacates the premises, Landlord shall return to Tenant his security deposit, with accrued interest, less any deductions Landlord is entitled to make under subparagraph (a) of this Paragraph and Paragraph 17. If any deductions are made, Landlord shall also give Tenant a written itemized statement of such deductions and explanations thereof. No deductions shall be made, however, for any repairs not listed in the statement required by subparagraph (c).

12. Landlord's Obligation to Repair and Maintain Premises

a) Landlord shall maintain the building and grounds appurtenant to the dwelling unit in a decent, safe, and sanitary condition, and shall comply with all state and local laws, regulations, and ordinances concerning the condition of dwelling units.

b) Landlord shall take reasonable measures to maintain security on the premises and the building and grounds appurtenant thereto to protect tenant and other occupants and guests of the premises from burglary, robbery, and other crimes. Tenant agrees to use reasonable care in utilizing such security measures.

c) As repairs are now needed to comply with this paragraph, Landlord specifically agrees to complete the following repairs by the following dates:

Repair   Date

_____

_____

_____

_____

_____

d) If Landlord substantially fails to comply with any duty imposed by this paragraph, Tenant's duty to pay rent shall abate until such failure is remedied. This subparagraph shall apply to defects within Tenant's dwelling unit only if Tenant has notified Landlord or his agent of such defects and has given Landlord a reasonable time to make repairs. The remedy provided by this subparagraph shall not be exclusive of any other remedy provided by law to Tenant for Landlord's violation of this Agreement.

13. Subleasing

Tenant shall not assign this Agreement or sublet the dwelling unit without the written consent of Landlord. Such consent shall not be withheld without good reason relating to the prospective tenant's ability to comply with the provisions of this Agreement. This paragraph shall not prevent tenant from accommodating guests for reasonable periods.

14. Failure to Pay Rent

If Tenant is unable to pay rent when due, but on or before such due date he gives Landlord or his agent written notice that he is unable to pay said rent on time and the reasons therefore, Landlord shall attempt to work out with Tenant a procedure for paying such rent as soon as possible. If, after 10 days, Landlord and Tenant are unable to work out such a procedure, Landlord may serve a notice to pay rent or vacate within 3 days, as provided by California Code of Civil Procedure Section 1161.

15. Destruction of Premises

If the premises become partially or totally destroyed during the term of this Agreement, either party may thereupon terminate this Agreement upon reasonable notice.

16. Tenant's Termination for Good Cause

Upon 30 days written notice, for good cause, Tenant may terminate this Agreement and vacate the premises. Said notice shall state good cause for termination. Good cause shall include, but not be limited to, entry into active duty with U.S. military services, employment in another community, and loss of the main source of income used to pay the rent.

17. Termination

Upon termination of this Agreement, Tenant shall vacate the premises, remove all personal property belonging to him, and leave the premises as clean as he found them (normal wear and tear excepted).

18. Lawsuits

If either party commences a lawsuit against the other to enforce any provision of this Agreement, the successful party shall be awarded court costs from the other. Landlord specifically waives any right to recover treble or other punitive damages pursuant to California Code of Civil Procedure Section 1174.

19. Notices

All notices and rent provided by this Agreement shall be in writing and shall be given to the other party as follows:
To the Tenant: at the premises.
To the Landlord: at _____

20. Holdovers

If Tenant holds over upon termination of this Agreement and Landlord accepts Tenant's tender of the monthly rent provided by this Agreement, this Agreement shall continue to be binding on the parties as a month-to-month agreement.

WHEREFORE We, the undersigned, do hereby execute and agree to this Lease.

LANDLORDS: TENANTS:

_____   _____
(signature)   (signature)

_____   _____
(date of signature)   (date of signature)

_____   _____
(signature)   (signature)

_____   _____
(date of signature)   (date of signature)

credit, or, if you can't return it, taking a loss and saying better luck or judgment next time. Moving is being uprooted, having to make a million plans and adjustments, spending a considerable sum of money, doing lots of just plain hard work. So you naturally enough want ways of somehow evening this balance between you, as an individual tenant, and the more powerful landlord.

Many people around the country have found that tenant co-operative action is the answer. Activities have varied from hanging out sheets saying "This building is a lemon," to picketing, to petitions to landlords, to withholding a rent increase (Senator Edward Brooke and Representative John Conyers, Jr., were in on that), to setting up associations and electing committees to meet regularly with landlords to discuss grievances. Middle- and upper-income families, though they've shunned the more militant tactics of poverty groups (such as becoming squatters), have learned that tenants together have some clout. They've won some rounds, lost some, and had partial victories in between.

One of the main objects of these organized tenant groups has been to reverse the one-sided, pro-landlord bias of the apartment lease. Gilbert Cornfield, a labor and civil rights lawyer who has represented tenant unions in Chicago, has argued that the present standard lease violates tenants' rights to negotiate as individuals, and therefore it is an unconstitutional use of government power for the courts to enforce the terms of the lease.

Emily Jane Goodman, in *The Tenant Survival Book,* points out that in a different tenant-landlord relationship, the relationship between a landlord and his commercial and industrial tenants, both parties have equal bargaining power. She says that "legally it's doubtful whether the standard lease constitutes a contract. However, tenants are caught in the worst of both worlds. You are bound by the terms of the 'contract' but enjoy none of the legal benefits of a contract. This is because a contract requires a certain meeting of the minds, free of coercion or duress, with certain warranties, representation and exchange being made . . . but you have to live somewhere. It is a landlord's market. You have to sign a take-it-or-leave-it lease, if any . . ."

To see what a lease would be if it were equitable to both sides see the one drawn up by the National Housing and Economic Development Law Project in California, reproduced with their permission on pages 148–49.

And until the balance is changed to represent both sides, let this thought console you. You know the situation. You know how to get the minimum protection available, and that the lease you signed isn't necessarily as all-powerful as it says. You know that individuals caught in a bad landlord-tenant relationship have banded together and succeeded in correcting some wrongs. But most of all, millions of us rent apartments year after year without any major complaints, and enjoy letting the landlord worry about keeping the lawn mowed, the snow plowed, and the hallways clean, while we enjoy our apartments.

24

How a Stamp Can Help You Find Happiness, Or: Scouting a Community via the Mail

"The respondents who reported that they are unhappy in the new city were much more likely to also say they had no information about the city prior to the move."
—Stella R. Jones, Ph.D. candidate at Indiana Central College, from her research on the effects on wives of moving

You've just made the big decision: you will accept that job offer in a different city, or you will take the transfer to the company's newest branch operation, or you're going to try changing your luck by changing where you live. The reasons don't matter; what is important is that the more you know about where you're moving to the easier it will be to find your way around, get the best housing for your budget, find a nice little restaurant to take the place of your current favorite where all the waiters know you like your salads with oil and vinegar, and overcome the feelings of loneliness that assail you when you realize that you're not as casual about your roots as you thought you were.

How do you go about getting more information than even the natives know? There are some time-tested ways, of course. If your company is helping you make the move you get all the advice available from them. (However, your idea of the sporting life may be a lot more sporting than theirs—or you may simply want to know what alternatives you have.) If you're in the academic community you write or phone the housing bureau of your new college or university. If you're a member of a professional or fraternal group, a union, or a club that has branches in other cities you ask them if they've got material available.

You also thumb through the pages of your alumni directory to see if you recognize any casual friends or at least acquaintances who are living in what will be your new home town. And you mentally thumb through your list of relatives, regretting that you haven't been very conscientious about going to family reunions. Who knows, Aunt Millie or Uncle John might have third cousins or friends who've moved to Oklahoma City, or Boston, or St. Paul.

All good ideas, but there is something else you can do that will provide all kinds of useful and fascinating information. Write to the Chamber of Commerce of the city you're moving to, or the city that is the hub of the metropolitan area you're moving to, and ask them for information. What comes back is valuable even if you have other sources.

I tested this theory by doing just that—writing to the Chambers of Commerce of a representative sample of major cities in the United States. And since I've moved something like thirty times around the country (after which I stopped counting) plus one move to London for a year and back to New York, with children at various ages from infants to teen-agers, I consider myself something of a veteran. Yet I found suggestions and ideas in the information sent that I'm sure I wouldn't have thought to ask about.

I also discovered that I had many misconceptions about the climate in various parts of the country—misconceptions that would certainly have led me to discard some of the clothing I might have needed. For instance, I thought south meant hot. But the brochure from Atlanta told me that Atlanta, with an otherwise equable climate, is cold enough in the winter to have occasional snow flurries and freezing rain or an icy glaze. And the average temperature in Dallas is 66°—scarcely what I would call hot. Other information sent—not by every Chamber of Commerce but by enough at least to remind me of all the things I would need to know if moving—were:

Maps of the cities and surrounding areas including road maps, maps of the subway transportation system, maps which named neighborhoods (North Gate, Central District) so that you could see where areas were in relation to the center of the city, or to parks or lakes;

Booklets and even a few good-size paperback books, describing the apartments and houses available in the different neighborhoods, with prices, facilities, sometimes pictures and/or floor plans;

Lists of public, private, and parochial schools, including the opening dates of the local school year;

Local laws governing car insurance needed and requirements for driver's licenses —a most useful thing to know, especially when, as in Indiana, you have to surrender your out-of-state license within five days of your arrival and take a visual test and pass a written examination before you can get an Indiana license;

Phone numbers of local medical societies;

Emergency numbers for medical and dental services;

Hours of customer service at banks (closing hours varied between 3 and 4 P.M.);

The location, hours, and phone number of visitor information centers;

Names and addresses of local newspapers, very useful if you wanted to get a look at their classified section, particularly the real estate and employment sections (Houston sent an entire classified advertising section from the Houston *Chronicle;* Dallas sent a card that could be redeemed on arrival for a two-week complimentary subscription to the local newspapers);

Voting procedures, and requirements (and sometimes the names and addresses of the headquarters of the two major parties);

Residences for business and professional women, or for students (San Francisco sent a brochure from the local "San Francisco Roommates Bureau");

Lists of real estate agents;

Booklets, usually beautifully illustrated, describing local recreational facilities: museums, concert halls, stadiums, ice skating rinks, lakes, beaches, camping sites and/or ski areas, which would be especially consoling if, just as you planned to move, your town had finished the neighborhood playground, or your local campus had just announced its most outstanding concert series, or your roses had never bloomed so magnificently.

Some cities included charts of the approximate costs of various major expenses in their areas, including taxes, and how they compared with other major cities, so at least you'd get some idea of how your budget would have to be stretched or squeezed. If you saw that food costs were lower than you had been accustomed to paying you could get an idea as to whether you might be able to spend a bit more for housing, for instance.

Naturally, every city likes to put its best features and neighborhoods forward. If you were from a foreign country and you received the packets you would get the impression that amusements were endless and uncrowded, and that all of the United States consisted of gracious houses on wide, tree-lined streets or handsome apartment complexes grouped around a swimming pool alternating with tall buildings that overlook magnificent views of the countryside. Fortunately, you have a healthy grain of built-in skepticism based on previous experiences translating a copywriter's imaginative prose into a builder's reality—so you won't be fooled.

If you do decide you want to do a little advance scouting by mail, write a letter to the Chamber of Commerce or comparable group. Here are the things your letter should include in order to get full information.

Your age, sex, marital and family status: "I'm a single woman in my late twenties" or "We're a couple in our early thirties with two children age ten and two."

The price level of the apartment or house you will be interested in: "I am interested in renting an apartment in a moderate price range" or "We are looking for a house in a medium-to-upper-medium-income community." (I favor this approach even if you are considering an upper-income community; since most agents will attempt to sell you a higher-price house anyway, you might as well see what's in the lower price range. I also favor not specifying what you mean by "moderate," since this varies from community to community.)

Your preference as to neighborhood: "I will be working at XYZ Company, and would like to find an apartment within walking distance if possible, or at least where public transportation is available and I won't have to travel more than one half hour each way" or "We prefer a suburban community that is as unspoiled and natural as possible, and are willing to go a little farther to shop if necessary."

The size of house or apartment you prefer: "I want a one-bedroom apartment" or "a three-bedroom, two-bath house."

Information about the cost of living: "Any information about the cost of living in your area would be much appreciated."

Even if you don't use half of the information sent to you, you will still get a "feeling" for the community you're going to, and some of the strangeness will have worn off before you starting filling your packing cases. Psychologically you will have begun to adjust to your new environment, and that will make the ultimate adjustment easier. And you will dazzle your new neighbors with your knowledge of the community.

Happy hunting.

25

How to Play Your Cards in the Real Estate Poker Game

"Say what you will about the devil—he's a hustler!"
—Proverb in a Chinese fortune cookie

He may never have read Freud, heard of motivation research, or had a single course in psychology. But when it comes to analyzing your dream, knowing your weak points, and being sensitive to your moods and desires, a good real estate salesman is a combination radar set, barometer, and volt meter. He has acquired his knowledge by dealing with many customers, attending sales meetings and pep talks, and listening to older and wiser heads in his office—and he means to use that knowledge.

He is not necessarily your enemy. In fact, he can be very useful. But he has a job to do—namely to sell you a house—and unless he does that job *his* monthly mortgage payments may be in jeopardy. So he has learned to do his job as skillfully as possible.

You, on the other hand, have to watch out for your own interests, and to do this you have to understand his technique so you can develop your own defenses against it. This is particularly true if this is the first time you're buying a house, you feel your ignorance is showing through, and the real estate salesman is as friendly and as reassuring as your Uncle Charlie.

The first thing to remember is that he is not your Uncle Charlie. Even with your best interests at heart he does not represent you; his heart, in fact, belongs to the seller for the very crass but honest reason that it is the seller who is going to pay a commission for having his house sold. (Since the commission is a percentage of the selling price it is to the salesman's and the seller's advantage to get the highest possible price—a viewpoint you don't share, naturally.)

The second thing to remember is that the salesman is competing with the other men in his office, and the other salesmen in the offices down the street or in other developments. He is expected to "produce," i.e., sell. When he does he earns not only commissions but also bonuses, nice fat bonuses, and sometimes even vacation trips to resort areas with all expenses paid for two. So he not only wants to sell you a house—he wants to sell you the most house you can afford.

How does he go about it? He learns to appeal to the romantic, emotional inner you, the inner you that the rational you may not be aware of. You think you know exactly how much you're going to spend, how important such things as plumbing and conveniences are, how impervious you are to flattery or suggestions. He knows better.

He knows very well, in fact, that what he has to sell is not a house but a dream. He paints a picture of your children romping and thriving in open spaces and fresh air, of the two of you entertaining at wonderfully casual and intimate dinner parties, of a haven of peace and quiet to return to every day after the mouse race has been run. And as you see yourself in that picture you forget that the house is near a major highway or freeway that pollutes the air; that the kitchen is so antiquated you may be cooking, not eating, by candlelight; that your haven of peace and quiet comes equipped with fifty thousand neighborhood children and dogs who prefer your yard to all others.

The process starts when you first enter his office. He has learned how touchy people are on the subject of money, and so he probably won't ask you what your income is. Instead he'll ask "about how much do you have to use for the purchase of a house?" Then he'll take a rough guess (mentally) as to how much house you can really afford, which will be more than you intend to spend.

After more questioning to get some idea as to what you're looking for, from specifics like "We must have three bedrooms" to generalities like "We want a house with some charm," you will begin a friendship which may or may not endure, but will start off on the best of terms with some guided tours of local houses. Rarely will you find a more agreeable traveling companion and tour guide. You'll get no arguments or differences of opinion, for your salesman is a devout believer in "the customer is always right" maxim. He also espouses the power of positive thinking. He wouldn't dream of arguing with you when you say, disappointedly, "But you have to walk all through the house to get to the kitchen," or "The bedrooms are so small." He will more or less agree with what you've said—"Yes, you do have to go through the house, but what a kitchen! Did you notice all those built-in appliances, and the big window so you could keep an eye on the children when they were playing in the yard?" or "The bedrooms are small, but you spend so little time in the bedroom. Most of your time is spent in the living room, and you really couldn't ask for a more spacious living room, especially with all that wall space for placing furniture."

In between viewing houses he'll be pointing out some of the plus features of the neighborhood: the wide streets, or the charming small lanes; the nearness to beach or park, or the absence of traffic because you're nicely tucked away in a corner far from recreation areas; the handsome shade trees because it's a nice old neighborhood, or the advantage of moving into a new area because you can plant all the things you prefer. And in the meantime he's listening and cataloguing your likes and dislikes, learning more and more about what really turns you on in houses—which may be quite different from what you think.

He's also pursuing further a question he originally may have raised in his office—why you want to buy. If you say you're expecting a baby in three months and you're living in a one-room apartment he'll know that you are very susceptible to pressure, because you're anxious to move and get settled.

What houses will he take you to see? Naturally the ones in his inventory that come closest to what you've said you wanted—but with some important limitations. If he's been given a three-month exclusive on a house and he hasn't sold it in two and a half months you can be sure he'll take you to see that house first, if it at all fits your description. With an exclusive he doesn't have to split commissions, so that of course is the house he's going to push.

He will also start at the bottom of your price range, take you to a few houses, and save for last one which costs several thousand dollars more than you planned to spend—working on the theory that when you fall in love with the house you will figure out a way to afford it. Very often he won't tell you the price of the more expensive house until you've been through it.

There will, of course, be quite a contrast between the first house and the last, and he'll let you bask in the joy of discovery, the feeling that at last, after you were beginning to give up hope, here is something you really like. You'll ask the price and he'll slur over it quickly, pointing out that though it sounds like more, it's really only another $15 or $20 a week, which you'll scarcely miss in the beginning, and which will make absolutely no difference to you several years from now when you will have probably gotten a raise. He'll bring out some well-tested arguments that have worked before: "After all, you live in a house for a long time, so it's very important to get what you want" . . . "After all, a house is the biggest investment you'll ever make, so isn't it worth a few extra dollars to be happy and have no regrets?" . . . "After all, what better way to spend your money than guaranteeing the comfort of your family. You won't miss the few dollars."

And all during this getting-to-know-you period he will be quietly testing you to judge how near you are to buying, setting up what is known in the trade as "trial closes." If he gets good vibrations from you when you're in a house he'll sense it immediately and say, "This is what you're looking for" or "You like this, don't you?" If your answer is yes he's got his pen ready, urging you to write a check for the deposit right away.

Sometimes your vibrations won't be so strong, but he'll recognize them: "Now, let's see, we could put the two boys together in this room until we add heat to that enclosed porch and make it another room" or "We really could get along without a garage" or "We really were going to look around a bit more but . . ." Then he'll answer with a trial close that's a little less direct, but a close just the same: "Would you like me to help you arrange financing?" or "A savings and loan association near my office may be able to get you a good mortgage on this house; they know the neighborhood well."

If you still hesitate he'll try to pin you down—to find out your particular objections and overcome them. If it's price, he'll ask at what price you would buy and then say he's willing to discuss this with the seller, but of course your *returnable* deposit will help get the ball rolling. If it's some physical detail, such as you had your heart set on a washer and dryer on the first floor, he'll point out that with a little rearranging the pantry could be converted into a laundry room, and that he thinks the seller would make an allowance so that you could have that done. If he thinks you're really on the verge he'll remind you that just because the house or the neighborhood is so desirable there are bound to be other buyers; if you don't act quickly you will lose out and regret it.

Now it's possible that all the things he says are true. He may indeed be able to get concessions from the seller; the house may indeed be just right for you; there may be other buyers and you may be sorry if you don't act quickly. But that's not the point—the real point is that this is a very important decision, and you want to make it as rationally as possible, without being pressured. So you want to be able to outpsych your friendly real estate salesman, so that the choice you make is your choice and a good choice.

How to do it? Some homework is necessary—the square labeled "Start" in the great real estate game is your budget. How much house can you afford, the absolute maximum, allowing for all the extras (discussed in Chapter 26) that Mr. Real Estate Salesman will never mention? This is the figure to keep in mind when you're out house-hunting. If you think you're going to forget it, or weaken, borrow your kindergartner's crayons, print the amount in big red numbers, and attach it to your car, so you'll see that figure each time you drive to the real estate office.

Next, do a little psychic probing of your own. What do you really want in a house and what are you willing to trade off to get it? Is spaciousness more important than a modern kitchen? Is the sight of a neighbor's lamp across the street more important than lots of land? Is living close to work or family more important than a larger house? Most of all, more important to whom? Who will be doing the trading off? Will you, the wife, resent that big back yard that your husband loves when you have to wash dishes in a stained old sink? Will you, the husband, resent that extra breakfast room when you're caught in a commuter's crush every night on your way home?

Real estate salesmen are adept at sensing and exploiting these differences between husband and wife; they tend to take the wife's side, counting on her to become an ally in selling the house to the husband. Buying a house can be full of psychological hazards that lead to, at the least, bitter quarrels, and at the worst, bad decisions. If possible, "rehearse" your changed living patterns ahead of time so that you can avoid difficulties and, not incidentally, present a united front to the salesman.

Of course, the better informed you are the better you are able to judge houses and salesmen. More homework is in order. Go to your local bookstore or library to take out and read some books on what makes a good house, from the structural and design features of the building itself to the neighborhood it's in, which will affect its value not only for the present but also for the future. And if you know the neighborhood you'd like it's a good idea to drive around and "case" it, noticing how well kept the houses are; where any commercial buildings are located that might attract traffic or pollute the air; where and what kind of shopping areas there are, since a prosperous shopping area shows a neighborhood with stability and a future.

Should you go to a large real estate office or a small one? Sometimes you have no choice—if a particular house is listed with only one agency that's the agency you'll go to. But large and small each have their advantages. The large agencies are more apt to have more extensive listings, more experienced salesmen (though they may be more high-pressure too), and better contacts for financing, which can sometimes make the difference between being able or not able to buy a house.

In smaller agencies, on the other hand, you are liable to get more flexibility. If you deal with the broker who owns the agency (a man you may never even get to see in a large agency) he can sometimes cut his commission to help you and the buyer arrive at a mutually agreeable price. In either case it's a good idea to deal with an agency that is firmly rooted in the neighborhood and specializes in residential housing—if they want to stay in business they have to have satisfied customers who will recommend them to other buyers and sellers. So they are going to go more out of their way to live up to their agreements and to see that you get a fair deal. If you have any doubts about an agency check first with the Better Business Bureau.

Timing can be important. If you've been troubled by a negligent landlord or a nasty one, you will naturally think of buying a house so that you can be king in your own castle. Though your annoyance is understandable it would be a mistake to let your emotions and a desire for either escape or revenge or both pique you into buying a house quickly. A house may not be forever, but it is for quite a while, and the best time to buy it is when you're not in a hurry and not under pressure.

When you're thinking of timing remember too that the worst real estate "season" is winter, when houses aren't bejeweled with rose bushes and lilacs and lovely leafy trees and you can see them unadorned. (After all, though you fall in love with the daffodils you have to remember that they will be only a passing affair while the septic tank is going to be a year-round companion.) Knowing this, many sellers keep their houses off the market until spring, when they are aided not only by the flowers but also by the fact that the holiday seasons are over, people can plan to move without interrupting their children's schooling, and it's just plain easier to get around. So if winter looking can fit into your plans, you may find a bargain—if you don't you still have the prime spring selling season in front of you.

No matter when you look, however, remember that your first job is to reinforce your sales resistance. Before you fall in love with the fireplace, head straight for the cellar where you can see the things that you're going to have to depend on—the heating system, the plumbing, and the wiring. Your salesman, of course, will try to head you in a different direction, but just say that ever since you were a little child you've been fascinated by things mechanical, and that's what you want to look at first.

The salesman will follow you into the cellar reluctantly—or into the heater room, or wherever the "guts" of the house are hidden. But he will answer your questions if you insist, and you should insist and be very specific on what you want to know. "Isn't that a repaired joint on that pipe—when did it leak?" "What do those stains on the wall mean, was there ever a flood?" etc. You should follow this procedure throughout the house. Your best bet, of course, would be to ask the questions from the owner, who would know that the stains on the wall came from the heavy rains in the spring of '68. And just because he *would* know, and would probably tell you, the salesman has told him to go visit his in-laws, or at least stay hidden, during your visit.

You, however, can try to get him out of his seclusion by asking for on-the-spot answers to your questions. If you do get to talk to him you will find him less skillful or less willing to slide over your legitimate questions.

If you're buying a development house you won't be able to get answers from an individual owner, but it will be even more important to get answers, *in writing*, from the developer or builder. Salesmen on these projects are often simply professional development promoters hired for the project, and they have no stake in the community whatsoever. They have been known to make promises—"Of course those cabinets will be straightened before you move in," "Of course the lawn will be completely seeded," "Of course the driveway will be paved"—that sell houses but make for unhappy homeowners. Unless you have it in writing, the broker or builder or developer can always say that the salesman wasn't authorized to make such promises, and you are left to do the undone.

Which brings up the whole question of professional help. Even if you've read every book on the library shelf, you should still invest in a *professional* appraisal of a house you're thinking of buying. Notice the emphasis on "professional"; your well-meaning relatives or friends are really no substitute. Buying a house is too important a decision to be left to amateurs. The fee for the service may save you more than you spend if any structural defects are uncovered; if none are you will be repaid in peace of mind.

If you are worried about losing the house to someone else (which may turn out to be a blessing in disguise if there is something wrong) you can protect yourself by placing a deposit and agreeing to sign a contract but stating, in writing, that the deposit and agreement to enter a contract are conditional on getting approval of the house's condition from an appraiser and approval of the contract from your attorney.

Of course, if you've gotten this far the chemistry is there—you like the house and you are probably on good terms, or even buddy-buddy, with the salesman. Since he no longer has to sell you he can really become valuable in helping you get the best possible mortgage for the house. Then you can invite him over for a drink after you've moved in and tell him you do agree that a large living room makes up for a small bedroom, especially when there's that beautiful lilac bush just outside the living room window.

· 26 ·

How to Be Happy Though a Homeowner with a Mortgage

"The love for comfort, that stealthy thing that enters the house a guest, and then becomes a host, and then a master."
—Kahlil Gibran

On the one hand there's that dream you have—a crackling fireplace, a swimming pool, a view outdoors of lawns, trees, flowers, and indoors of washers, dryers, mixers, lush carpets, and handsome furniture.

On the other hand there's the reality of your should-be-bigger bank account, should-be-bigger paycheck, and should-be-smaller taxes. The first question you ask yourself when you think of buying a house is, how much house can I afford?

The answer depends on whether you like conventional or unconventional wisdom.

Conventional wisdom says the price of your house shouldn't be more than two and a half to three times the family's take-home pay. (You know, that miserable pittance left after city, county, state, and federal tax collectors have taken a juicy slice right off the top.) And it has to be income that will continue, which means a wife with an outside job has to intend to continue that job. (I shun the phrase "working wife," with its implication that "at home" wives aren't working. All wives I know are working, whether at home or at jobs.) Overtime pay and bonuses can't be counted on either, unless there is a guarantee they will continue well into the foreseeable future. So, if your income *after taxes* is $15,000, you should be able to afford a house that costs about $37,000 to $45,000.

You should be—but are you? *Before* you consider the question, automatically add anywhere from 1 per cent to 3 per cent annually for maintenance, depending on how old and in what state of repair your house is, and how handy you are at making repairs or alterations. And if this is your first house add on anywhere from several hundred to several thousand dollars for some of the things you may need (or want) right away—furniture and appliances. There isn't much point in moving into a house without allowing for a minimum of furniture, and, as noted earlier, you will be under social pressure to have certain living standards. You must also have a little fund for things you never needed before—garden tools, for instance, and snow shovels. And there are always miscellaneous items, like towel racks, that you take for granted in your apartment but may not be in your house.

If you want to be very hardheaded about it, here's the advice of Chris Dahl, a banker who's had much experience with families who've suffered financial and psychological penalties from overestimating how much house they could afford. "The limit for the price of a house should be what you can afford if a crisis comes up. A rule of thumb is, if I lose my job can some income that I have or my savings carry the house until the crisis is over?"

This is the conservative viewpoint, for those who are happier living conservatively, who consider their future prospects somewhat limited, or who choose to live life in a low key.

But there are other viewpoints. If your job and promotion prospects are good, you may feel it's not only worthwhile, but even sensible to buy more house than you can afford at the moment. You will struggle for a few years, but you won't have to go through the trauma and expense of looking again in a few years, your children's schooling won't be disrupted, and you'll be able to maintain the friendships and relationships that you establish.

It could also be very important to be in a neighborhood where you meet the kind of people who could help you with your career. It's not unheard of for insurance agents, lawyers, and businessmen to meet neighbors on their commuter trains, or at the hardware store or the Parent-Teachers' meetings—neighbors who are good prospects as clients or customers. And there's nothing wrong with the idea either.

And democratic country though we are, there are still many instances where it's important to have a home that makes the right impression, if entertaining is part of the job. After all, no less an authority on making money than Aristotle Onassis has been quoted as saying that whatever else you can't afford, you are wise to spend money on where you live.

So how much house you can afford depends on the "non-financial" price you're willing to pay, as well as the dollars-and-cents price. The price is always too high if you aren't happy with your choice: if you find yourself horribly in debt and being owned by your house instead of vice versa; or if you buy a house you really don't like because it was cheap and you're living in it unhappily ever after. The important thing is to make the choice *consciously,* so that you are psychologically prepared to do without dining room furniture for a few years to buy the house that you're in love with, or to accept the morning line-up at the single bathroom door as the price of living in a house that's well within your means.

THE HIGH ROAD VS. THE LOW ROAD, OR: THE DOWN PAYMENT HASSLE

Once you've decided how much house suits your needs you're going to want a marriage of convenience between you and some kindly financial institution. They must share your love for a house enough to lend you the money you'll need. And you're going to be faced with many questions you may never have had to think about before. In the hopes of making your life easier I've tried to anticipate these questions and give you some of the answers.

Q. What is a mortgage anyhow?

A. A mortgage is a contract between you and a friendly lending institution. Their part of the contract is a loan—the mortgage—of a specified sum at a specified rate of interest for a specified length of time, for instance, $25,000 for twenty-five years at 8 per cent interest. Your part of the contract is paying back the loan, or paying off the mortgage, according to the terms agreed on. Typically you may sign two documents: a note or bond which is your promise to pay, plus the mortgage paper (in the jargon of the real estate trade often called a "security instrument") by which you pledge the house (or condominium) as security for the loan. Though you may like to think of the house as yours, and you do get title to it, the lender protects himself by having a lien against it. The lien means you can't sell the house until you pay off the mortgage. Furthermore, if you don't meet the terms of the mortgage, i.e., if you stop making payments, the lender can foreclose the mortgage and take over the house.

Q. That scares me. How big a mortgage will I need?

A. That depends on how big a down payment you can make. Your mortgage is the difference between the down payment and the price of the house, plus—and as you'll see in a moment, it is a big plus—interest paid on the loan and some money set aside by the lender in an escrow account to pay taxes and hazard insurance. For instance, if you want to buy a $35,000 house, and you have $10,000 cash to put down, you will need a mortgage of $25,000.

Q. How do I pay it off?

A. You make monthly payments just as if you were paying rent. How much you pay each month is determined by how long a period of time your mortgage covers. Let's say your $25,000 mortgage is for twenty years, at 7½ per cent. A long time ago some very smart mathematicians took $25,000, added on 7½ per cent for each of the twenty years, added on to that some taxes and insurance, prorated the whole business for each month of the twenty years, and came up with your monthly mortgage payments.

Q. How nice. Does it make a difference whether I take a twenty-, thirty-, or thirty-five-year mortgage?

A. Yes, it does make a difference—and a big difference in dollars and cents. Mortgages and that prorated monthly business are very tricky. Since you pay interest for the life of the loan (mortgage) the longer the mortgage the more interest you pay. Over a period of years this mounts up considerably. For instance, the interest on a $25,000 mortgage at 7½ per cent will add up to $24,336 in twenty years. In thirty years at 7½ per cent it will add up to $37,931. The difference between these two is $14,595—enough to buy a lot of beautiful furniture to put in the house. So you see that if you bought a $35,000 house with $10,000 down and a mortgage of $25,000, at the end of twenty years the house actually cost $59,336.*

Another interesting point about interest. Your payments at the start are mostly interest, not principal. (You're paying a percentage on what you owe—and in the beginning you owe all of it. But as you pay off more and more, you pay interest on

---

* This is not quite as bad as it looks since the interest is tax-deductible.

less and less, and the amount that goes to pay off the principal keeps going up. So if you sell your house after five years you have paid off very little of the principal. You won't get much from the sale for a down payment on your next house.)

Q. Does this mean that I'm always better off with a big down payment and a short-term mortgage?

A. It does seem that way, doesn't it? In fact, *conventional wisdom* says put as much money as possible into the down payment, have the smallest possible mortgage as a result, and take it for as short a term as possible (most mortgages run from twenty to thirty years). And there's no denying that this is the most economical way to buy; you'll pay out the smallest amount of interest.

Unconventional wisdom says that's true, *but* there are other factors to be considered besides the total amount of money to be saved. There's the time of your life factor: when will you have to be paying out the money? With a short-term mortgage your monthly payments are higher, though the house may cost less over the long run. With a long-term mortgage, however, your monthly payments are going to be a lot easier to meet, at a time in your life when your earnings have not yet reached a peak, and your expenses, if you have small children, are heavy. A wife who is only working at home isn't bringing in extra income; if she is working outside much of her salary goes for child care. The difference between the two amounts could be the difference betweeen having a washer and dryer or having to hang the wash outside; between having a newer, more reliable car or an older car that always develops pneumonia on chilly mornings.

There's also the possibility that you could invest some of that down payment money, and that your investment would bring in a higher return than the money saved in interest on the mortgage. And, should you decide to sell the house and have someone take over the mortgage—a likely possibility—the range of buyers would be broader for a mortgage that had lower monthly payments.

There are arguments on both sides. Which side appeals to you doesn't depend on whether you are conventional or unconventional, but *how you foresee your future*.

Consider Arnold and Helen, for instance, who've just started their careers in a government agency that has a regional office in their city. They like their jobs and plan to work their way up the government career ladder in the agency. They want to remain near Helen's family, so that Helen's mother will be available for baby-sitting when they decide to start their family. They've been saving the money they got as wedding presents and they've decided to pay about a third down on a house they want to buy, and take a twenty-year mortgage. They feel their income is guaranteed, and even if Helen has to stop working on her job for a year or two, they will have enough to meet their monthly payments. They don't anticipate they're going to get rich in government jobs, so they want to pay off their house during their prime earning years, so that when they retire they will own their house free and clear.

Pat and Robert couldn't disagree more. They hate the thought of being in the same place ten years from now—they're not even sure where they want to be five years from now. Though they're currently Easterners they want to resettle on the West Coast someday, preferably in Oregon or Washington. Bob's company has offices there and after several years of learning the business he plans to ask for a transfer. Because they don't like apartment living and because they have to entertain a great deal, they are buying a house, but putting in as little money as possible.

They feel their spare cash is better off in a savings account earning interest and available to them when they need it.

If you are anxious to put down roots and expect they'll stay solidly rooted for some time you'll look on your house as a long-term investment and think it's worthwhile to put funds into it. If, on the other hand, you want a house but not forever or not *that* house forever, you'll be better off buying with as little cash as possible and lower monthly payments. In either case you may guess wrong (crystal balls are never guaranteed), but in the meantime you make the best choice you can, based on your best judgment—and no one can do better than that.

Q. Where can I get a mortgage?

A. Several places. Savings and loan associations provide the bulk of mortgage money, but mutual savings banks, commercial banks, life insurance companies, and mortgage companies are also good sources of funds. If you're fortunate enough to belong to a credit union that grants mortgages you may find it a very good source for a mortgage on advantageous terms. All these lending institutions arrange several types of mortgages: conventional; insured by the Federal Housing Administration (FHA); or insured by the Veterans Administration (VA).

Q. What's the difference between them?

A. Generally speaking (the mortgage market is changing so that these are only general guidelines; when you are ready to buy you will, of course, get the most recent information), conventional mortgages require larger down-payments (maybe up to 20 per cent of the purchase price), are for a shorter term (perhaps twenty years), and have a *prepayment penalty clause*, i.e., if you want to pay off part of the mortgage before the term of the loan is reached, you must pay a penalty for doing so.

Mortgages guaranteed by the Federal Housing Administration (the guarantee, by the way, is to protect the *lender* if you default, not to protect you) require a much smaller down payment (from 5 to 10 per cent), are for a longer term (perhaps thirty to thirty-five years), and have a much smaller prepayment penalty. There is also an upper limit on the price of the house. In 1973 it was about $37,000.

Mortgages guaranteed by the Veterans Administration offer the most generous terms of all (virtually no down payment), thirty to thirty-five-year mortgages, and no prepayment penalty. They too have upper limits on the price of a house; about the same as the FHA's or less. They are, naturally, available only to veterans.

Conventional mortgages are usually the easiest to get and the fastest—*if* you have the down payment. In recent years FHA approval on mortgages has been so bogged down in red tape that many lenders have been reluctant even to try to get FHA mortgages. (In addition, charges of corruption and scandals have made lenders leery of FHA mortgages.) Buyers with good credit rating who lacked the down payment sometimes lost out on houses they wanted because it took so long to get FHA mortgage approval. Now new companies, private mortgage insurers, have come into the mortgage field. They make guarantees to the mortgage lender, whether a bank, insurance company, or whoever, so it's sure of getting its money even if the borrower defaults. This has made it possible for buyers with good credit rating to get terms comparable to FHA terms, i.e., 5 to 10 per cent or less as down payment, without the FHA hassle.

Q. What's the best buy in a mortgage?

A. That's difficult to answer. Conditions are different around the country, depending on state laws, individual practices at lending institutions, the availability of mortgage money, possible changes in FHA and VA terms and regulations. However, when you need a mortgage you can get the best buy only if you shop around among banks, insurance companies, and mortgage lenders, comparing the terms, rates, and options available. Since it's one of the most important purchases you'll ever make, and since you'll be paying for it for a long time, you just have to explore all possibilities so you're sure you're making the correct decision.

Q. What is an "open-end" mortgage?

A. A mortgage that allows you, after you've paid part of your loan, to borrow up to a given amount stated in the contract, still using your house as security. For instance, after you've paid about $5,000 on your $25,000 mortgage, you might be able to borrow another $5,000 to add a bathroom or remodel or some other worthwhile purpose. The additional loan would be added on to your present monthly payments.

Q. What will this additional money or refinancing cost?

A. That depends on the going interest rate at the time you want to refinance. If rates are lower the new loan will cost less; if rates have gone up, you will pay more. Sometimes, however, you can get a *split* rate, i.e., your old mortgage stays at the same rate, but the new part of the loan is at a higher rate. If interest rates have gone up since your first mortgage loan was made, however, you may have to refinance the whole mortgage at the higher rate.

Q. What is a package mortgage, where can I get one, and do I want it?

A. A package mortgage is usually offered by a developer who finances the houses in his development. Sometimes, because of his borrowing power, he can offer you better terms than you could get on your own. And the package allows you to include the cost of some appliances and other extras, such as carpeting, in your monthly payments. Adding these on to the mortgage means you're paying for them over the same extended period of time—say twenty years—and that has its drawbacks. Long, long after the dog has chewed a hole in the carpeting, or you've replaced the washer, you may still be paying for them.

Admittedly, at the time you buy the package you may be so short of cash that it's the only way you can get the extras. And admittedly the price of the appliances may be lower than the price you would pay at a store. *But* the store model may be superior or simply have features more to your taste than the one the developer offers. And you have no guarantee that the builder or developer will service the appliance; he may, in fact, be building three hundred miles away and have forgotten your town when the washer floods the floor for the first, but not the last, time. If you can manage it you are better off buying on your own. If you don't have cash look for the best credit terms you can get. Almost any of them will be cheaper than paying for an appliance or carpeting over the life of your mortgate.

Q. What are second mortgages?

A. You should know what second mortgages are, but avoid them as you would avoid poison ivy, snarling dogs, and dark streets on rainy nights in strange cities. A second mortgage is just what the name implies, another loan with your house as security on top of your first loan or mortgage. It means two monthly payments, not one—and if you could afford this amount you would be better off simply getting a larger first mortgage, especially considering that even if you pay off the first, if you miss payments on the second (which is always more expensive) your house can be foreclosed and you can lose it. Second mortgages are considered so risky that both the FHA and the VA require you to certify that you don't have such a mortgage before you can be approved for an FHA or a VA mortgage.

Q. I've heard talk about "points." What are they?

A. Sorry to say these are not like Brownie or Cub Scout points for tying marvelous knots or selling lots of cookies to raise money for some good cause. Many states have so-called usury laws that prohibit lenders from charging more than a set interest rate. On the statute books this sounds like a good idea that would save would-be homeowners money by maintaining a low interest rate. In real life it doesn't quite work that way. Interest rates are not just controlled by the government—they are also subject to the laws of supply and demand. When lots of people want to borrow, so the demand for money is high in relation to the supply available ("tight" money, as the economists say), interest rates go up. Lenders are understandably reluctant to lend at less than the going interest rate, but—since they can't charge more than the law will allow for mortgage loans—they get around this whole thing by charging "points."

To get back to your question—*a "point" is a charge equal to 1 per cent of a loan.* For instance, three points on your $25,000 mortgage would be $750. Points *cannot be charged to buyers on FHA or VA mortgages,* but a seller or a builder who gets FHA or VA loans for buyers of his houses can pay the points to the lending institution that finances the mortgages he'll offer. In all probability he will simply add these costs to the selling price, so you are still paying for points, though indirectly.

Q. What are closing costs?

A. Just when you think you've got everything arranged: you've found the house, you've got the commitment for the mortgage, you've even figured out how you'll manage to eat for the next few years—someone comes along and says, "of course you've allowed for closing costs."

"Closing costs?" you say. "What are they; do I really need them, and if so, can't they wait until next year?"

Unfortunately they can't wait, and unfortunately you must have them. They are the fees that go along with every transfer of property, and they have kept generations of lawyers, notary publics, title company employees, and other courtiers in the real estate kingdom well fed for many years. Closing costs include title insurance to protect the lender, *but not you,* against the possibility that someone else has a claim you don't know about against the house you've just bought; lawyer's fees for various chores while you were getting ready to buy; a processing fee (sometimes called an origination fee) that is the lender's price for arranging the loan, having the house appraised, your credit checked; and some miscellaneous fees, such as notary charges and recording fees.

No matter where you live or buy you're going to have to pay some or all of these, grouped under that all-inclusive umbrella, "closing fees." However, the cost does vary, depending on the schedule set by the state you live in, the fees charged by the lawyer, the kind of mortgage you have. Unless you like unpleasant shocks at the last moment it doesn't hurt to find out ahead of time about what the total cost will be, so you can be prepared with aspirin, tranquilizer, and checkbook. For a

$15,000 to $20,000 mortgage the fee could easily be $600 to $800—and the scale goes up from there.

Notice that the bank that holds the mortgage thinks it's important to have title insurance to protects its investment. You, no less than the bank, need the same kind of title insurance. After all, though the bank owns most of the house in the beginning, you too own at least a brick or two and some blades of grass the minute you put in your down payment. And in five years you don't want some stranger to walk up to your door and say he is planning to build a road across your lawn because he has the right of access, or he's come to collect for the estate of his grandfather who was a master plumber never paid by the previous owner for installing a bathroom.

Presumably all this was settled when someone searched the title to your house and found that you owned it without any of these obligations. If a long-lost heir does turn up, however, the company that sells you title insurance guarantees they will fight for your rights—and if they lose you will be compensated for any losses. Some states require this title insurance for owners, others don't. Better have your lawyer check it. The cost runs about $3.50 to $5 per $1,000 of coverage, and it's a one-time fee.

Q. What is mortgage insurance? Should I have it?

A. Mortgage insurance is life insurance for the head of the household. It will pay the unpaid balance of the mortgage if the head of the household dies. Without such insurance there's the possibility that the family wouldn't be able to meet the mortgage payments and might lose the house or be forced to sell at the worst possible time. With such insurance the family is at least guaranteed a place to live. Should they decide to sell, since the mortgage has been paid, any money that results from the sale of the house belongs to the family.

Q. Wouldn't it just be easier to pack a bikini, a sheepskin, a supply of candles, and a packet of seeds and go find a nice, warm, well-ventilated cave somewhere?

A. You're undoubtedly right.

But since that's not possible, you'll cope, and probably cope well.

Remember—the first house is the hardest.

Do's and Don'ts in Dealing with Contractors

"Fly-by-night contractors who think they can make a fast buck from unsuspecting homeowners and get away with it should realize that defrauding a consumer is a crime and will be punished accordingly."

—Bess Myerson, formerly Commissioner, Department of Consumer Affairs, New York City

Even if you're a charter member of the do-it-yourself club there comes a time when a home remodeling project is just too big, too time-consuming, or beyond your expertise. You decide to hire a contractor to do the job. And, realizing that you will literally have to live with the results for a long time, you know you have to proceed with caution. Here are some basics, the result of interviews with contractors and with homeowners who've had both good and bad experiences. Checking these do's and don'ts before you get started could save you much grief.

DO'S

1. *Do* know what you want, or think you want. Roughhewn, or finished? A place for tools, sewing, television, a bar? Will it be a recreation room, a workroom, a place just for the children, or a combination of some or all of these?

2. *Do* look around for the materials and equipment you'll need. Visit appliance stores, lumberyards, home equipment centers so you'll get some idea of what your remodeling bill will be. You won't buy anything, you may annoy a few salesmen, but you'll be much more knowledgeable when you talk with a contractor. You'll have some idea of costs, which won't be lost on him.

3. *Do* ask friends and relatives for names of good contractors—but take a look at what they've had done. Their definition of a "good job" may be quite different from yours.

4. *Do* get bids from several contractors so you have a standard of comparison. (You'll learn a little bit from each one.)

5. *Do* check out the contractors with a local trade association if there is one, or the Chamber of Commerce, a consumer agency, the Better Business Bureau, even your bank, or better yet, his bank.

6. *Do* be sure the contractor you choose has insurance covering workmen's compensation, property damage, and personal liability. He should be able to prove this by showing you a certificate of insurance if you ask for it.

7. *Do* settle in advance the condition of your house, lawn, and yard when the job is completed. If not, you may be stuck with lots of debris. "Broom clean" is the usual phrase, and it means everything removed and the house left swept clean.

8. *Do* specify the year and the model that you want if you are buying appliances through the contractor and they're included in the total price. He may automatically order the standard model (since he's paying), which is cheaper. But what you want is the deluxe model, which is better.

9. *Do* check that your contract has a clause freeing you from liability if he goes bankrupt before the job is completed. Under existing mechanic's lien laws, even though you've paid the contractor in full you can still be liable for payments to subcontractors or mechanics (craftsmen) if the contractor didn't pay them. (If during the course of the work one of the subcontractors asks for money, run, don't walk, to the contractor's bank and find out if he's in trouble. If he is you should know about it so you don't get stuck with a half-completed job.)

10. *Do* keep an eye on things as they go along, especially in the beginning of each phase. For instance, if some, but not all, of your kitchen cabinets are to be torn down, be sure the workmen know where to start and *where to stop*. If you don't watch you may find all kitchen closets on the floor before you know it.

DON'TS

1. *Don't* expect your contractor to be an architect. Know what you want and be realistic about what changes you can make or add in the space available.

2. *Don't* ignore the contractor's advice about materials and appliances. He may know, based on his experience, that some materials aren't suitable for some purposes or don't wear well. Ask him his reason for his opinions, however, to be sure they're not based solely on saving himself time and effort.

3. *Don't* automatically choose the lowest bidder; he may have underestimated the work involved. If so, he's going to be very unhappy and may try to recoup his losses by using inferior materials or (since he's usually working on several jobs at once) making you low man on the totem pole when it comes to assigning workmen. The highest bidder isn't necessarily the best either. You're going to have to use your judgment, trust your instincts and cross your fingers, pray, or do whatever you think is effective to propitiate the malevolent spirits that delight in lousing up home remodeling jobs.

4. *Don't* expect an ironclad completion date. An experienced contractor, especially if you have an old house, knows that all kinds of things operate against a precise completion date. He may chip away a plaster wall only to find a solid brick

wall behind it. He must also allow for the vagaries of suppliers, weather, temperamental workmen, and delays by city, county, and town officials. He will, however, allow for all these things in giving you an *approximate* date, and barring major catastrophes or strikes over which he has no control, you can hold him to this deadline.

5. *Don't* think you're bound to get a better price by telling one contractor what another contractor has bid. It could be that Mr. A., with whom you are dealing at the moment, had planned a lower price than the one you mention, and with a quick flicker of his eyelids he immediately raises his quote.

6. *Don't* sign a contract until you've checked it with your lawyer, your mortgage company, or someone in the home improvement section of your bank if you're paying for it with a bank loan. And regardless of which of these options you choose, be sure to read the contract carefully yourself, so you're sure you know what you're getting, or getting into. If you've been dealing with a representative of the contractor be sure the contractor's name is on the contract so that he's responsible for the contract's fulfillment. If not, he might later claim he wasn't responsible for a salesman's commitment.

7. *Don't* deal with the contractor's workmen directly: in other words, don't become foreman. If you think a workman is using the wrong finish or the wrong color paint, ignore his assurances that it will look "exactly the way you want it, lady (or Mac)" when he's finished. Call the contractor and make him responsible. If you can't reach the contractor insist that the man stop. Better to have a delay than find yourself with navy blue walls or blond cabinets when you'd had your heart set on pale blue walls and walnut cabinets.

Finally, how can you be sure of complete satisfaction? The best rule of thumb is not the rule of thumb but the rule of purse. Customarily contractors get a minimum down payment—something like 10 per cent of the total cost of the contract—before they start. (Sometimes you may arrange for progress payments, but this is rare unless it's a major job, such as rebuilding after a fire for instance, or adding a complete wing to a house.) The remainder of the price is paid on completion—but if you want to keep some control it's worthwhile to withhold a little money, perhaps fifty to several hundred dollars, depending on the original price, for a short time. Then, when you're sure the roof doesn't leak after a heavy rainfall, or the floor tiles don't buckle or the wallpaper doesn't buckle, you can finish the payment.

Faith, hope, and caution—but the greatest of these is caution.

· 28 ·

Home Is Where the Furniture Is—Some Buying Pointers and Pitfalls

"A house that does not have one worn, comfy chair in it is soulless."
—May Sarton, former furniture columnist

Ever wonder why some decorative objects are advertised as "conversation pieces?" The implication is that your friends will walk in, notice the decoration, and start talking about your exquisite taste or your talent for finding rare and unusual things. But any kind of furniture is a conversation piece when you're going to buy it, and the usual opening remark is "I know what I like—but I can't afford it." Furniture is one of the most costly investments you'll make in your lifetime, and one of the most difficult. There are so many obstacles: lack of experience, lack of information, and of course lack of money. That's on your side, or, as the economists like to say, on the demand side. On the supply side there's the—to put it charitably—poorly organized, inefficient furniture industry with *its* obstacles: shortages of raw materials, problems with shipments and paperwork, and a dearth of skilled craftsmen. All in all, it can add up to a big pain in your purse and your psyche.

But there's no need to suffer unnecessarily. There are things you can do to ease the pain and the burden, accepting what is almost inevitable since it won't do you much good to be up-tight, and coping well with those things that you can do something about. It's important to understand, first of all, that the buying process is fraught with all kinds of psychological pitfalls. Furniture is not like a dress or a suit—if you make a mistake you can't wear it a few times and then quietly donate it to your favorite charity, somewhat easing your conscience if not your bankbook. When you buy a chair that's uncomfortable or drapes that aren't the right color, you have to sit on or look at the damn things for a long time, and they are a constant reminder of your frailty. The situation can be exacerbated if there were two of you doing the choosing and you didn't agree. It's difficult for the person who was right to resist saying "I told you so," and then the conversation piece may turn into a "quarrel piece."

Next, you should accept the fact that unless you're fantastically lucky you're going to make mistakes, and you can prepare yourself to deal with them. It helps to know that those beautifully decorated model rooms you see in department stores and furniture showrooms don't spring full-blown from the mind of an interior designer. They are the result of weeks of planning, plus hours or even days spent with several strong and patient men on hand, whose only job is to move the chairs, couches, and lamps from here to there and maybe back again until the decorator has gotten the best effect. Yet even with all that help and variety of furniture and accessories to choose from designers sometimes make mistakes that end up in the clearance corner (where you can buy them at a bargain price if they suit your needs).

If professionals, with all that backup, accept the idea that mistakes are inevitable, you should do likewise. Our friend from Chapter 2, Dr. Fensterheim, the behavioral therapist, suggests comparing your mistakes to looking at a partially filled glass. Would you say the glass is half full, or half empty? What if your choice wasn't perfect? Was it 50 per cent wrong, or 50 per cent right? Just acknowledge that you're not the supreme shopper—no one is—and go on from there. You will build your confidence, profit from your mistakes, and you *will* gain expertise.

Suppose, however, you worry because you know you've made the wrong decision in the past, and you feel you were talked into this decision by a very persuasive salesman—against your better judgment. Your lack of sales resistance may be based on your fear of revealing ignorance by asking questions, a trait that can be especially hazardous when it comes to furniture, since it is a specialized kind of knowledge that you aren't likely to have acquired. If this is your problem you should, says Dr. Fensterheim, set up a program of deliberate exercises to overcome this feeling.

Start by going to places where you wouldn't be expected to know the facts and asking questions—an art gallery, perhaps, or an equipment showroom. Next, go and ask questions in places where you do have a little knowledge—an automobile showroom, where you could ask about some detail of the car's construction, or a restaurant, where you could ask how a particular dish has been made. If you feel yourself getting anxious about what people will think of you for being so uninformed or unsophisticated, stop, think, and ask yourself, "Why should this worry me?" Say "a plague on the pagans," or some such thing, and continue to ask questions. You'll soon learn that the ceiling won't immediately start to crumble if you reveal your ignorance, and though you may not always get a good response, you will feel good about yourself, because *you* will be in control.

Actually, it's been my experience that people usually love to have a chance to show off their knowledge and are flattered if you ask questions about their work. It's also been my experience that if they're huffy about it, or annoyed and curt, it's often because they don't want to reveal their ignorance. If a furniture salesman won't answer questions he may not know the answer, or he may not be helpful—and in either case, who needs him? Find somebody else. It's your money and your furniture and you're entitled to both information and courtesy.

Now, to go over to the supply side for a moment, so you know what you're up against on that score. As a quick look around at your friends and colleagues will confirm, more and more people, single, married, and somewhere in between, are busy setting up households and buying furniture. At the same time, as furniture manufacturers point out with sorrow and bitterness, there are fewer and fewer craftsmen, it's more and more difficult to get raw materials or finished fabrics, production lines get fouled up when something doesn't arrive on time, and the net result to dealers and consumers is delay and more delay. Waiting time for furniture can be anywhere from *several months to a year* from the day you fall in love with a sample on the salesroom floor to the day of delivery. This of course has to be in the back of your head as you plan for your furniture shopping.

Which brings up the question of a philosophy of furnishing. There are two extremes: the buy only the best even if you have to sit on the floor while admiring your magnificent carved dining-room table vs. the early orange crate plus late hand-me-down but every corner filled school, and all the range of choices in between. Your own temperament, life-stage, and life-style enter into the decision, plus other considerations—two-legged or perhaps four-legged ones. It hardly pays to have exquisite light-colored fabrics and fine wood unless they can be kept beyond the reach and natural devastation of small children and/or large dogs.

Most of us, with imported champagne tastes and domestic beer pocketbooks, end up compromising, not only because of our budget but also because we don't want to live in or raise children in a world circumscribed by "keep off the furniture" signs. (Even if we could, dogs and cats can't read and neighborhood children, of course, are not as well behaved as ours.)

WHERE TO SHOP—
SOME CHOICES

If budget is your primary limitation the most reasonable plan is not to stint on the basics—bed, couch, a comfortable reading chair, good lights, and a sturdy dining room table and chairs—and to count on acquiring the other pieces along the way. How far you can stretch your money depends on where you choose to shop and how you go about shopping. The place to start isn't necessarily the place where you will finish, i.e., the department stores and furniture showrooms. This is where you want to spend time "just looking": strolling around, scanning price tags, noticing differences in workmanship, and making mental notes on attractive decorating ideas. As you go from store to store you'll soon learn which ones seem to offer better values than others, have better-informed or more helpful salespeople, and carry more stock in the kind of furniture you're interested in.

There are some advantages in buying from a regular furniture store or a department store. You will have an extensive selection of price ranges, styles, and fabrics. Since you're buying from a sample you may have your choice of kinds of filling for cushions (feather or rubber, for instance), and you may even have options like extra cushions or legs with casters. You're much more likely to have knowledgeable salespeople and you may even have the free advice of an interior designer. You may even be able, if you make a mistake, to return the furniture (see box on page 177). If you have a regular charge account you can, without risking your credit rating too much, space out some of your payments so that you pay no interest. Or you may be able to take advantage of an actual plan for extended credit with no interest for three months or so. (Beware, however, of a revolving credit plan with interest of 18 per cent or more—you can do better than that by borrowing from a bank—see Chapter 5.)

There are drawbacks, however—and the biggest one is price. On medium-price furniture you will probably be able to do better at discount houses, clearance centers, and warehouse outlets (we'll get to this in a minute). And since you're buying from a sample, delivery, as I said earlier, can be anywhere from a month to almost a year, and will probably average at least four months.

So, after shopping the showrooms and furniture floors and getting some "feel" for prices and values, you should have a look at other places to buy furniture. One of the first places to try is the clearance sections of the very same furniture and department stores. Here you will find the samples, odd pieces, returned pieces, canceled orders, and mistakes that other people have made. These are marked down, sometimes quite drastically, the defects are often minor—sometimes nothing more than dirt—and if you find what you need you can get really good furniture at bargain prices.

(This is a good way to buy rugs, particularly odd-size rugs and end-of-broadloom rolls left over from wall-to-wall installations. When these ends are taking up space needed for new rugs the store will often sell the leftovers at very reduced prices, though they may add on a small charge for binding any unfinished edges. If you find a very large size you like you can, with the help of large heavy scissors or a linoleum cutter and some heavy corrugated cardboard to protect your floors, cut down the large rug yourself into room-size rugs plus smaller rugs or hallway runner. Shaggy rugs with rubberized backings won't need any binding, and other weaves can usually be used unbound until they are cleaned and can be bound, fairly cheaply, by the rug cleaner.)

Next stop is the furniture discount centers. Several major department stores and furniture stores now operate clearance centers in major shopping areas around the country. Many of them started as extensions of the in-store clearance center but are now stocked not only with pieces left over from the stores but also with new and fresh pieces. These may be last year's models, a line of furniture from a small manufacturer, or even some manufacturer's leftovers. If they have what you want you can get a good buy.

Another kind of discount operation is the so-called "warehouse furniture center," known as the supermarket of the furniture business. You give up some of the services of the regular furniture or department store—model rooms for ideas, a decorating and sales staff for help and advice, regular charge account privileges, and free delivery service. You also have a more limited range of styles and fabrics to choose from. In exchange, however, you get lower prices, anywhere from 10 to 20 per cent. Even more, they offer immediate delivery—in fact, if you want to, and have a few sturdy friends or in-laws, you can cart away the furniture yourself from the warehouse stores, a real advantage.

However, buying from these stores does have some disadvantages which you should be aware of, since they either cut down somewhat on how much you save or present other problems, as follows:

1. They are not really wholesalers, but a different kind of retailer. In California three of the subsidiaries of Levitz Furniture Corporation were barred by the Los Angeles Superior Court from representing that they were not retail furniture dealers and saying that they sold furniture direct from the manufacturer to the consumer, unless this was actually the case in a particular transaction. They were also barred from saying their furniture was offered at a saving of a given percentage, unless that percentage was based on the prevailing market price in the area

for the furniture in the three months preceding the ad. And they also were barred from falsely saying that prices had been "slashed" or that they were holding a "discontinued furniture sale."

While Levitz, one of the largest furniture chains (it has about fifty stores in twenty-three states), probably won't use such tactics again, there is nothing to say that other, smaller stores (much harder to police) won't indulge in such tactics. What it boils down to is that only wholesalers of furniture really buy directly from the manufacturer, in most cases, and that when you buy at a discount center you are getting savings passed on to you by a large chain's buying power, or because you are giving up some services that more traditional stores offer. You still have to do comparison shopping to make sure the store's prices are competitive with those of other stores; there are differences in price among the various types of discount houses, so it always pays to shop around.

2. They don't offer charge accounts, so if you're not going to pay cash, you have to use a bank charge plan, such as Bank Americard or Master Charge. You are then paying 18 or more per cent interest—certainly a higher rate than the no-interest regular charge account or some of the extended-payment plans that some department or furniture stores offer. (A better arrangement would be a bank or credit union loan; see Chapter 5.)

3. Furniture is usually sold as is, final sale. If it doesn't fit or looks terrible you are still stuck with it.

4. You have to read the ads, the price tags, and the pre-printed "list price" or "manufacturer's suggested retail price" tags themselves with care. The "list price" given is a dubious figure, usually put on for the sole purpose of being a base from which the retailer can advertise "20% or 30% off list price," or "off manufacturer's suggested retail price." The ads will specify "walnut finish," or "oak finish," or "maple finish," which is definitely *not* the same thing as walnut, oak, or maple.

If you are a member of a buying co-operative through your union, church, or credit union you already know of the savings you're able to get on many items of furniture. If you're not, and you're a member of an organized group, you might discuss with them the possibility of affiliating with a buying service. Requirements are usually a minimum of one hundred members and a willingness to distribute free brochures and other literature supplied by the service to your members. When it comes to furniture the services refer you to a group of co-operating dealers who give you an agreed-on and presumably better price on various pieces of furniture than you can get elsewhere. Possibilities for saving are very much there—but you have to know comparable prices and value to be sure you are getting a bargain. (For information about affiliating write to Mr. Gerald A. Lerner, General Manager, Rollins Buying Service, United Buying Service, 747 Third Avenue, New York, or Ms. Mary Lee, President, Better Buying Service, 400 Madison Avenue, both N.Y. 10017.)

BEFORE YOU BUY— SOME LAST-MINUTE WARNINGS

After you've surveyed the field, but before you actually put some cash on the line, in any kind of store, you should consider how the furniture you buy will adapt to inevitable changes in your life or your life-style. (If you want a quick guideline you might keep this in mind—at this stage in your life be wary of buying anything that is untested by time, can't be rolled up, unplugged, or taken through a narrow doorway.)

Consider, for instance, the possibility that you might move. If you're an apartment dweller the odds are very high, but even if you're a house dweller they're still high. (You may remember, as noted in Chapter 21, that the average American family moves once every seven years.) So if you want to be practical the key word for furniture shopping should be "adaptability." And adaptability in several ways.

Size. How about that 9-foot couch, or those 10-foot bookcases that you like? Will they fit into the elevators in the newer apartment buildings, which seem to be getting smaller and smaller? (You may think architects and builders think of these things, but I can tell you—as a fascinated member of a jury that decided a lawsuit between a builder and a contractor—that little "details" like this are sometimes overlooked.) If you're moving into a house, will the big pieces get through ordinary doorways and can they be maneuvered in narrow hallways? If not, you'll have a major problem on your hands. Even if they can be maneuvered successfully minor casualties—chipped paint off the door and scratches on the furniture—are almost inevitable.

Even furniture that is promoted as "easily moved" has its problems: wall-mounted bookcases, for instance, that consist of brackets, shelves, and supports. They seem sensible, but have a drawback that's not obvious. Sometimes new buildings have inside walls that can't support the weight of bookshelves. In older buildings the beams supporting the walls could be strong but the plaster might crumble so badly that the wall would have to be redone completely, at your expense, if you move out.

Convertibility. If you're "filling in" with inexpensive things after buying the major pieces you'll want furniture that can be converted to other uses later. Outdoor furniture is a fine choice for dining areas, and can serve its purpose nobly and attractively until you buy your dream house in the middle of your dream acreage. (You can very often get excellent buys in such furniture at the end of the summer selling season.) Fold-up wood and canvas chairs can move easily from living room or dining room to den, as you get more prosperous. A set of nesting tables can be used separately as lamp tables. Open-style desks can double as dining-room tables or sideboards and become children's desks later.

"Shift-ability." Wall-to-wall carpeting looks luxurious, and makes a room seem full even if you don't have much furniture. But it has drawbacks for young families. Murphy's law says that if you have a pet who is thoroughly housebroken he will have the one accident of his career in the middle of the one room that has wall-to-wall carpeting. And of course the kids will inevitably throw up on that rug and the neighbor's little boy will ride his new tricycle through before you know what's happening. If you really want the wall-to-wall effect consider substituting a "room-fit" rug. The rug is cut to fit the size and shape of your room as if it were wall-to-wall, but it isn't installed permanently. What you save on installation costs may be spent on cutting and seaming to get the size and shape rug that you want. But this rug can be picked up and sent out for cleaning, can be turned for spreading the wear more evenly, and can be taken along if you move.

Resalability. If you aren't passionately attached to a particular period of furniture keep in mind the experience of people who've lovingly bought and even more lovingly spent days, nights, and weekends restoring and refininshing antique or unusual pieces. Then they decide to move from San Francisco to Philadelphia or vice versa and don't want to take their furniture. Inevitably, there are few problems selling the conventional pieces, but either no one wants the fine pieces, or no one is willing to begin to pay for the hours of work put into restoring them. It's always easier to "mass-market" the mass-market pieces of furniture that fit almost anyone's taste and budget.

Which brings up the question of the trend-setting pieces that are featured in home-decorating magazines. One year they're all shiny steel and glass, the next year chrome and marble; then plastic or laminated cardboard. When you see the pacemakers in the pages of the magazines, gorgeously set with just the right rugs, drapes, lamps, pillows, assorted art objects and plants, of course they look beautiful. Ditto for the furniture actually on display in model rooms. But would they still look stunning in your conventional apartment, with your plain end-of-the-roll carpet and the drapes you inherited from your Aunt Helen? How will you feel about those blazing colors and plastic and steel several years from now? Remember that plastic can't be scraped and refinished, as can wood, though it can be recovered.

Remember, too, that new materials have not yet withstood the test of time. No one can be quite sure how long or how well they will last. When synthetic carpets were first introduced, for instance, they wore very badly. Though the defects were corrected people who bought them in the guinea-pig stage got a bad buy. Furthermore, there is much controversy surrounding the flammability of many of the plastics being used in cushions in furniture and in underlays for rugs. Some of these plastics flare up instantly, give off intense heat rapidly, produce great amounts of dense smoke, and, perhaps most dangerous of all, release poisonous gases and chemicals.

What to Do If You Goof

What if the ultimate catastrophe occurs? You wait and wait, the delivery is fouled up twice, and finally, when the couch or chair arrives you hate it. Hold on before you get ready to jump out the window. It could be that you are simply accustomed to things as they were, and you're feeling upset because things are different. It could be that the new piece simply looks bare and as soon as you get the tables and lamps that are going to complement it it will look as beautiful as you had anticipated. It could be that it's a fine piece but you're going to have to change plans and put it in a different place than you had originally foreseen. It could be that you will need a different color paint on the wall or different wallpaper.

Or it could be that you really have made a serious mistake. If you're desperately unhappy call the store, explain your plight (you're not the first one it's happened to), and ask if they can take it back. Be prepared to take a loss; how much varies from store to store but can range from 10 per cent plus carting charges to 50 per cent.

You always have the option of advertising and trying to sell a piece you don't like. Resign yourself to the fact that, even if it's brand-new, you're going to take a loss. Furniture depreciates a minimum of 20 to 30 per cent as soon as it leaves the store and is classified as "used." How much of a loss will depend on what you're selling, the market in your neighborhood or area, the time of the year, your selling skill, and just plain luck. It's one occasion, however, when honesty isn't necessarily the best policy. Better to fudge just a little bit about your reason for selling—if you say you just don't like it in your living room but it's really a handsome piece you'll only prejudice your own case.

Far better to murmur under your breath that your husband's mother is moving from a house to an apartment and giving you a new set of furniture, or your father is remarrying and moving into his new wife's house and giving you some family furniture that you're sentimental about, or some such reason. If you're not the type who can carry this off well get a friend who is, and let him or her sell the piece and intimate all kinds of things (divorce, murder, mayhem) that make the sale logical.

SOME FINAL WORDS OF EXPERIENCE-BASED WISDOM

There's many a slip, usually about a dozen in assorted colors, between promise of delivery and a truck really pulling up to your door. The in-store pickup service gets two yellow ones, the trucking company gets three pink ones, the expediter gets the light blue, etc., and they all get lost in the mail, on the truck, or in some clerk's file. Which means that you stay home from work, miss an important meeting, or otherwise doublecross your life for the deliveryman who doesn't show.

Or he does show and brings in a piece with scratches, a door hanging on half a hinge, a table with a cracked leg, or a chair with the wrong upholstery. This is bad enough, but the error is often compounded by stores that are careless or indifferent about making adjustments (though their billing departments are always careful to see that you get the bill promptly). You have better things to do than waste your time dealing with couldn't-care-less furniture and adjustment departments. Unfortunately there is no way of setting up a foolproof system to prevent such errors, but you can at least minimize the possibilities.

1. Check with the Better Business Bureau, with a consumer affairs office or agency, and with friends, neighbors, and co-workers to learn about their experiences with various stores. If you learn that one store is particularly guilty of shoddy treatment avoid it, even if it may cost you a bit more to go elsewhere.

2. When you're placing your order ask the salesman for his most pessimistic, off-the-record estimate of the reliability of delivery schedules.

3. Plan to do some follow-up on your own. If it's the store's practice to notify you in advance (and it should be) what day delivery is scheduled, doublecheck with the delivery department yourself. Insist on speaking to the chief expediter or whoever oversees the delivery schedule, and get him to confirm the date you've been given. If you can't speak to him directly tell the person you are talking to that you'll be happy to hold the line while he checks. (You can spend the time cleaning a file, changing your nail polish, or updating your address book.)

Cheer yourself with the thought that your chances of having everything go well are just as good as your chances of having some things go wrong and, human memory being what it is, as you sit on your good choices and look around at your pleasant homey surroundings you'll forget the anxiety and the trouble and be able just to relax and enjoy things.

· 29 ·

How to Get the Best Car, at the Lowest Cost, with the Least Hassle

"Thinking of buying a new car? Instead of kicking the tires, open the glove compartment and get out the owner's manual."
—Virginia Knauer, Director of the Office of Consumer Affairs (Quoted in the September 1, 1973 "Consumer News" Bulletin.)

You're a rational creature, right? You know that buying a car is a major expense and a major investment, something that has to be done carefully. You know there are two parts of the expense: the price of the car itself and the cost of financing the car, unless you are planning to pay cash. You make up your mind to get the best price and the best financing; to make cold, calculating, intelligent choices.

You shop around. You spend weeks looking into car prices, reading newspaper advertisements, comparing "good deals" at various showrooms. You're very happy when you get a dealer to drop his first-quoted price by $50 to $100.

Then, one day, maybe after you've just met someone and think the romance would thrive better under the aegis of a shiny new car; or after you've waited half an hour in freezing weather for a crowded bus; or after you've heard that funny "plink" that reminds you of the time you caused a major traffic jam when the car broke down with just such a "plink"—you wander into a showroom. And there it sits, the car of your dreams, the beautiful, highly polished, luxuriously upholstered chariot you'd envisioned. Your solemn resolutions become a speck of dust that floats silently in the air and out the revolving door. You want that car and you want it yesterday.

Experienced car salesmen say they can almost smell when a person is bitten by the "get it now" bug. Naturally they press to complete the sale on the spot, because they know that if you're psychologically ready you'll take accessories you don't really want, luxury features you know you can live without, a different color than the one you had in mind, and their financing, just to be able to drive away as soon as possible.

This fever can be contagious. If you've ever wondered why car salesmen are sometimes almost arrogantly independent it's because they know the fever is in the air. When a particularly popular car model is on the floor, a "hot item," they'll be able to sell that particular car four or five times right off the floor. Then, when you come back to make the final arrangements your salesman will say something like "I didn't know it but the manager had already sold it" or "I couldn't let you have that one—between you and me the head of the shop told me he's not sure the carburetor is working right." He knows he can get away with this because you are so smitten with new-car fever you will end up spending anywhere from several hundred to several thousand dollars more than you had planned on, just because you fell in love.

PLANNING TO EXERT
A POUND OF PREVENTION

What can you do to resist these very basic and all-too-human impulses? Just knowing about them is the first step, so that you can exert some control over the situation. Plus deciding *in advance* how much you should spend, what kind of car is best, and what financing possibilities are open to you. Let's consider these one by one.

How much should you spend really means—unless you are buying for cash—how big a loan can you undertake, considering both monthly payments and the time for which they're incurred. This will depend on what debts you are carrying at the moment, for how long, and what plans you have for the next few years. One possible rule of thumb: if you have average expenses your monthly car payments shouldn't be more than half your monthly payments for your mortgage or your rent. In other words, if your rent is $250 a month you can afford—if you're not heavily in debt—to pay about $100 to $125 on a car.

But, as any car owner will tell you, you are due for a shock as you find out that the initial price is just the beginning of a car's cost. From the moment you pull up to your front door or apartment house entrance, depreciation, like a silent plague, is busy eroding your car's value. Even if you did nothing more than admire the car as it sat in the driveway, and only took it out for a round-the-block ride once a week on Tuesday at five o'clock, it would still go down, down, down in value, especially in the first few years. A Department of Transportation study showed that in 1972 a standard-size car, operated in a fairly typical suburban community, would depreciate $1,226 the first year, even if it was kept in plastic in a garage. But you don't keep it in plastic in a garage, and operating and maintenance costs are also nibbling away at your bankroll. It's important to decide in advance how much you can spend, including operating costs and maintenance, because it will affect your decision on type and size of car and optional equipment. The costs of driving a car vary considerably, and are changing rapidly at this writing, but if you live in an area such as New York City you would pay much more, since insurance, garages, tools, and other expenses would be higher, than you would pay in, for instance, a small town in Texas.

For our purposes I'm going to discuss the low-priced and medium-priced cars, from the subcompacts to the full-size standards, and since you have many choices even in this price bracket the discussion will have to be somewhat general. They range in price from about $2,500 to $4,500, plus optional equipment that can easily add $1,000 or more to the basic price. They range in size from about 163 inches long and 70 inches wide for the subcompacts to about 230 inches long and 80 inches wide for the full-size standards. You may have your choice of two doors or four doors and various engines, from the four cylinders in some subcompacts to eight cylinders in the medium or full size, plus all kinds of options.

What size do you need? One factor is the kind of driving you do. If you scoot around in flat, level country, and don't customarily carry very heavy loads, you can get along fine with a smaller, lighter car. But if you drive frequently in hilly country and load your car heavily, you will need a larger, more powerful car. Another factor is economy. Naturally the bigger cars offer more head and leg room, a smoother ride, more luggage space—but they also mean bigger bills for repairs, maintenance, and above all for gas. Weight, in fact, is the biggest factor in savings on gas. Road tests have shown that as the weight of the car goes up the miles per gallon go down, from about twenty or more miles to a gallon for the cars weighing about 2,5000 pounds to about ten–twelve miles per gallon in the 4,500 class. (There are other factors at work here—more powerful engines, air conditioning, and automatic transmission also cut mileage, but the more-weight-fewer-miles-per-gallon ratio is generally valid.)

Safety is another and very important factor to consider when choosing a car. The National Traffic and Motor Vehicle Safety Act requires that manufacturers state in the owner's manual some things that influence safety, such as the car's stopping distance, acceleration and passing ability, and the tire reserve load. In other words, how long it will take your car to stop after you've applied the brakes, how fast it will be able to pick up speed and pass another car, and how often you can load your car with passengers, suitcases, baby gear, logs, or stuff from the farmer's market before the tires begin to wear out and you have the danger of a flat tire and a skid off the road, or worse.

You should also know that tests by the Insurance Institute for Highway Safety and the National Safety Bureau showed that small cars are more apt to be damaged in a crash than large cars. In fact, the National Safety Bureau survey of accidents found that severe injury or death was often in proportion to the size of the car. Therefore you certainly want to balance the economy of the subcompact car against the greater safety of the larger cars, and if possible get the intermediate, or the larger compacts. Other safety factors you might want to consider are two-door sedans, if you have children who ride in the rear seats. If you drive alone at night it might be worthwhile to have power door locks that are controlled from the front seat, if they are possible on a model you're considering.

After you've decided on the basis of use, safety, and economy the size car you'll need, you can decide on some of the other features. Tires will be one of your first questions. Most models come with the correct size tire to carry their rated load at normal inflation. However, a set of four oversize, blackwall tires plus a spare costs about $15 to $20 extra and, if available, is worth the additional expenditure for its extra margin of safety. Many cars now come with radial tires as standard equipment; they are considered stronger and longer-lasting than the other tires and should be considered as a desirable option if they're not standard.

And after deciding on the tires you still have to pick and choose among various other kinds of optional equipment. The problem is not just the basic price, but whether they are worth having at all.

Automatic transmission, at about $250, is getting to be a standard item on most cars. If it isn't included it's definitely worth having, particularly if you do much driving in heavy traffic. If you have the choice, get *disc brakes,* usually power-operated. They cost about $70 to $80 and help you to stop the car with less swerving, though no faster than with ordinary brakes. They also respond better even when they're soaking wet—a help if you drive over rutted roads that collect puddles in the rain.

Power steering, at about $100, makes parking easier if you do lots of in and out driving. However, it may require some additional maintenance—and a mechanic who knows how to maintain it.

The most popular option—and for people in a hot, sticky part of the country it may not even be considered an option any more—is *air conditioning,* which can add a *minimum* of several hundred dollars to the price of the car. If you think it's worth it you're better off getting a factory-installed unit rather than adding on a unit later. The factory unit is integrated into the car's system and will be more efficient. Incidentally an air conditioner will be more effective in a light-colored car, especially if it has a light-colored roof, since light colors don't absorb the sun's rays as much as dark colors do. Salesmen will probably try to persuade you to take tinted glass—at about another $50—saying that it makes the air conditioner more efficient. True, but it also impairs night vision, so it's definitely something you can get along without.

KEY TO CONTENTMENT—
THE WHEELER-DEALER

Just as important—in fact, maybe more important—than knowing something about the car you want is knowing a great deal about the dealer you are going to buy from. He can make the difference between reasonable happiness and utter frustration. If you have your choice between two fairly similar cars and one is sold by a better dealer than the other, it's really no choice—you should be guided by the dealer rather than the car. Why? Because a car is a complicated and intricate mechanism that requires careful assembly. For want of a nut tightened here or a screw left out there, you can get a dashboard rattle that will drive you out of your mind—or a serious defect that can literally endanger your life and the lives of your passengers. It's up to your dealer and his service department to make all the adjustments needed in a new car, both for the life of your warranty and after. If you're dissatisfied, you and your dealer are going to have a poor relationship, to say the least.

There are many things a poor dealer can do to cause you anguish, from the first moment on. He can try to finagle on the price in your contract—one reason you must read it carefully before you sign, and be sure all the figures are in and as agreed upon, before you sign. He can deliver your car with scratches or without being sure it's been properly serviced. He can refuse to make the minor adjustments usually needed. He can fail to live up to the warranty. The whole question of your rights under the warranty can be a real hassle if he wants to be difficult or if he's just plain inefficient. You can be, in this day of shortages of skilled mechanics, at the mercy of a dealer's service department. If the department is good you're in luck; if it's poor you can write to the manufacturer, complain bitterly to the dealer or the manager of the agency, write to the president of the company or to Ralph Nader. But in the meantime *you* are greatly inconvenienced.

(Many dealers are less than ecstatic about making repairs under the warranty, since they may feel that the manufacturer isn't paying them enough for the work they have to do, and they could make more money putting the same time into work being done for private customers. If their competitors are looking for future business they may oblige you by taking on your work, in the expectation that you will stay with them after the warranty expires. But then again, if they are already very busy they may be just as happy if you go somewhere else.)

Since so much is at stake in this potential love-hate relationship you have to shop around for a dealer. One basis for choosing is his reputation in the community, so of course you'll want to check on it. You could start with your Better Business Bureau and/or your local consumer protection agencies, and then go on to relatives, friends, neighbors. Ask them how long they've had to wait for routine service and for emergency repairs. Then check the following items with the dealer:

1. Hours of the service department, particularly the hours that are convenient for you, i.e., before and after work and weekends.

2. The kind of equipment they have for diagnosing a car's troubles.

3. The number of mechanics in the service department and their qualifications.

4. How long customers have to wait for routine service and what equipment and personnel are available for emergency service.

5. Do they have a pickup and a delivery service?

6. Will they lend you a car while yours is being repaired?

NOW THE CRUCIAL PART— ## FINDING THE MONEY

You have pretty well decided on the size car you want, the price range, the options, maybe even the dealer. Now you've got to get the wherewithal. You have several choices.

You can pay cash. As always, this is the cheapest, since you save the interest on the loan, which can be anywhere from several hundred to several thousand dollars, depending on the size and length of the loan. A one-year loan is going to cost less than a three-year loan, $2,000 less than $3,500, etc. However, you have to balance this savings against the interest you lose if you don't have the money in the bank. Also, this earned interest becomes part of your income, while interest payments on the loan are deductible.

You can borrow from a credit union if you're a member. Their terms are usually very favorable and many add on life insurance at no extra cost, so that if you should die or become disabled the loan will be paid in full. (Other lenders some-times charge for this kind of insurance; it pays to ask about it.)

You can borrow from a bank. Usually this is the most advantageous arrangement and certainly the first place you should check if you're not a credit union member. Many banks offer a variety of auto loan plans, with different interest rates, depend-ing on whether you will use the car as security, or some other asset, such as a sav-ings account, stocks, or bonds. Different banks offer different loan plans, so don't assume they are all alike. It will pay to shop around and see where you can get the best terms. If the bank where you have your checking account also offers auto-mobile loans they may be willing to deduct the monthly payment from your ac-count automatically, saving you the time and trouble of writing a check. The one thing to beware of is a payment plan that requires a ballon payment at the end, i.e., a payment that is sometimes several hundred dollars higher than the previous payments. If you can't meet this payment the bank will offer to finance it for you—but there you are, in debt again for another six months to a year. A plan with equal payments that you can budget for is much better.

You can finance it through the dealer. This is usually the most expensive, de-spite the dealer's claim that he can get you "bank terms." If you didn't know better you might be persuaded to take it, since it's so easy with that lovely car sitting there, and there's the terrible temptation to get the whole business over with at that moment. Resist. It costs too much. And if you have a good credit rating it can be quite simple to arrange for a bank loan with a delay of a few days or at the most a week. You may be able to make all arrangements by phone or mail, which is certainly little enough trouble for a saving of several hundred dollars at least.

A word of caution: Don't announce to the dealer that you're not considering his finance plan. Many dealers get a rebate or commission of perhaps $150 to $200 for every loan they arrange through the finance company they work with. A dealer will be much chummier if he has that commission in his mind's eye. He may even make more of a concession on the price of the car, or what he is willing to give you on a trade-in on your old car, if he thinks he is also going to do the financing. Just say you are going to borrow the money (you don't have to say from whom) and let it go at that. When the price has been set you can announce—at the very last minute—that you have arranged bank financing.

Now that you know where you're going to get the money for a car it's time to decide what kind of car you want—and with how many options.

Time to buy? Almost, but not quite. You should go in forearmed with some knowledge of car pricing, starting with the fact that by law the sticker or list price must be pasted to the rear left window of a new car. This is not the selling price—it's the price from which you start bargaining. And the best way to bargain is to know what the dealer has had to pay, so you can judge how much he can cut his price and still make a reasonable profit, so he can remain in business.

Consumers Union has worked out a formula, as follows, that will help you get the dealer's cost before he has to add on something to pay for his overhead (rent, heat, phone, etc.), his advertising, and saleman's commission. The formula goes like this: To calculate the dealer's cost, take the bottom figure on the official price sticker and subtract the transportation charge, also listed on the sticker. Then, for a do-mestic subcompact or compact sedan or compact specialty car, multiply by .85. For all intermediates, multiply by .815. For full-sized cars, multiply by .78. Finally, add back the freight charge, and you have the dealer's cost within about 1 per cent. (The markup on imports varies too widely to allow the use of such a formula.) The optional equipment can also be the subject of bargaining; you might be able to get from 5 to 20 per cent less than the list price.

But there is also the possibility of buying through a car broker—and it's a possibility that can definitely save you money.

BUYING THROUGH A CAR BROKER: PRO—AND SOME CON

Buying through a car broker isn't difficult; here's how it works. You write to an organization such as Car/Puter, 1603 Bushwick Avenue, Brooklyn, New York 11207; United Buying Service, 1855 Broadway, New York, New York 10023; D & J Enterprises, 130 Scotts Drive, Holland, Michigan 49423; or Masterson Auto Sales, 1957 Chestnut, San Francisco, California 94123. You tell them what model, color, and optional features you want in a car and send along a small fee (about $7 to $9).

In a few days you get from them a computer printout that tells you the dealer price and the sticker price (by law the sticker or list price must be pasted to the rear left window of a new car) of the car or cars you're interested in. With this information you are in a fine bargaining position with a car dealer. You know where he's starting from and how much margin he has to lower this price in order to save you some money. Of course, he has to make a profit or he'd go out of business—but he can make more or less, depending on how shrewd a bargainer you are.

Car/Puter will do more than send you a computer printout. Through a company called United Auto Brokers, Arnold Wonsever, president and founder of Car/Puter, makes it possible for you to buy the car of your choice (with the possible exception of the most luxurious American-made cars) for about $125 (in 1973) above the factory price paid by the dealer for the car and the optional features. Dealers in cities all around the country co-operate with United Auto Brokers, so when you place your order with United Auto Brokers they turn your name over to a dealer in your neighborhood who has agreed to sell you a car on these terms.

The brokers make their money on the commission paid to them by the co-operating dealers. The dealers make their money several ways: though they have less profit per car, they sell more cars; they can cut down on other expenses, such as advertising and salesmen; they may get handsome bonuses, such as free vacations from manufacturers, for achieving high sales. So you don't have to worry about taking chickens out of the pots of the dealers—they really make more than a hundred dollars or so on their cars while still saving you money.

How much money can they save you? That depends. Less on the stripped-down, comparatively low-cost car, more on the medium- and medium-to-high-priced car. The range can be from several hundred to close to a thousand dollars, depending on what you want to buy.

Are there problems? There have been published reports from individuals who bought from car brokers, and from the regular dealers—not surprisingly, their opinions differ. (Incidentally, if you haven't read in your local newspapers about buying a car through a broker don't be surprised. When the business started many newspapers, who depended on their advertising revenue from regular car dealers, refused to accept ads from Car/Puter. The regular dealers were understandably upset by the competition, especially since it revealed that their own selling and pricing practices had more in common with the bazaars in Middle Eastern countries than with the typical American retail showroom. However, consumer columnists, TV shows, and just plain word of mouth have spread the gospel. The situation may change, since Car/Puter has filed an anti-trust complaint against *Reader's Digest*, General Motors, Ford, Chrysler, and American Motors.)

Regular car dealers say that the dealers who've signed with car brokers won't service the cars they sell at these reduced prices. The broker dealers have emphatically denied these charges and said that when a car is brought into a repair shop, particularly if it's the shop of a large broker dealer, the service manager has no idea what the customer paid for the car or under what arrangement he bought it.

Regular car dealers have also said that the broker dealers will try to raise their profit by "building the deal," i.e., once the customer has arrived in the showroom he will be encouraged to buy options like air conditioners, a burglar alarm, or undercoating—and at inflated prices. The broker dealers have also denied these charges.

The Best Time to Buy a Car

Are there good, better, and best times of the year to buy a car? If you have a choice there certainly are. Emotions, the model cars, the weather, contests among dealers, even the day of the month, all have their effect on the price of a car. If you take them into account you may be able to save yourself anywhere from $100 to as high as $500–$600, depending on what car you buy, when you buy it, and how long you intend to keep it.

In general, the most advantageous time to buy is right after the new models roll onto the dealers' floors in the fall. Dealers need the room, and buying fever is in the air, so that otherwise cautious people are looking at last year's new cars—which they formerly loved—as if the cars had suddenly broken out with a bad case of flat tires and peeling paint. Dealers and manufacturers may be willing to give discounts up to 20 to 40 per cent off the list price (check this) for cars that are still on the showroom floor. The great advantage of this is that the discount can equal or even be more than the depreciations that set in as soon as the new models are for sale.

Luck, the selling year, and your own flexibility will influence how good a buy you can get. If the dealer's been lucky, or smart, or both, or if it's been a busy year, the dealer may have few or no cars left, and he will shave his discount accordingly. Or he may have only cars left in bilious colors that are loaded with extras that you don't need or want—in which case you won't have a deal.

This is where you have to be flexible. If you are determined to buy one particular make of car and you don't find it "left over," you can't take advantage of the bargain time. But if you can decide on a size and price range and are willing to buy one of several makes as long as it meets your other requirements, you will get a good deal.

A variation of this scheme is the end-of-summer buying time, before the new models are out and when dealers aren't sure how well the new cars will capture the public's fancy. Again, they are willing to bargain on price, though they may not give quite as high a discount, since there are more buyers competing for these leftovers. As a result the smaller discount could mean that what you save by buying a leftover could be less than the amount that the car will depreciate just as soon as the new models come out. So, *unless you are planning to keep your car at least three to four years to offset this depreciation,* you won't get a bargain.

The next best buying time is early January on into February, especially in the parts of the country where winter is then at its peak. Walk into a showroom the day after a blizzard and the dealer will greet you as if you just descended from heaven in answer to his prayers. And he may be spurred by an incentive plan from the manufacturer, who dangles a contest prize—anything from a rebate on each sale to a vacation in the sun—for salesmen who meet or beat a sales quota. After this you may get your best deal in early spring—perhaps around income tax time when manufacturers are again offering incentives to get the spring selling season started. Finally, you may do better if you shop around the end of the month—particularly on the last selling day of the month if the dealer and salesmen are part of a factory promotion plan or contest that offers them incentives for meeting or beating monthly sales figures.

Incidentally, foreign cars don't have these seasonal patterns, partly because they don't have annual model changeovers and partly because foreign-car buyers have never been as new-model- or style-conscious. But even with foreign cars it may be possible to get a better deal in December, when all car buying is at its lowest ebb.

One thing to keep in mind—if you are planning to trade in your old car, don't mention this fact until you get a price from the dealer. If he doesn't know you are planning a trade-in he won't count on "making up" a lower new car price by offering less on a trade-in. Bargain first—then talk trade-in.

Nevertheless, some people who've bought through brokers have run into such problems as slow delivery, or having to drive a good distance to find a dealer who is part of the plan. And out-of-state dealers can't take some of the minor burdens off your hands, such as transferring your insurance if you already have a car, or supplying dealer plates until the new ones are available.

Repairs are another matter. They depend on the warranty of the manufacturer and whether it is to be honored by the selling dealer or by any dealer who is authorized to sell that manufacturer's cars. But slow delivery and troubles with repairs can occur even when you've ordered a car and—should you be so foolish and you wouldn't be—paid the list price for it.

So there seem to be few if any strong arguments against buying through a broker, and many strong money arguments for using one. Even the cost of the printout, if you decide not to buy through a broker, will be redeemed by your informed and therefore superior bargaining power.

Interestingly enough there are some dealers who have a foot in both camps: they are regular dealers when customers come in "off the street" and participating dealers when customers are referred by a buying service. The result is that two customers can buy the identical car on the identical day for a different price—depending on the arrangement they have with the dealers!

Needless to say, you'd rather be the customer who gets the lower price. And why not? Now that you've got the know-how you'll enjoy your car even more with the thought that you got the best buy.

30

Insurance—A Matter of Death and Life

"I'm convinced that the average life insurance policy is substantially less readable than Einstein's basic work on relativity."
—Dr. Herbert S. Denenberg, former insurance professor and Insurance Commissioner of the State of Pennsylvania

I'm all for a relaxed approach to life and life's money problems when possible. It's not possible when buying life insurance. The trouble with making a mistake is that you're not around to make corrections, and it's your survivors who have to move out of the roomy apartment into a cramped one, take an unsuitable job, or forgo a good education.

First let's get our terms straight. Life insurance is a misnomer. The correct name is death insurance. What we are talking about is insurance against what would happen to a family's income if the main breadwinner dies. Why isn't it called death insurance? Because all of us, for good healthy psychological reasons, resist the idea of death. Psychologically, therefore, it's much more pleasant to buy—and much easier to sell—"life" insurance. The words themselves have a cheery ring, as if they were assuring us that we would live, especially if we buy a policy that offers benefits we're going to enjoy as we live: savings, investment, low-cost loans. The trillion-dollar life insurance industry understands this very well—it didn't get that big and prosperous talking about death.

Second, let's remember that the insurance industry has made it just about impossible for the average intelligent person to arrive at a correct decision. Insurance policies are so complicated that just about everyone outside the field, and even some in it, can't understand them. Methods of figuring costs and benefits are equally unintelligible so buyers can't make valid cost comparisons. Government regulatory bodies are frequently non-existent, weak, or indifferently administered. No wonder millions of families have bought the wrong kind of life insurance and spent too much to get too little. Fortunately, as a result of pressure from consumer advocates both in and out of government, the situation is beginning to change. Beginning to change—but you still must do your homework to find out what's best for you and how to go about getting it.

As a start rid yourself of the assumption that if you don't understand an insurance plan or a particular policy there's something wrong with you. Instead, remember that confusion, obfuscation, and sometimes deliberately misleading information used to be the name of the game—but the rules are changing. You, in particular, are not willing to play it that way. If you can't understand some fine point in the fine print the fault might lie with the agent, the policy, the company, or the explanation—but not with you. After all, it's your money and it's up to the salesman, otherwise known as the agent, to prove to you—in dollars and cents—why something is in your best interests. If he can't do this, in writing, love him dearly if he's your brother-in-law, or have a beer with him if he's a jolly fellow—but look elsewhere for your insurance.

Since I know some very nice and very honest insurance agents let me say a few words right here about the life and hard time of an insurance agent. He's selling something that will cost you money and not bring an immediate gain, and that's not easy. (It's not like selling you a shiny red convertible that he can deliver to your door for instant happiness.) He has to come and see you when you're free, which means he spends his nights and weekends working, and that's not fun. And he has been expensively and carefully indoctrinated to believe in the superiority of straight life insurance, so that's what he tries to sell.

And that's where the trouble lies—what he sells. Remember that the whole industry is based on actuarial tables that predict quite accurately the percentage of the population that will die at any given age, though the tables can't name the individuals within that percentage who will be the unlucky ones. It's on the basis of these tables, plus their knowledge of the costs of doing business, that the insurance companies establish the charges for their various plans and policies. Remember too that basic insurance needs don't vary too much from similar family to similar family. So you would think that the sales package and prices among various companies would also show some similarity. That's what you would think, but it hasn't worked that way. Instead, surveys have shown that the agents come up with startlingly different proposals that don't provide survivors with the kind of income they would need to maintain their standards of living and cost too much for the protection they do offer. Only one of fifteen agents in one survey, for instance, recommended *term insurance*, though this is undoubtedly the best buy for young families with small children.

This brings us to the very heart of the problem. The first thing you should know about life insurance, if you're only in an early lap of your race toward fame and fortune, is that what you need is term insurance—and that may be the last thing the insurance agent pulls out of his briefcase. Why? Because, as I've noted before, he's been trained to sell the other kind of policy, known variously as straight life, whole life, or permanent life. Straight life is more profitable for insurance companies, not only because you pay a higher premium* but also because they have the use of some of your money to invest in other enterprises that can be very lucrative. (And also because, and perhaps not incidentally, the agent earns about 50

---

* "Premium" is a good example of the kind of doubletalk that insurance companies use. According to the dictionary a premium is something you *get*, a "prize, bonus or award." But in insuranceland a premium is *what you pay*.

per cent commission on a straight life policy and only about 25 per cent commission on a term policy.)

But of course you want to know *why* you need term insurance, why it's better than straight life, and the answers to many other questions about insurance before you need to make a decision. So maybe this is the time to ask the questions, set out the answers, and let you do the deciding. Let's start at the very beginning and go through the whole bit.

Q: Who needs life insurance? Does everyone?

A: No. If you're single with no dependents, or married with no children yet and each of you is financially independent, there's no need to have insurance. But you do need insurance if you have dependents whose income would be reduced sharply if the family's main support were to die. This used to be the man in the family, but that's not necessarily the case any more. It might be a divorced mother supporting her children. Some of the illustrations I'll use will be based on the "typical" family —a husband, a non-working wife, and a dependent child or two. But the principles involved will apply in exactly the same way regardless of who brings home the bacon and who is dependent on getting that bacon.

Q: What are my choices?

A: You have two options: you buy either term or straight life. Term has only one purpose—to provide benefits for survivors in case of death, and it's sold on that basis, namely protection. Straight life provides protection and in addition has what's called "cash value." A part of your premium goes into a fund that accumulates for you, though at a slow rate. The insurance company even pays you interest on the money in this cash value fund—though at a lower rate than you could get elsewhere. So with straight life you get protection plus savings or investment.

Q: That sounds like a good deal. Is there a hitch?

A: There is—the price. Straight life costs more than term; so much more that most experts in the insurance field think it's a bad bargain. For instance, at age thirty-five a man could get a $25,000, five-year insurance policy for about $135 per year, while a straight life policy of only $10,000 would cost him $235. For five years (and then at a slightly higher rate for the next five years, more of this in a moment) *the term policy would give him two and a half times the protection for $100 less per year.*

Q: That sounds outrageous, not to say ridiculous. How do the insurance companies explain this difference in price?

A: They point out the advantages of buying a policy that builds a cash value† as you and the policy grow old together. As the cash value builds you have an automatic savings account, with interest, without worrying your good-looking head about making deposits in the bank. Furthermore the interest is tax-free. And just to add a dollop of whipped cream to this gorgeous financial concoction, you can borrow against your cash value at any time at an interest rate lower than the prevalent bank rate.

So why am I being such a spoilsport and saying a cash value policy is a bad buy?

---

† Where does the cash value come from? It's *your* money. Straight life is paid for in equal premiums (level premiums, as some insurance agents say) for the duration of the policy, twenty years, for instance. But it costs less to insure you when you're younger, because the risks are lower. The difference between what you are paying and the cost of insuring you goes into your account as the policy's cash value—an oversimplified explanation but that's the general idea.

Because there a few things insurance companies don't go out of their way to bring to your attention.

1. The cash value builds very, very slowly. On a $50,000 policy, for instance, it could be only $5 per $1,000 of insurance or about $250 the first year, going up to about $137 per $1,000 or $6,850 plus interest by the tenth year. You would accumulate much more than this by just saving the difference between the premiums of the two kinds of policies and letting a savings bank compound the interest on these savings for you. Let's say you bought a $50,000 term policy when you were twenty-five, and deposited the difference in a savings account earning an average of 6 per cent annually. In ten years you would have spent about $3,600 on insurance and accumulated a savings account of about $6,500. For the same expenditure on straight life your policy would have a cash value of about $4,300. (I use approximate figures since these values change depending on individual companies, ways of computing interest, etc.)

2. The only way you can get your cash value is to give up your protection by canceling your policy. Compare this with being able to withdraw your savings any time you need them—even if you have to sacrifice some interest by doing so.

3. You can also borrow against your savings account, though admittedly not as cheaply as you can borrow against your cash value. And the interest on such a passbook loan is deductible from your income, so the loan may not cost as much it seems. And in the meantime, your insurance protection hasn't changed one penny. But—

4. When you borrow against the cash value of your life policy your insurance protection is reduced by the amount of your loan. Let's say you have a $50,000 policy which has accumulated a cash value of $10,000. You borrow against the $10,000. Now you're insured only for $40,000.

5. You lose your cash value when you die. Suppose a meteor comes out of the sky and hits you on the head after you've had your $50,000 policy for ten years and it has a cash value of $10,000. Your survivors get $50,000—and that's all. If you had a $50,000 term policy and a savings account accumulated with the money you saved by buying term insurance your survivors would get the $50,000 plus the savings account.

Q: What you say makes sense, and I hate to admit this, but I'm afraid I just wouldn't save the money. I'd spend it.

A: You're not the only one. So let someone else be your conscience and offer you saving grace. Get your employer to deduct money from your salary and put it in savings bonds or a bank account. Or let your bank transfer money from your checking account to a savings account before you can get your eager hands on it.

Q: How much insurance do I need? Someone has said it should be about three to four times my yearly income.

A: There's no valid rule of thumb because each family's circumstances differ. The only guideline is what you think your dependents will need to maintain the standard of living you'd like them to have. You will probably feel that your family should have enough to maintain a household and provide income for the surviving spouse and children until they are on their own, including a college education if that's what they want. If a wife is at home now taking care of small children but planning to return to work the insurance might also cover tuition for *her* education or re-education so that her earning power would increase with better skills.

Q: How do I estimate this amount?

A: Start by going to your local Social Security office and getting a pre-printed "Request for Statement of Earnings" postcard. If you can't get to your local SSA office a letter or postcard to the same address stating what you want will do just as well. When they return a printout of your earnings your local office will be able to tell you what your survivors' monthly income would be if you died. (They use a rather complicated formula so it's not something you can estimate easily yourself.) This survivors' monthly income is the base from which you start your estimate. Next, write down what your family spends each year and multiply this figure by the number of years it will take until the family becomes self-supporting. The total you get will be the amount of insurance that you need. Here's a vastly oversimplified example to show you how it works.

Let's suppose you are a man of thirty-five with a wife age twenty-eight and two children age five and three. You are now spending about $20,000 per year. Let's say you want to provide for your family for fifteen years. This means you want to leave them $300,000—$20,000×15. (There's no allowance for inflation. Since the nation's best economists still haven't figured out how to allow for it I know better than even to make an attempt.)

Q: I'm overcome, crushed, and I don't see where that money could come from. Where could it come from?

A: Two sources: Social Security, which might amount to $250 a month or $3,000 a year (depending on your salary, number of years employed, etc.), plus your insurance policy, placed in a savings banks and earning 6 per cent per year, simple interest. An insurance policy for $250,000, earning 6 per cent simple interest would return $15,000, giving your survivors an annual income of $18,000 before taxes. (The Social Security income is not taxable, which would be a help.) So you need an insurance policy of $250,000 if you want your family to live in their present style. Let's cut it back just a bit and say you decide to buy $200,000 of life insurance. Depending on the type of term policy, the company you bought it from, and other factors, you would have to pay about $930 or more annually for a five-year renewable and convertible term policy, and about $850 or more for a decreasing balance term policy. (I'll get to the explanation of these terms in a minute.) These are certainly considerable sums, but they are something you have to consider when planning your budget if you want your family to be protected. If you feel they are quite unrealistic invest in your wife's earning power by helping her find and keep a job that she likes while the two of you manage your household and child care. (But you'll still need insurance—more of this later.)

Q: Okay, I'm sold on the idea of insurance and term insurance as well. Now tell me something about term policies.

A: There are two kind of term policies: renewable and convertible, and decreasing balance. When you buy a renewable policy—a very popular choice for young families, by the way, because it's adaptable to their changing needs—you buy term insurance for a given period (or term), usually five years, with the option to renew at the end of five years. If you want a policy for say, $100,000, you pay the same premium for the five-year period. When you renew, say for another five-year period, you pay a higher premium for the next five years for the same $100,000 coverage, because you've become somewhat more of a risk. The same thing happens for the ensuing five years, etc. (See Table 1, page 193.)

Table 1

$100,000 five-year renewable and convertible term policy from a non-participating company. Benefits remain at $100,000.

Annual premium: at age 35—$465

Renewed: at age 40—$ 630, annual premium

```
          45—   920
          50— 1,395
          55— 2,150
```

$100,000 twenty-year decreasing balance term. Annual premium, $425, stays level but the benefits decrease according to the following schedule.

```
Year 5 through 8—$80,000
     9   "   12— 60,000
    13   "   16— 40,000
    17   "   20— 20,000
```

With a renewable and convertible policy you have the option of shifting, i.e., converting your term policy to straight life up to a specified age, such as sixty or sixty-five. There does come a point in your life when, if you decide you want to continue to have insurance, it will pay you to convert to a life policy. This decision can be postponed until you are beginning to think about planning for your later middle years and possible retirement. However, when you're starting your insurance program you want to be sure that you have the option to convert. The great advantage of this option is that you don't have to take a physical examination or complete a medical questionnaire. If you've developed a few aches and creaks along the way they won't result in higher premiums because an insurer considers you more of a risk.

Another possibility is decreasing term. With this type of policy you pay the same annual premium but your amount of coverage declines as you become more of a risk. The idea behind this is that your need for protection goes down as your family gets older and closer to self-sufficiency, your house is partially paid for, and so on.

You can buy your term policy from a company that offers either participating or non-participating policies. In a participating company you participate in the profits of the company through dividends; in a non-participating company you do not. Naturally you pay a higher premium for the chance to share. Policies from a participating company may or may not be better buys; the dividends are not guaranteed. If you are considering a participating company ask to see the dividend record of the past in order to get some idea—but of course the past doesn't necessarily predict the future.

Q: How about taxes? Won't taxes cut down on the amount my family will get if I die?

A: You're right—insurance is subject to estate taxes. The answer is to let your wife take out the policy or to make a gift to her of an already existent policy. She should pay the premium out of her own bank account, so that it's quite clear that she owns the policy, whether she bought it outright or received it as a gift. If payment comes out of a joint account the Internal Revenue Service may doubt that the policy really belongs to a wife, and may then decide it's subject to estate taxes.

Q: We have children but we both work. Doesn't that mean we'll need less insurance?

A: Yes—and no. The real question if you have children is, what would happen to the surviving parent if either one of you died? Would you be able to continue your present household setup or would you have to arrange for child care at considerable additional expense? What would happen to your standard of living if you became a one-paycheck family? If you know there would be a drastic change you should both carry insurance; probably decreasing term insurance would be best.

Q: Are all term policies the same or would it pay to shop around?

A: Good question. A survey by the state of Pennsylvania's Insurance Department showed that costs can vary from company to company by as much as 140 per cent for essentially the same coverage. Yes—it pays to shop around!

Q: Is there anything else I should consider when deciding on a policy?

A: Yes, the caliber and qualifications of the agent. A good agent knows his company's policies, record on dividends, quickness and ease of settling claims. He keeps up with new developments that may save you money and tells you about them. He keeps in touch with you—and not only when premiums are due—and makes sure your insurance needs haven't changed. In short, a good agent works at being a good agent year-round, year after year. This just about rules out part-timers, who simply don't have the time, even if they have the motivation, to do a good job in a field which is complicated and probably due for changes in the next few years.

You should know, though insurance companies certainly don't publicize the fact, that the industry has one of the highest turnover rates in the business world. What's the good of "trusting your agent because he knows the field" when chances are better than 50 per cent that, if he's new, he won't be around in a few years? An agent who suspects he isn't going to stay in the field very long isn't going to worry about your long-run benefits—he'll be much more concerned about his short-run commission. So you have to be wary of new agents and look for someone who will sacrifice present income for possible future gain from you as a customer for other kinds of insurance if he is a broker or works for a company that has a "multiple line" (auto, liability, health).‡

Q: What are my chances of finding such an agent?

A: Not as good as they should be, but getting better as the industry gets more and more concerned about pressure from consumers. However, you don't have to depend on the agent's noble motives. You can simply state clearly that you've considered your needs and your budget and you are firm in your conviction that term insurance is your best buy. Assure him that if he isn't prepared to tell you what kinds of term insurance he offers he might as well tell a few jokes and leave. But— a little sweetener—if he is prepared to sell you term insurance you can probably arrange matters fairly quickly, freeing him to go out and talk to other prospects. (A smaller commission sold after only one visit may be more profitable than a larger commission sold after numerous visits and he knows this.) If he still thinks he can persuade you that straight life is best forget it and try another agent.

Q: Is there anything else I should watch out for?

A: Yes, you have to know something about the company whose policy you're buying. First thing to remember is, as I mentioned before, policies can vary as much as 140 per cent in costs without a comparable variation in protection. But you also have to know something about the stability of the company: what good is a low-

‡ Legally, there are differences between agents and brokers. Technically, the broker represents you, the buyer, while the agent represents the insurance company. They both serve the same purpose in the insurance scheme of things.

cost policy with good benefits if it's out of business when the time comes to collect? You also want a company that has a record for paying claims promptly and with a minimum of difficulty. *Best's Reports,* the most widely recognized and reliable industry reporting service, gives life insurance companies one of four recommendations: most substantial, very substantial, substantial, and considerable. Obviously you want to buy from a company with the highest rating. Interestingly enough the companies with the better financial ratings are also those that offer the best policy buys—a cheering thought. You also want to make sure the company is licensed by your state. If you know, or suspect, that your state's insurance department is lax about regulating business find out if the company is also licensed to sell in New York State, which has very strict regulations.

Q: Must I buy insurance through an agent or are there other sources?*

A: Yes, there are other sources, both good and bad. Good sources are your employer, union, professional association, credit union, or church or fraternal group. But just because such policies are available doesn't mean you buy blindly, without checking in the same way that you would check a policy from an agent. You'll also want to know what happens to the policy if you leave the company or drop out of the association, etc. Will you be able to continue on your own and at what price? Beware of buying insurance that's sold only through the mail—it may be unregulated and your chances of being bilked are very high.

Q: How should I pay the premium—all at once or in installments?

A: If possible, all at once. The company may charge a rate of interest if you pay on the installment plan.

Q: Ouch. I already have a straight life policy. Should I switch to a term policy?

A: Ouch. That's a very difficult question to answer; it would be impossible to lay down a ground rule since the situation would vary so much depending on the type of policy, how much was involved, how long you'd had it, whether you'd borrowed against the cash value. You would have to sit down with your insurance agent and see, in dollars and cents, if you would be better off by switching *at this point.* However, there are two things to keep in mind. In New York, with its very rigorous insurance laws, the savings banks' brochures on insurance carry this warning: "BEWARE OF SWAPPING [their capitals] old life insurance policies for new. By swapping you may have to pay a higher rate for the same protection. Remember, too, there are early restrictions on all new life insurance policies. Savings Bank Life Insurance recommends extreme caution in surrendering any existing life insurance." In Pennsylvania there is a regulation that requires that you get expert advice *in writing* from the insurance agent that a proposed switch would be advantageous.

Here's one consoling thought—life insurance is one gamble it pays you to lose. Plan to buy the best possible insurance and throw all that money away by living, in perfect health, to be 105.

Should You Buy Insurance from Friends and Relatives?

Who comes around to sell you life insurance? Very often it's your cousin Joe, who hasn't been out of college very long and has decided on a career as a life insurance

---

* If you live or work in New York, Massachusetts, or Connecticut you can buy low-cost insurance through a mutual savings bank. You can't buy enough to have all the protection you need, but for the amount you can get it's a good buy.

agent. Or it's a cousin of a cousin or a friend of a friend of a friend. (One of the things a new agent has to do, often, is draw up a list of prospects. The best place to start such a list is with friends and relatives who will find it very difficult, if not impossible, to say, "No, you can't come and see me.")

This has obvious advantages for cousin Joe or friend Willy, and some advantages for you too—if you operate on the assumption that you are more likely to get an honest opinion and a good deal from a relative or a friend, even a distant friend. You are the only one who can really make a judgment about this. But when you are debating with yourself, keep in mind that relationships in families and among friends are delicate and extend beyond the few individuals involved in an insurance sale.

Suppose you say okay to cousin Joe, "you can come over and at least talk to me about insurance, but I'm warning you that I probably won't buy." You really mean it, but cousin Joe doesn't believe that you mean it. He is quite annoyed when you don't buy, but he has learned not to show his annoyance. Aunt Sophie, however, is furious, and from then on a chill develops between the two families that takes some of the warmth out of future family parties.

Or suppose that you do buy from cousin Joe, or friend Willy, and they sell you what they honestly believe is the best policy for you *among the options offered by the company they represent*. And suppose you find out later that a much better policy was available from a different company. Then how would you feel toward cousin or friend? Would the chill emanate from your side of the table?

There is another consideration. In order for an insurance agent to make an evaluation of your insurance needs he has to know most if not all of the intimate details of your financial life. You have to tell him your income, how much money you have in the bank, what stocks and bonds you own, the value of your house, the size of your mortgage, the value of any life insurance you may have from your employer, and potential pension benefits. To round out this picture of what would happen to your family if you, the husband, died, you should also consider how much your wife could make if she returned to work or continued working—and even her chances of remarrying. Of course he's been instructed to be discreet—but are you sure you want to discuss these matters with friends and relatives?

31

To Your Health, and
to Your Health Plan

"I enjoy convalescence. It is the part that makes
the illness worthwhile."
                                  —George Bernard Shaw

Remember what happened the day they had the orientation meeting to tell you about the company's group health insurance plan? You overslept, missed your morning coffee, and found it very difficult to concentrate as the assistant personnel director explained all the details of the plan. You took the policy home, glanced at it, made a mental note that you really would read it carefully someday—then filed it along with your other insurance papers. Somehow or other the day for reading it carefully has never come. Or if it has, it's only *after* you've been charged for something you were sure you were covered for.

Since misery loves company you'll be glad to know that you are typical of the group health insurance plan subscriber. You're sure you're never going to be seriously sick because you rarely catch colds; you know the health insurance plan covers you for just about everything because it's a "comprehensive" plan; you don't see why you should bother your head with all that fine print when Miss Collins in Personnel is superefficient and a real angel besides, so you just know she'll take care of everything.

Unfortunately, as administrators of health plans will hasten to tell you, this is an unhealthy attitude that may very well cause you a pain where it really hurts—in your wallet. Their desks are piled high daily with cases of employees who didn't understand the health plan and who then (literally) had to pay the consequences. At the worst, these consequences can run into several hundred dollars; at the least they cause delays of weeks or even months in settling claims, plus piles of paperwork for everyone—including you.

Whether you are covered by a policy that pays doctor bills or hospital bills, or both, or by a policy that allows you to join a group plan that includes medical care from the group's corps of doctors and services, you may be guilty of one of these common errors (as gleaned from administrators' files).

1. You go to a doctor without asking him if he is a member of the corps of doc-

tors available through your health plan. Then you discover, after using him, that he is not a member, and you must pay the bill.

2. You don't check your policy for some special benefits, such as payment for X rays. You pay out of your own pocket and unwittingly lose a benefit you're entitled to.

3. You need a service that isn't available through one of the doctors included in your group health plan. You are allowed to make other arrangements for the service with a promise of reimbursement. You arrange for the service but don't check the fee. Then you find that the doctor's fee is more than you're allowed through your health plan. You, of course, must make up the difference.

4. You're not aware that there are sometimes waiting periods before you're eligible for certain benefits—maternity, for instance, or the removal of a child's tonsils or treatment of an allergy you had before becoming part of the plan. (Under Blue Cross, for instance, in 1973 the waiting period was ten months for maternity; six months for removal of tonsils and adenoids, and eleven months for pre-existing conditions.) Or, conversely, you believe there is a waiting period when this provision has in fact been waived for the group that you became eligible to join in your new job. If you don't know of the waiting period you run the risk of incurring expenses the health plan won't pay for; if the waiting period has been waived you forgo treatment that you are really eligible for, because you think you must wait.

5. You neglect to add wives, husbands, children, or other eligible dependents to your coverage. Conversely, when you have a change in status, e.g., a legal separation or a divorce, you continue to pay for dependents when you shouldn't.

6. You don't check on the kind of accommodations you're entitled to in a hospital. You are placed in a private room and discover when you're billed that your health plan only covered the cost of a semi-private room.

7. You assume you are covered by the group health plan just because you have joined a company and been told that the company has such a plan and you are entitled to benefits. You neglect to file an application and miss out on coverage. (Hard to believe this happens but it does.)

8. You forget to investigate the possibility of continuing in a health plan after you've resigned from your job and can no longer be a member through that particular group. Admittedly joining as an individual is more costly than being part of a plan, but usually it is still cheaper than not belonging to any kind of plan, and well worth looking into. Or, you neglect to rejoin within the time limit given you— not difficult to overlook if you are moving, particularly to a different city or state— and then incur penalties or forfeit the right altogether.

Of course, you're not able to foresee all the emergencies or illnesses that might arise. That's why administrators stress that the time to check on coverage is long before you have any expenses. At that point you're under no pressure and you can pay attention to what you are and are not entitled to, what papers you will need to substantiate claims, what services are only partially covered. In general you'll find— from self-interest if no other reason—that administrators are only too glad to spend time explaining because it will spare them endless phone calls, digging into files, filling out forms in quadruplicate. You'll save yourself lots of time and trouble too.

In addition to saving money on your doctor and hospital bills there are other possibilities for saving. For instance:

1. Keep records of all your medical bills and expenses for tax purposes. You

may, after checking the Internal Revenue Service's directions for completing your tax form, find that you can deduct not only doctor bills but also money paid to dentists, opticians, chiropodists, physiotherapists, registered and/or practical nurses. You may be able to deduct for prescription drugs and for some patent medicines such as aspirin, cough medicine, nose drops, perhaps even rubbing alcohol, tonics, or vitamins—if their use was prescribed by a doctor.

2. Check to see if you can deduct for health and hospital insurance policies that your employer didn't pay for. For instance, if your children went to a day nursery, private school, or camp that offered or required payment for health services or health insurance fees these fees may be deductible. So too may money spent on transportation to and from doctors' offices and hospitals or convalescent homes.

(Since you can't possibly remember all these miscellaneous expenses the thing to do, to make life easier, is to keep records during the year. If you're a perfectly organized neatnik you probably already have a nice little book in which you make entries by item, price or fee, and date. If you're not a neatnik just get yourself a large manila envelope and whenever you pay out some money that may be a medical deduction jot it down on whatever little slip of paper you have handy and throw it in the manila envelope. It will all be there for sorting when tax time comes around.)

3. Look into your medical expenses toward the end of the year, especially if they've been higher than usual. If you find you've already exceeded your limit for tax purposes, see if you can't postpone further medical expenses until the start of the new year. You might, for example, be able to postpone dental treatment or new eyeglasses.

4. Keep records of when you and/or your children have had various immunization shots, X rays, and eye examinations. These records will prove useful should you move, change schools, or go on trips out of the country. But they will also prove useful in helping you avoid the need for duplicating the shots and examinations—and the fees—since you will know exactly when the last exam or immunization took place.

5. Discuss what the charge will be before you incur medical bills. It's charming to be delicate about money matters—but not where the medical and dental professions are concerned. Doctors have certain standards by which they set their fees, despite their contention that every patient is different and no case is "routine." They may not be too happy about it but they are becoming accustomed to having patients ask about fees, and you might as well support this new, cost-conscious trend. The fee may be set by a variety of components: the service you're going to get; the value put on this service by the doctor which in turn is influenced by the value of the service as determined by his local, county, or state medical society; the neighborhood, area, or region of the country in which he practices. It may or may not include some special charges—which brings up the next point.

6. Check on what additional charges may be part of a particular medical bill. Will there be fees for laboratory tests? If the service includes an operation will there be fees for the services of an anesthesiologist? If it's a maternity charge will the fee include office visits before the birth and care after the delivery?

7. Discuss payment methods with your doctor. Though you can't expect him to change his fees (the idea of charging a sliding scale depending on the patient's income is pretty much dead since insurance plans began to cover medical bills) you

may be able to arrange a schedule of payments that will be easier on your budget if not your bank balance.

8. Check on the services you're going to get from a hospital or convalescent home. Will there be extra charges for intensive care? In a maternity case, will you be billed for infant care even if you are nursing your baby and caring for it under a rooming-in arrangement? What charges are there for laboratory tests during a hospital stay?

9. Ask your doctor to prescribe drugs by their generic name where possible, i.e., by the name given them to identify the chemicals of which they're composed. When these chemicals are compounded by drug manufacturers they are given a trade or brand name, which varies with the manufacturer. The action of the compounds is identical, however, if the formula and method of compounding it is identical. In general, if you can buy a drug by its generic name, rather than its brand name, you will save money.

10. Don't throw your money away by neglecting to follow the doctor's orders. Though it may sound foolish one of doctors' most common complaints against patients is that patients spend a good deal of time and money to get a doctor's advice and then ignore that advice. If patients don't like the medicine, or hate to stay in bed, or begin to feel a little better they will blithely ignore what the doctor has ordered—and then wonder why they've had a relapse, or why they aren't getting better faster.

11. Practice preventive medicine—since the best way to save money on health care is not to get sick. And use psychology to bolster your good intentions. If you know you are overweight, or underexercised, or creating an ecological disaster on your lungs by smoking, develop a way of helping yourself overcome these health hazards. Promise yourself a new tennis racket if you make a point of playing indoors regularly during the winter. Find a method of dieting that agrees with you, even if no one in your office or Women's Lib group or Parent-Teachers Association ever heard of it. Join a Smokers Anonymous group or form one to help you give up the habit without feeling guilty that you didn't have enough will power to do it on your own.

Be kind to yourself and your body. Be your own health maintenance organization—and splurge with the money you save on doctor and hospital bills.

· 32 ·

The New Landed Gentry: Should You Belong?

"There isn't a single mosquito here. They're all married."
—Vacation home salesman to prospective buyer

You wouldn't believe it. You really wouldn't believe it until you realized what was at stake. Selling land in recreation areas to those of us who dream of a little place in the country or at the seashore is a $6-billion industry; and the men who sell the subdivided pieces of the land have a taste for hand-tailored suits, long vacations, and Cadillacs. Their "piece of the action" can be as high as $50,000 a year—and to earn it through commissions they've been known to use sales tactics like these:

The two-way radio ploy: While a development salesman and prospects are driving toward a lot in a car with a two-way radio, the salesman checks with the development's office to see if the lot is still available. The office tells him it was sold that morning, but an equally desirable lot may still be unsold. By coincidence it is. The salesman then takes the prospects to the lot and urges them to put a "hold" on it, to discourage other buyers and to enable them to look at the government-required property report. No commitment on their part, just "protection." They succumb, and he can announce on the radio that now another lot is on "hold" —for the benefit of other salesmen and the prospects being driven around in their cars. They will of course reciprocate the favor.

(He neglects to mention that by law he should have shown them the property report before he showed them the lot. And he knows they have now made a psychological if not financial commitment and are well on the way to becoming buyers.)

The decoy drama: Company employees posing as prospects happen to come and look at a lot just as the salesman is showing it. In full view and more important in full earshot the "prospects" discuss the lot's advantages (maybe even mentioning a few minor disadvantages to increase their authenticity) and consider buying it.

The "buddy" bit: The salesman is a jolly fellow who gets you talking about yourself, your jobs, your children, your hobbies. In a short time you are buddies, and since you are his buddy he lets you share his professional secrets. The lots have been selling well, and in no time at all it's inevitable that any lot you buy is going to become more valuable. Of course he can't tell everyone this, but if you buy today and come back in two years he will double your money. So it really doesn't matter to you that the beach isn't cleared or the lodge or ski lift isn't built yet.

(What he doesn't tell you is that two years from now he will be enjoying a holiday with that good-looking receptionist you saw in the development office, or he'll be thousands of miles away selling lots in the Caribbean or in Spain. Furthermore, if he ever did see you again he would not only look at you with a blank stare but also with an expression that made you feel as if he had a sensitive nose and you had a piece of overripe Limburger cheese in your coat pocket.)

These are the more sensational and illegal tactics, but there are others that aren't quite so outlandish, but still calculated to make you buy before thinking.

A favorite one is the dinner at an elegant restaurant featuring a pre-dinner cocktail; fresh fruit cup, slides of the development taken from its most favorable angle; breast of chicken, more slides; a yummy parfait, and then a speech or two about the development. There are salesmen at each table, and—in a variation of the two-way radio ploy—every now and then a salesman will confer with an officer of the company in whispers. The officer will then announce over a loudspeaker, "Delete lots 521 and 522 from the available list."

A more deluxe version is the free weekend at the site of the development. You are put up at the local motel and amid a smorgasbord of visits to the various attractions, the skating rink, the lake, the lodge, or the places where these attractions are *going to be,* you are given a hard sell. If you comment on the distance from the lake the salesman assures you that it only seems far—on a beautiful day you'll welcome the walk. If you say there are too many large rocks on the land he says they will make lovely walls for your property. If you get bitten by insects he will say they are rare—due to an unusually wet spring. He has been carefully trained to overcome all your objections with a sales pitch he has memorized so well you don't realize it isn't spontaneous—and he's very good at his trade.

So good in fact that recent land sales investigations, after more than five thousand complaints had been received by the federal government, revealed that customers had been sold land in Florida at $4,000 an acre even though much of it was under water during the rainy season; had bought land halfway up a mountain and so covered with rocks it could never be built on; or had bought land to escape city noise and crowding only to find themselves with neighbors three or four feet away, sharing the same inadequate or non-existent sewer system.

Many if not most of the companies in the field are reputable, but even the reputable ones claim they can't always control their salesmen. And there are many fly-by-night developers who have successfully bilked customers, even sophisticated customers who admitted with chagrin at the land sales hearings that they should have known better and not been so trusting.

How could this be, you say. There ought to be a law! The trouble is, there is a law, the Interstate Land Sales Disclosure Act. It's been around since 1969, when the federal government undertook the responsibility for regulating the sale of lots smaller than five acres in subdivisions containing fifty or more lots. The developer of such subdivided land included under a common promotional plan has to file a prospectus with the Federal Housing and Urban Development Department and has to give a prospective buyer a printed Property Report. This report gives the buyer much of the information he needs to make an intelligent decision. (For a copy of the Property Report see pages 206–9.)

How come then that complaints continued to pour into the government's Office of Interstate Land Sales Registration? Partly because a law is only as good as the means to enforce it, and for a time there were only two inspectors, although later eight more were added (and the number has increased considerably since then). Still, that was a tiny force to check on complaints that were then coming in at the rate of fifty or more a week from different parts of the country. Since 1972, under a new administrator, enforcement has become much stronger after public hearings not only revealed the depth of the chicanery and fraud involved but also warned the public about the hazards and pressures of land sales. Some of the companies have been indicted but there is little possibility that those who were cheated will ever get their money back. In the fall of 1974 OILSR also began to use the services of the Inspector-General's Office of the Department of Housing and Urban Development to enforce legislation.

As always, however, laws on the books aren't enough, especially if there isn't sufficient staff to see that they are tightly enforced. So, as a buyer, you have to be your own lawyer to the extent that you know your rights. And you also have to be your own investment counselor and accountant to know how to evaluate some of the advice you're getting.

LAND AS AN INVESTMENT: GOOD, BAD, OR SO-SO?

One of the biggest hazards is assuming that your salesman is right when he tells you an investment in land will inevitably be an investment that will pay off. He will tell you, and correctly, that the supply of land is fixed but the demand is rising. He will add that the value of recreational land is part of this trend, only more so, since rising incomes mean more people are looking for vacation spots they can call their own. Also true—in general and in the long run. But there is no guarantee that the land *you own* is going to rise in value at any particular moment in time. Nor is there any guarantee that it won't decline in value if any one of a number of things happens: pollution of the lake near your property; a storm washing away big chunks of your beach; a vote against a bond issue that would put a much-needed highway near your property to end unbearable traffic jams, or, conversely, a highway built near your property that makes the area as crowded as the city you are escaping from.

Buying land is a highly speculative process. Lucky or shrewd people have made millions; but even experts, such as developers, have been known to lose—even to go bankrupt. Unimproved land, that is, land without power, water, and sewers, can be the riskiest investment of all. The pleasure of the most breathtaking, most spectacular view of mountains or ocean, the balmiest breeze, or the most peaceful meadow is apt to pall if you have no water, no sanitary facilities, no electricity, no telephone.

Furthermore, while you are waiting for these amenities to be installed you still have to pay land taxes, you may have some insurance bills, and you'll want to go and look at your property occasionally to see if nature has done any damage during a storm, or if improvements are being put in as promised by a developer. All these things cost money or time or both. An executive of the research-oriented Urban Land Institute has estimated that unimproved land must double in value in about five years just to meet the expenses of carrying the property. And this estimate doesn't include an allowance for lawyer's fees, a broker's commission if he sells the land, and taxes on profits.

Even reputable builders and developers have a way of sending out, as part of their information package, a list of "resales of property" showing the profit made on original investments. These bona fide lists enumerate seller, date purchased, purchase price, date sold, selling price, *gross profit,* and profit percentage. They don't mention that you must subtract, from the gross profit, fees you pay as buyer and then as seller, taxes, miscellaneous expenses such as long-distance calls, trips to the site to show it, advertising, or special assessments you may have had to pay while you were the owner.

This is not to say that it isn't possible to make money speculating on land, nor to deny that some individuals have done very well. It's just to point out that if it's investments you are interested in there are alternatives to land speculation. They range from almost completely carefree and safe investments, such as leaving your money in a savings account, to buying highly speculative "go-go" stocks. All could very well involve less time and effort than buying land. To buy because you intend to build a lovely summer home is one thing; to buy because you intend to become an overnight millionaire (or at least thousand-aire) is quite another.

You have to be very clear as to your purpose, or you will be much easier prey for the $50,000 buddy-buddy salesman who knows how to appeal to the tiny little bit of greed that squiggles around in the souls of most of us. It's this little bit of greed, and perhaps the conviction that this once you're just a bit smarter than the next person, that he appeals to when he says he's not allowed to tell everyone, but he will tell *you* he's sure your lot will double in value in a few years. He will, he assures you, be happy to sell it for you then if you'll close the deal now, today.

If he can't appeal to greed he'll rely on his ability to confuse you thoroughly with a welter of papers that have to be signed but are just "red tape," or "not too important." Among them could very well be a waiver getting you to sign away your rights to a refund if you haven't been shown the property report at least forty-eight hours before you are to sign a contract to buy. You may not find out until it's too late that you don't have title to your land, or that you have no protection against the developer's default, or any one of any number of other basic rights that you might take for granted.

Finally, what may be the best ploy of all is summed up by one developer, who says, "Our salesmen don't sell the land, they sell the dream." If the salesman can't appeal to the squiggle of lust for profit in your soul he will appeal to that soft blue cloud that surrounds the squiggle. As you look at the bare, rock-strewn lot he sketches a picture of a spacious house with the family all gathered around the fireplace, or barbecuing steaks around an outdoor barbecue pit, or just drinking in warm sun and cold beer as the birds sing nearby. Perhaps he'll even have a deer tiptoeing into the picture—or at the very least a rabbit.

Who could remember, at such a delicate moment, to ask how near the water supply is, or how good the septic tanks?

Obviously, there are real hazards in becoming landed gentry, and you need to grow a special pair of antennae so that you'll be sensitive to the ploys that developers and salesmen use. But you should also:

1. Check with your state consumer protection agency to find out if the company selling land you're interested in has been registered to sell the land, so that they've had at least to pass state inspection. If your state has no such agency write to the Office of Interstate Land Sales Registration, Department of Housing and Urban Development, Washington, D.C. 20411, and ask them.

2. Go and have a look at the land itself, which will at least give you some idea of what you're buying. Note that I say "some idea," because just looking doesn't tell you about prior claims on the land, or the quality of the soil for building, or the accessibility of drinking water.

3. Drive around on your own to get a feeling about the area outside of the immediate development. Then go and talk to local real estate brokers, if possible, to get some idea of comparable property values in the adjacent areas.

4. STUDY the property report that the developer is required by law to give you before you sign a contract. (If there are false statements in it he is liable for prosecution.) For a sample of the report, see pages 206–9.

5. Check on the local shopping facilities; go and have a look to see if you would like to buy their meats, groceries, produce. Are they adequate not only for the area as it is but also as it will be? If not, are there any plans to expand the facilities? (See also Chapter 33, page 210.)

6. Check on who is going to manage the development, particularly the septic tanks and the sewage system, after the development is completely sold. A local homeowners' association, even with all the good will in the world, may be composed of people with no technical knowledge—very important since community health is involved—and poor judgment. And without good will there may be bickering, confusion, and delays. Very often the developer sets up a separate corporation to handle the affairs of the community; this may be profitable for him but not necessarily good for the homeowners. An alternative now being used in some places is to have an independent agency such as a local bank become the trustee of a corporation that is responsible for the operation of the sewer system. Such an arrangement means that someone is always available and responsible, winter and summer.

7. Don't sign anything until you've thought it over at leisure and are certain you want to invest in property and take on the responsibility of a second home. (See the next chapter for some problems you may not have considered.)

8. Beware of contracts-for-deeds. Most land companies sell on an installment loan basis by means of a contract-for-deed or land contract. The company remains as owner of the property until you've made all the payments. If you default the developer can cancel the contract and *keep everything you've paid in*. This contract-for-deed can hurt your ownership of the land even if you're prepared to complete the payments. If the developer has sold your note or installment contract to a sales finance company or other lender you are now responsible to this other lender—even if the developer doesn't keep his part of his contract with you. If the developer defaults on his debts—it's been known to happen—his creditors could put a lien on your property which you would have to pay off before you could own it free and clear. You might be better off arranging your own financing for the property perhaps with a bank loan, so that you owned the deed right from the beginning. Con-

PROPERTY REPORT
NOTICE AND DISCLAIMER BY OFFICE OF
INTERSTATE LAND SALES REGISTRATION,
U.S. DEPARTMENT OF HOUSING AND URBAN DEVELOPMENT

The Interstate Land Sales Full Disclosure Act specifically prohibits any representation to the effect that the Federal Government has in any way passed upon the merits of, or given approval to this subdivision, or passed upon the value, if any, of the property.

It is unlawful for anyone to make, or cause to be made to any prospective purchaser, any representation contrary to the foregoing or any representations which differ from the statements in this property report. If any such representations are made, please notify the Office of Interstate Land Sales Registration at the following address:

> Office of Interstate Land Sales Registration
> HUD Building, 451 Seventh Street SW.,
> Washington, D.C. 20410

Inspect the property and read all documents. Seek professional advice. Unless you received this property report prior to or at the time you enter into a contract, you may void the contract by notice to the seller.

Unless you acknowledge in writing on a waiver of purchaser's revocation rights form that you have read and understood the property report and that you have personally inspected the lot prior to signing your contract, you may revoke your contract within 48 hours from the signing of your contract, if you received the property report less than 48 hours prior to signing such contract.

1. Name (s) of Developer:

   Address:

2. Name of Subdivision:

   Location: County, State of

   (a) Effective date of Property Report

IMPORTANT READ CAREFULLY

Name of subdivision:

By signing this receipt you acknowledge that you have received a copy of the property report prepared pursuant to the Rules and Regulations of the Office of Interstate Land Registration, U.S. Department of Housing and Urban Development.

Received by _____

Street Address _____

Date _____

City _____ State _____

Zip _____

Notwithstanding your signature by which you acknowledged that you received the Property Report you still have other important rights under the Interstate Land Sales Full Disclosure Act.

---

3. List names and populations of surrounding communities and list distances over paved and unpaved roads to the subdivision.

Name of community	Population	Distance over paved roads	Unpaved roads	Total
a.				
b.				
c.				
d.				
e.				

4. Complete all items under this paragraph regardless of whether the sale will be an installment or cash sale.
   a. Will the sales contract be recordable? Yes or No?
   b. In the absence of recording the contract or deed, could third parties or creditors of any person having an interest in the land acquire title to the property free of any obligation to deliver a deed? Yes or No?____ Explain_____
   c. State whether and/or when the contract or deed will be recorded, and who will record it. State who will bear the costs of recordation, and the amount if those costs are to be borne by the purchaser.
   d. What provision, if any, has been made for refunds if buyer defaults? If none, and the buyer's payments are to be retained, state whether his loss will be limited to the amount of his payments to date, or whether he will be responsible to the developer or his assignees for additional damages or for the balance of his contract.
   e. State prepayment penalties or privileges, if any.

5. Is there a blanket mortgage or other lien on the subdivision or portion thereof in which the subject property is located? Yes or No? If yes, list below and describe arrangements, if any, for protecting interests of the buyer or lessee if the developer defaults in payment of the lien obligation. If there is such a blanket lien, describe arrangements for release to a buyer of individual lots when the full purchase price is paid.

Type of lien	Effect on buyers if developer defaults
a. _____	_____
b. _____	_____
c. _____	_____

6. Does the offering contemplate leases of the property in addition to, or as distinguished from, sales? Yes or No? If yes, a lease addendum must be completed, attached, and made a part of the Property Report.

7. Is buyer or lessee to pay taxes, special assessments, or to make payments of any kind for the maintenance of common facilities in the subdivision (a) before taking title or signing of lease or (b) after taking title or signing of lease? If yes, complete the schedule below:

	Approximate amount of buyer's or lessee's annual payments
Taxes	$ _____
Special assessments	_____
Payments to property owner's association	_____
Other	_____
Specify	_____

8. a. Will buyer's down payment and installment payments be placed in escrow or otherwise set aside? Yes or No? If yes, with whom? If not, will title be held in trust or in escrow?
   b. Except for those property reservations which land developers commonly convey or dedicate to local bodies or public utilities for the purpose of bringing public services to the land being developed, will buyer receive a deed free of exceptions? Yes or No? If no, list all restrictions, easements, covenants, reservations and their effect upon buyer.
   c. List the permissible uses of the property based upon the restrictive covenants, and which are consistent with local zoning ordinances.
   d. List all existing or proposed unusual conditions relating to the location of the subdivision and to noise, safety or other nuisances which affect or might affect the subdivision.

9. List all recreational facilities currently available, proposed, or partly completed (e.g., swimming pools, golf courses, ski slopes, etc.) and complete the following information for each facility:

i Facility	ii % Complete	iii Estimated completion date	iv Financial assurance of completion	v Developer obligated?	vi Buyer's costs or assessments

State who will own the facilities.

10. State availability of the following in the subdivision: State any estimated costs or assessments to buyer or lessee. If only proposed or partly completed, state estimated completion date, state provisions to assure completion, and give an estimate of all costs to buyer or lessee, including maintenance costs.

a. Roads:
   1. Access:
      Paved
      Unpaved
   2. Road system within the subdivision:
      Paved
      Unpaved
b. Utilities:
   1. Water
   2. Electricity
   3. Gas
   4. Telephone
   5. Sewage disposal
   6. Drainage and flood control
   7. Television
c. Municipal services:
   1. Fire protection
   2. Police protection
   3. Garbage and trash collection
   4. Public schools:
      i.   Elementary school
      ii. Junior high school
      iii. High school
   5. Medical and dental facilities:
      i. Hospital facilities
      ii. Physicians and dentists
   6. Public transportation
   7. U.S. postal service

11. Will the water supply be adequate to serve the anticipated population of the area?

12. Is any drainage of surface water or use of fill necessary to make lots suitable for construction of a one-story residential structure? Yes or No? If yes, state whether any provision has been made for drainage or fill and give estimate of any costs buyer would incur.

13. State whether shopping facilities are available in the subdivision; if not, state the distance in miles to such facilities and whether public transportation is available.

14. Approximately how many homes were occupied as of___(insert date of filing)?

15. a. State elevation of the highest and lowest lots in the subdivision and briefly describe topography and physical characteristics of the property.
    b. State in inches the average annual rainfall and, if applicable, the average annual snowfall for the subdivision of the area in which it is located.
    c. State temperature ranges for summer and winter, including highs, lows, and means.

16. Will any subsurface improvement or special foundation work be necessary to construct one-story residential or commercial structures in the land? Yes or No? If yes, state if any provision has been made and estimate any costs buyer would incur.

17. State whether there is physical access (by conventional automobile) over legal rights-of-way to all lots and common facilities in the subdivision. State whether the access will be by public or private roads and streets and whether they will be maintained by public or private funds.

18. Has land in the subdivision been platted of record? Yes or No? If not, has it been surveyed? Yes or No? If not, state estimated cost to buyer to obtain a survey.

19. Have the corners of each individual lot been staked or marked so that the purchaser can identify his lot? If not, state the estimated cost to the purchaser to obtain a survey and to have the corners of his lot staked or marked.

20. Does the developer have a program in effect to control soil erosion, sedimentation and flooding throughout the entire subdivision? Yes or No? Describe the program, if any. Has the plan been approved or must the plan be approved by officials responsible for the regulation of land development? Yes or No? Is the developer obligated to comply with the plan? Yes or No?

Include the following information at the end of the property report:

Special Risk Factors

(a) The future value of land is very uncertain; do NOT count on appreciation.

(b) You may be required to pay the full amount of your obligation to a bank or other third party to whom the developer may assign your contract or note, even though the developer may have failed to fulfill promises he has made.

(c) Resale of your lot may be subject to the developer's restrictions, such as limitations to the rights of other parties to enter the subdivision unaccompanied, membership prerequisites or approval requirements, or developer's first right of refusal. You should check your contract for such restrictions and also note whether your lien or any other liens on the property would affect your right to sell your lot.

(d) You should consider the competition which you may experience from the developer in attempting to resell your lot and the possibility that real estate brokers may not be interested in listing your lot.

(e) Changing land development and land use regulations by government agencies may affect your ability to obtain licenses or permits or otherwise affect your ability to use the land.

Financial Statements

You should carefully review the attached financial statements of the developer (see exhibit A).

Signature of the Senior Executive Officer of the Developer

_____

(title)

Lease Addendum

1. State term of lease.

2. Will the lease be recordable? Yes or No?

3. Is there any prohibition or penalty against the lessee for recording the lease? Yes or No? If yes, explain.

4. Can the owner's or developer's creditors or others acquire title to the property free of any obligation to continue the lease? Yes or No? Explain.

5. Describe whether rental payments are flat sums or graduated. Describe any provisions for increase of rental payments during the term of the lease.

6. Are there any provisions in lease prohibiting assignment and/or subletting? Yes or No? If yes, describe.

7. Summarize termination provisions in the lease.

8. Does the lease prohibit the lessee from mortgaging or otherwise encumbering the leasehold? Yes or No?

9. Will lessee be permitted to remove improvement when lease expires?

sider also, if a bank loan isn't feasible, having the developer put your money in an escrow account and letting a trustee hold the deed until you've paid off your loan from the developer. Obviously, this is a tricky business, which points to the importance of the next point.

9. Above all, don't sign anything until you've had the contract reviewed by your own lawyer.

Above is a sample of a property report that you should get from a developer. Not all reports will follow this one precisely, since developments vary as to location, size, facilities offered, terms, etc. But this should give you some idea of what information should, by law, be in the report the salesman or the developer gives you. (Source: p. 23890, Federal Register, Vol. 38, No. 170, Tuesday, September 4, 1973.)

33

Leisure House: Second Home or Second Headache?

"It probably figures out to $300 a weekend for the privilege of mowing a second lawn."
　　　—Corporate executive discussing his second home in a resort community on the Pacific Ocean near San Francisco

What picture enters your mind when you think of a vacation home? Do you smile happily at that lovely vision of enjoying the home on weekends and vacations—and that other vision of enjoying your trip to the bank to deposit the money that tenants pay for using the house when you're not there?

The income you can get from renting a second home is always a strong selling point among vacation home salesmen. Somehow you get the idea that all tenants are either two young female elementary school teachers, or high-level bank executives with artistic wives and well-behaved children.

And while these lovely people are tending your property, sweeping your rugs, and watering your lawn they are helping you pay off your mortgage. Furthermore, they offer you tax advantages: depreciation on the house itself, on the furniture they are so carefully using, plus deductions for other expenses such as utilities and repairs.

It all sounds wonderful when the salesman talks about it, stressing the many families in his development who have practically become kissing cousins of their tenants.

And sometimes it does work out that way.

But even when all is well in this best of all possible landlord-tenant worlds, the salesman may neglect to mention that tenants do not drop from the heavens —they have to be found. And the finding means you have to advertise, which costs money. If you don't want to advertise you have to rent through an agent, and agents charge fees, perhaps 10 to 15 per cent of the annual rental.

If you want to save the agent's fee you have to be on the property to show it, to explain where the dish towels are and how to turn on the oven pilot when the winds blows it out. And even if you pay an agent you still may want to have a look at who is going to be sleeping in your bed and sitting in your chair. The trips back and forth cost money.

Of course, you have to go and clean the house before the people arrive (you don't want them to think you're a slob). What can often be much worse, you have to go and clean up after the tenants have gone, when you may discover what really big slobs some otherwise very nice people can be. As one executive put it, "Though you ask tenants not to leave food every time you have tenants you go back and find three-week-old oysters in the refrigerator and a crusty casserole in the oven."

(When we worked in London for a year we rented an apartment, or as the British say, a "flat," that had been occupied previously by a diplomat. Despite the fact that the apartment had been gone over once by a cleaning woman we found pots that hadn't been scrubbed in months, all kinds of crumbs from diplomatic parties behind the sofa cushions, and a checkbook full of stubs hidden under the mattress!)

Well-mannered tenants do a certain amount of damage simply because anyone living in a house wears and tears it down a bit. But there are also not-so-well-mannered tenants who can do real damage—letting water overflow in bathtubs or abusing the plumbing—that will run into hundreds of dollars of repairs.

THE QUESTION OF INSURANCE—
IT CAN BE A PROBLEM

This brings up the question of insurance. You will need some kind of insurance against fire, other natural perils such as storms, floods, erosion, etc., tenant damage, and vandalism. You'll need it, but there's no guarantee that you can get it; there's no law compelling an insurance company to give you coverage. If the company thinks you are in a high-risk situation—a very isolated spot, for instance, or one where floods or violent windstorms are not unknown—you may not be able to buy insurance or it may be so expensive you'll think it's not worth it.

And a growing insurance problem is security, not against nature, but against *people*. Back in the good old days "security" for a second home meant being sure you had enough liquor on hand if people dropped in unexpectedly, plus the makings of a meal if they decided to stay for dinner. Unfortunately this is no longer the case. Whether you buy a house in an isolated spot or in a small community of private (non-development) homes you have to think of protecting your property against theft and vandalism when it's unoccupied.

One possibility, depending on where your house is, is getting a retiree or a local high school student to look in on your property for you. This means of course that you have to keep him informed of your comings and goings, and you have to be sure he is discreet as well as trustworthy. Naturally you will either want to or have to pay for this service in some way. It may be no more than generous gifts at Christmastime or reciprocating the favor. If you're planning to pay someone for regular checkups, however, you'll have to add this cost on to your other expenses for the vacation house. (Even these precautions aren't always enough. There have been instances reported in the newspapers of thieves pulling up to a house with a moving van and removing the furniture while neighbors watched, thinking that the whole operation was perfectly legitimate.)

This arrangement is, of course, in addition to the local police force, whose job it is to protect property. But though they may be very conscientious, they can be almost powerless against vandalism, and only too often vandalism by young people living near or even in the community itself. Sometimes the vandals are simply young lovers looking for a cozy spot to continue their romance, and they do a minimum of damage once they've gotten into the house. Sometimes they are kids out for a "thrill," who will take only things that appeal to them—all the peanuts in the bowl on the coffee table, some bathing suits, a camera, a TV set. Sometimes, for no apparent reason, they are wantonly destructive and smash windows, spill paint, and strew clothes around for the sheer pleasure of doing damage.

I've checked with insurance agents, local police, and people who own summer homes, and all say there isn't much, if anything, that can be done about this vandalism. More secure locks have often been looked on as a challenge by the vandals, who then do more damage to doors as they break in forcibly, instead of picking the locks. Some families in small communities of vacation homes, where everyone knows everyone else, have—by means of the grapevine—at least managed to get back their cameras and TV sets, though sometimes at the price of decidedly deteriorated relationships with neighbors whose children either were involved themselves or knew those involved. Most people have simply resigned themselves to accepting the fact that they may have their house broken into, and have compensated by not keeping anything of value on hand.

If you live in a development which has its own private guard system you are somewhat better off. Many of these developments have either a formal or an informal patrol—employees who drive around checking the property for fallen branches, fire hazards, litter, etc., and who also keep an eye on unoccupied property for possible damage by wind, rain, or storms. Though they can't prevent vandalism they do at least act as a deterrent; if you're on your own, you should see what kind of coverage you can get, if any. A local broker will probably be your best source. It's impossible to quote rates here, since they vary depending on the laws of individual states, the value of the house and its furnishings, the location of the house, and other factors. And you will have to add the cost, if you can get coverage, on to all your other second-home charges.

YOU—AS A BUSINESSMAN, CARETAKER, AND "SUMMER FOLK"

So a vacation house that's going to be rented out part of the time has to be looked at as a small business enterprise with a possible (and taxable) profit, and possible losses, not all of which will be covered by tax deductions or insurance. If you look on it as a business you have to decide if you really want to get into that business every year. Are you prepared to devote the time, effort, and money needed to keep the enterprise going? Can you afford to have some bad seasons and still meet the mortgage payments on the house? If you have a pressure job which involves travel or working over weekends sometimes, will you still be able to spare the time to make a trip to show your house? And how will you feel if you get there, clean and scrub like mad—and the prospective tenants don't call and don't come either?

How will you feel if you have bad luck and rent to careless tenants who, without actually destroying anything, make a mess of your house? Some of us can shrug these things off—but some of us feel absolutely devastated. Of course, you aren't going to put expensive furniture in the house, but you will still feel some pride of possession. Naturally you can't expect a salesman, who is touting the virtues of renting your house for income as an inducement to buy, to point out these little "details." But you will consider them because you want to look at the dark side before tying up cash that could be safely in a savings account earning interest.

Here's another thing to consider, while we're looking at the dark side. Having two houses is more expensive and more work than you think when you first fall in love with the idea. For no matter how simple the "shack," there is still some maintenance required. You have to have a path to get to the door, which means a certain amount of weed cutting or paving or snow removal, depending on the climate. You have to worry about the plumbing, even if all you have is an outhouse. You have to think of minor destructive factors, like squirrels, mildew, and mice; plus major factors, like floods from heavy rains or burst pipes; or catastrophes such as a fire or a hurricane. Even if you can get insurance *you* still have to go and clean up the damage, large or small. Property isn't something you can just walk away from—it has to be tended.

And again, no matter how simple you want to be, you are still running an establishment. You have to sweep the sand off the floor and the furniture once in a while, do a little laundry, wash a window or two if you want to see the gorgeous view you're paying for, and pound in a nail or two to keep the walls from sagging.

Above all, you have to shop to satisfy appetites increased by all that fresh air and exercise. Depending on where you have your second home, shopping can be a pleasure with supermarkets as good as or better than those you have near your "first" home, or it can be an exercise in frustration, with long lines in small stores not set up to handle the "summer folk" and tourist trade (except for higher prices at the height of the season, which you grumble about but pay because you have no alternative). And it's a standing joke, but told with a wry smile, that if you have two houses you can never remember which refrigerator has the eggs, and you always have two jars of mustard in one kitchen and none in the other. So before you are completely carried away by visions of yourself tanned and lean, or forever a happy family because your children have all those wonderful childhood memories of time spent in the vacation house, remember that time and trouble are involved as well as money.

Which leads us logically to the next step—if you do understand the risks and are willing to pay the price in time and trouble as well as cash, should you buy an individual property or should you buy into a development?

If you want an individual property—a country home—how to find one varies so much from one part of the country to another that it is quite beyond the scope of this book. (You might take a look at the pitfalls of buying a development house, however, since some of these same pitfalls will apply to individual homes.) But beware of anyone who says the whole idea isn't full of danger, that it's all a simple proposition that you'll never regret, since it's a one-to-one, person-to-person transaction. All "city slickers" don't live in the city and all "country bumpkins" aren't in the country. You are at a disadvantage because you don't know the territory, so despite the beautiful, peaceful surroundings it will pay you to be as cautious and cagey as the fox eluding the hounds.

But if you are considering buying into a community which has been or is being developed, there are advantages to be gained, and pitfalls to be wary of.

The first thing you have to decide is—are you buying the present or the future? You will pay less if you can wait but you are, in a sense, buying a pig in a poke. Even the most responsible developer has to contend with acts of God and man: strikes, delays in shipments, unseasonable weather, unusual snowfalls or rainstorms. The less responsible or less experienced developers have to contend with these plus their own lack of expertise. In either case you are the ultimate victim.

If the builder is reliable things will get straightened out eventually. If he's not reliable you may never get to swim in the pool, jog on the trail, or ski on the slopes. In fact, you may never even get to see your house, or if you do you may find yourself one of just a few families living in a desolate spot with no water or sewer lines—the actual fate of some unlucky families in a vacation development near Newnan, Georgia, when the project's developer had financial difficulties.

Your best bet, obviously, is to buy from a reputable and reliable builder who has other interests as well, or other developments, preferably in the same area. He will then be much more interested in staying within the bounds of good business practice, in complying with the requirements of federal, state, and local housing laws, and in seeing that the area remains stable. He will then also have a stake in the community and a reputation you can check on.

If you buy in a planned community you have the advantage of buying where there are provisions for roads, maintenance of grounds, fire-fighting equipment, clubhouses and other recreational facilities. If the development is near completion you can literally see how far away these facilities are (maps can be deceptive!). This advantage can be offset, of course, by the fact that the most desirable sites may already be gone—so timing is a factor and again you have to weigh the present against the future.

A planned community will also offer some supervision of your children by lifeguards at the swimming pool or lake. There will be opportunities for swimming lessons and, depending on the community, perhaps skiing, riding, or tennis lessons. As the communities develop they often offer more and more organized activities for children.

There will also be organized activities for you: "Masquerade parties, seasonal dances, other fun activities," to quote from a brochure describing one of many planned communities. This may be wonderful, or it may be a nuisance and a bore. So when you are considering a particular community take a look at the people who've come to look, just as you have, and who may be your future neighbors. Sit around the pool or lake if you can. Listen in on the group around the fireplace. Can you see yourself sharing "fun activities" with the group or others like them? What if they're not people you think you'd find compatible? It may be very difficult to escape from them in a planned community without being called a snob or being subject to community pressures. Despite the view and the facilities it might be the better part of valor to look elsewhere. Remember, you're buying the place to escape tension.

And finally, if commuting time is an important part of your schedule check with the state police, local police, and/or automobile clubs to find out what traffic conditions are really like. When the brochure for the property says that "the community is just two hours away," do they mean two hours by the light of the moon on a mild night at 2 A.M.? Or two hours average time on a hot summer afternoon when there are thousands of people just like you in their cars headed in the same direction. How about snowy days? Are the roads cleared quickly or will you be still driving over November's snowfall in late February? Have they neglected to mention that not only isn't the highway complete, but also there are no plans to complete it, since the one small town that has jurisdiction of the two-lane main street that the six-lane highway funnels into has no intention of widening that same main street? The slow traffic has proved to be a bonanza for the local gas stations, diners, and luncheonettes, and the town fathers know a good thing when they've got one.

However, when you've satisfied yourself that you've taken all possible precautions, looked into all possible hazards, and believe you've got a good deal—then why not go ahead? Life is short, and some time should be spent enjoying it.

34

Nag, Nag, Nag, Or:
How to Complain

"The buyer needs a thousand eyes, the seller but one."
—Old Chinese proverb

Remember when you used to hear "the consumer is king" and you'd give a cynical laugh? Uneasy lay the head that wore the crown. Not only uneasy, but also furious, frustrated, disillusioned, fighting mad—the natural reaction to the indifference or calculated neglect shown when you tried to find out why your new car broke down in the middle of the expressway at rush hour, or why the percolator made coffee that looked like weak tea, or why the couch that should have been delivered to Pittsburgh on Tuesday was en route to Falls City, Nebraska.

These multitudes of sins used to be covered by that good old Latin phrase *caveat emptor,* "let the buyer beware." But in the last decade or so a new Latin phrase has entered the language—to the dismay of many manufacturers, the delight of lawyers (new work representing either manufacturers or consumers), and the edification of customers. The phrase is *caveat venditor,* "let the seller beware," and it's a refreshing change.

(If you're interested in how all this came about you will remember the knight in consumer's armor, Ralph Nader, and his joust with the General Motors Corporation, using as his sword his book about cars, *Unsafe at Any Speed.* But there was also a series of court decisions that completely changed the laws governing the responsibilities of manufacturers for their products. A landmark case was Henningsen vs. Bloomfield Motors. Mrs. Helen Henningsen was driving a recently bought Plymouth when the steering wheel came off. The car ran into a brick wall and was completely wrecked; she suffered painful injuries. The case went all the way to the Supreme Court, which ruled that proof of negligence by the manufacturer was no longer necessary. Instead, there was an implied warranty that the car would operate properly. After this decision came a series of other court rulings that made manufacturers liable, as they had not been before, for the safety and correct operation of their products.)

In addition to its new legal clout consumerism has become a popular cause, even helping politicians get elected in some places. And consumer protection agencies have been set up or revitalized in many states, cities, counties, and towns around the nation. Attorney-general offices that used to perform fairly routine legal duties for their states have taken an active role in protecting consumer rights, from issuing injunctions against companies that pollute natural resources to getting refunds for consumers who've been bilked. At the very highest level the federal government set up an Office of Consumer Affairs, with an active executive director, a newsletter to consumers, and appearances before Congress and at legislative hearings.

On top of all this, many companies have adopted that ancient but honorable doctrine "if you can't lick 'em, join 'em," and have appointed vice-presidents to answer complaints, or have established consumer hot lines for consumers to call, or have instituted buyers' protection plans.

Has the millennium arrived? Is it okay to pick up your crown from the corner where you kicked it in disgust? Should you set it back on your head at a jaunty angle, and smile?

Not by a long shot.

There's no denying that the situation has improved greatly, but despite new laws and new attitudes, many drawbacks still exist.

First, while it's true there are many new consumer protection agencies at all levels, their effectiveness varies. All the laws on the books are no protection if a complaint requires investigation and there aren't enough investigators on the agency's staff to go out and investigate. Nor is the agency much of a threat if it has no real authority—if it can only recommend or mediate, rather than being able to use its legal powers of enforcement. Few consumer agencies have sufficient staff, funding, or power to do a complete job of consumer protection.

Second, there are drawbacks in some of the recent procedures that have been established. Arbitration, for instance, has been regaining favor as a fair method of settling disputes between buyer and seller. Under the usual arbitration proceedings both sides choose an impartial person to hear the complaint and settle the case. Both sides agree in advance to abide by the decision of the arbitrator. It can be a great time- and money-saver, since it avoids both the cost and the time involved in getting a case through the various legal steps. There's only one problem: arbitration depends on the co-operation of both sides, and the very companies that are the most flagrant violators of good business practices are the very companies that wouldn't be caught anywhere near an arbitration proceeding.

Finally, the Small Claims Court has been established or utilized as the place for consumers who can't pay legal fees to obtain justice. (In some states you can have a lawyer if you choose to but you can also represent yourself, and some states forbid lawyers.) But while the court has helped many who have used it, it too has limitations. Even the minimal procedures required to have a case heard require time, effort, and some knowledge by the person presenting the claim. In the meantime the company being sued may very well have a staff lawyer whose only job is to prepare the company's case. There are delays, postponements, rescheduling, chasing around to find true owners and correct addresses—all time-consuming for the person who wants to sue, while the company lawyer does it as part of his regular routine—and couldn't care less.

Worst of all, even when the consumer wins he may lose. A judgment in his favor is not good if the company has gone bankrupt, or left town, or the mechanic says he has no assets to pay with, though he's not bankrupt. And there is no compensation for time, trouble, expenses, which may have been considerable.

So, to be realistic, as consumers we're still in trouble, especially as our technology gets more complicated and our repair services and repairmen get scarcer and more expensive. We'd be better off looking at ourselves as court jesters and deciding how we can make the best of a bad situation. There are several approaches.

First, the buying itself. If you have a choice, buy the simple, not the complex. Stoves that look as if they require an engineer's license to operate, blenders that have thirty-two buttons, floor cleaners that wash, wax, mop, and pick up the baby's toys are to be avoided unless someone in the family has an engineer's license or a natural empathy with gadgets plus the time to get spare parts and put them in their proper place. (Even at repair centers you have no guarantee that the repairmen can make adjustments properly—sometimes the technology is beyond *them*.) If you must have the complicated gadget at least try to buy one that has been designed so repairs are relatively easy.

Second, buy only from reputable dealers, even if it may cost a bit more initially. They care, or they should care, enough about future business to make good on their products.

Third, never buy without checking the service department to see what kind of service you'll get if things go wrong. Watch out, in particular, for service guarantees when you buy through a mail order or catalogue order retailer. One way they may be keeping their prices low is by stinting on servicing.

Fourth, don't take anyone's *word* on guarantees, not even the sweetest, most obliging salesman, who may be so sweet just because he knows he's quitting next week to take a bicycle trip in Europe or a better-paying job at the license bureau. Get the guarantees in writing and read the fine print to be sure that what the large print guarantees isn't taken away by the fine print.

Fifth, be sure the guarantee or warranty (the two words are interchangeable) is complete and that you understand it. (If you don't, go on the assumption that it's not because you are stupid but because the guarantee is either purposely obscure or is badly written.) Check these points:

Is the entire product guaranteed or only parts of it? Is it the television set, or only the picture tube?

How long does the guarantee last: Ninety days, a year, a lifetime? And if it's a lifetime, whose lifetime—yours or the product's?

Is labor included? Some guarantees include labor, some only material, some both. Other guarantees promise labor and parts for a specified length of time and parts only after that. If the guarantee states that the defective part will be "replaced" at no charge it could mean only that the part itself will be replaced—perhaps by sending the part to you and leaving it up to you to do the replacing.

What alternatives are offered? Does the guarantee mean complete replacement, i.e., a new appliance, or does it mean repair only? The guarantee for something that has an estimated life, such as a tire, may be prorated. In that case you may be entitled to a new tire, less a deduction for the use you've already gotten from the defective tire.

Where and how will the guarantee be taken care of? Will you have to wrap everything three times and send it off to some remote corner of the country, or will you be able to take it to a local service station?

THE COMPLAINT PROCESS, OR:
HOW TO NAG EFFECTIVELY

Let's say you've taken all the precautions you possibly could and things go wrong anyway. (It happens. We used a moving company when we moved in 1965 that did a fine job, so when we had to move again in 1971 we called them again. A disaster. There was extensive damage to our furniture and we withheld part of the bill while we went through all the complaint procedures, up to and including the Small Claims Court. Eventually we settled out of court and about broke even, if you don't count thousands of man-hours spent hassling; plus the psychic satisfaction of winning against a company that thought it didn't have to pay attention to customers' bad treatment.) You have two possibilities: conventional and not so conventional.

The conventional route, in view of the new "pow" of consumer power, can be very effective. You arm yourself with your ammunition, the facts—the merchandise involved, the date you bought it, the model number or receipt if any, copies of canceled checks and repair bills. Then you begin the upward climb. You complain to the proper person in the store or at the dealer's. You send letters and make phone calls, keeping carbons of your letters and making a note of the name of the person you speak to. (This doesn't always work—some people in a department will either refuse to give you their names or will give you an incorrect name.)

If you don't get satisfaction at this lower level you take your file, which by now is nice and fat, and try somewhere else. Your local Better Business Bureau is a good bet, especially since their campaign, begun in 1971, to become more effective. They have added phone lines, personnel, and new programs to enhance their strength and value. If you have a local or state consumer protection agency they too should be brought into the act. Since these agencies often co-operate with each other a letter to one should also include a carbon copy sent to the other or others.

Other possibilities, depending on what's available, are the letters-to-the-editor column of local newspapers and a report to an action-line program on radio or television. (These are programs featuring a reporter who takes complaints from consumers and tries to do something about them. Usually he succeeds, since the program has a big audience and gets much publicity.)

If the problem is a major appliance that's taken sick—a refrigerator, washing machine, incinerator, or stove—and you've had no success with your local dealer or service center you can refer your complaint to the Major Appliance Consumer Action Panel (MACAP) at 20 Wacker Drive, Chicago, Illinois 60606, phone 312-236-3165, either by letter or by a collect call. This industry-wide group is the court of last resort, short of going to legal courts, for consumers who have complaints about their appliances.

Finally, of course, you can go to the Small Claims Court or even to the Civil Courts. However, for most of us the courts just aren't the answer—the Small Claims Court for the reasons already given on page 217 and the Civil Courts because though we have the legal right to use them there is nothing which guarantees us the more crucial ability to *pay* for them. In most cases the cost of a civil suit far outweighs the cost of the damage we've suffered.

No matter which route you choose, if the adjustment isn't quick, it is time-consuming, temper-fraying, ulcer-giving, and costly. How costly depends on how far you go. But even a minimum complaint involves phone calls, transportation (gas, fares, maybe parking fees), letters. There are other ways to complain, and sometimes they can be very effective, as friends of mine have proven.

Nancy B., for instance, twice resorted to tears when she didn't get furniture delivered in time, despite promises from the most reliable of stores. The first time she was a bride, expecting her in-laws for Christmas, and there was no couch to sit on; in fact, nothing to sit on. When she explained her plight, through the tears, the store sent her a couch on loan until her own was delivered two months later. The second time she was pregnant, had just moved to a larger apartment, and had no regular bed to sleep on. Again the tears, and the store came through with two sturdy cots until her bed was delivered.

Kathe S. bought a percolator that conked out after two weeks. She returned it, was promised quick repairs, and then spent many more weeks subsisting on instant coffee while she bombarded the store with phone calls and letters. Finally she decided to call in person; she was kept waiting for half an hour because the adjustment clerk was out to lunch, and then was told she would have to come back the next day because of a backlog. Kathe said calmly, in a room full of customers like herself, that she was so sick and tired of phoning, writing, and waiting that she could scream. In fact, she said, she would scream. And she did, standing there in the middle of the floor, quite calm, emitting loud scream after loud scream. Her repaired percolator was shipped to her that same day.

Louis H. bought tires that proved defective, and was unable to get any promises of adjustment via telephone. At the store he was shuffled from clerk to clerk, repeating his story each time and each time being told "That's not my department" or "That's not my responsibility" or "I just don't have the authority to give you a refund." Finally Louis saw the manager, safely separated from the staff behind a glass partition. Lou stood in front of the partition, banged his knuckles against it loudly, pointed to the manager, and said, "I'm not going away until I see *you*." In one second, Lou said, the manager came out from his sanctuary "pale and shaking" and authorized a refund.

However, the ultimate satisfaction-guaranteed consumer is my friend Seymour R. Seymour is now a communications analyst with the Department of Defense in the Pentagon, but he was a lieutenant colonel in the United States Air Force before his retirement. During World War II he was a pilot whose specialty was flying over the uncharted and unmarked North Pole and Alaskan regions. He pooh-poohs reports about his ability as a pilot, but generals used to request him if they had to fly these routes which were so treacherous, since there were no landmarks, and the pilot's instincts were often the only thing to rely on if a storm came up. Obviously such a man, though he is now and was then quiet-spoken and mild-mannered, isn't going to take runarounds lightly. (He says his attitude has nothing to do with his army years, but with the fact that he learned to be "tough" as a poor kid on the sidewalks of New York City, and doesn't like to be taken advantage of.)

And he rarely is, since he has worked out methods of resolving his complaints and proved them in action. When the upholstery in his expensive car wore out after only a year he complained to the manager of the car agency, got nowhere, and wrote to the national marketing vice-president in Detroit. The upholstery was replaced. He's also gotten refunds on carpets that wore poorly, quick delivery of a new car and an adjustment of an incorrect bill without having to go to court, and a refund on an insurance policy. He has some very definite ideas about how to proceed with complaints; they coincide with the view of others who've also proved their methods through successful action. Here's the consensus:

You must have a fair complaint and a reasonable one. Then your approach varies depending on the person or the store you are dealing with. If it's a small store you are probably dealing with the owner. When you ask for a refund or an adjustment you are almost literally taking money out of his pocket, and he will be understandably reluctant. It doesn't pay to lose your temper, but if you feel you are justified, by all means press your case and ask for a reasonable settlement. If the owner is intelligent he will appreciate that you are a regular customer and it's in his interest to keep your good will.

When you are dealing with a large company your approach should be totally different. Then you have to contend with several or even many levels. There's little point in telling your story in any detail at all to a clerk, no matter how sympathetic. He is under orders, has no flexibility, no authority to make adjustments.

Instead you should go to the highest level possible; the higher the level the greater the responsibility and the authority to cut through red tape and get something done. However, if you can't immediately get to the highest level—say a regional manager vs. a store manager—take advantage of the fact that the store manager is worried about what his boss will think about how the manager is doing his job. Take advantage of the local manager's realization (which you subtly convey) that you will have no hesitation, if you're not satisfied, about going over his head, which will surely cause him some difficulty at the home office.

One of the problems, when it comes to settling bills, is getting the attention of the billing department. (Seymour says he sometimes gets a mental picture, after repeated letters have brought no answers, that the billing department in many major stores is composed of intelligent apes who've been trained to slit open envelopes, take out checks, and throw everything else away. Furthermore, they are happy to do this for two bananas a day.)

One way to flag the billing department—sometimes the only way—is to abstain from paying the part of the bill that's in question. Always pay the remainder, which proves your good intentions and helps maintain your credit rating, but withhold some. Sooner or later, mostly later, the billing department will notice that something's wrong and get in touch with you, most often by way of a dunning letter. Then at least you are in a file handled by humans, not computers, and you can get to see someone who will straighten out the whole affair.

Where you decide to arrive at a settlement can be very important. Suppose you want to attract the attention of other customers as part of your strategy for applying pressure—a useful tactic in an automobile showroom, for instance. Pretend to lose your temper and raise your voice so you are playing to an attentive audience. (But keep your cool so you are sure you are getting the best possible deal.) The manager will want you to go into his office and talk things over quietly. You of course refuse because it's your nuisance value that's going to win your case.

On the other hand, when you are settling a credit error or something where the facts are in question you may want to give the manager the opportunity to back down graciously, in a relaxed atmosphere. Then you can be happy to accept his offer to discuss the affair quietly in his office.

Whenever you are writing letters make carbons and distribute them lavishly to where they will, by adding pressure, do the most good. Presidents of companies, for instance, when you're dealing with executives under them; consumer agencies; government officials in the agencies or departments that are interested in or responsible for the question you're dealing with; your state representatives; and your congressmen.

You might also send carbons to the Better Business Bureau; any consumer groups you're a member of or other similar groups such as block or tenant organizations; women's clubs; garden clubs—any place where there are people who would learn of your difficulties and might be customers of the same store or merchant. Just putting at the bottom of the letter all the people you've sent copies to (you might like to use the little symbol cc—carbon copy) can have a very salutary effect in hastening the pace of an adjustment.

Who should make the complaint, especially the personal complaint? In every household there seems to be one person who has an extra supply of adrenaline that starts spurting on just such occasions—and one who prefers to walk twenty paces behind and to say, if asked, "I don't even know him." Obviously the born fighter is the one who gets into the hassle; the silent partner can do his share by finding out where to go to complain, by writing letters, or by keeping the complaint file up to date. If both partners in a household are shy take along a friend who isn't until one or both of you learn to overcome your reticence.

The thing to remember is that we are living in a time when consumerism is no longer looked on as a passing fad nourished by crackpots, but as a very important movement that can affect a business where it hurts—in the balance sheet, where profits and losses show. You can think of yourself as fighting the good cause, not only for yourself but also for better products, better management (very often the upper echelons in a business don't know what the lower echelons are doing and are horrified when they find out), and better living. And you, as a consumer, will personally profit.

You can't beat that!

INDEX